# INSIDE THE IBM PC

Executive Editor:  David T. Culverwell
Production Editor/Text Design:  Paula Huber
Art Director/Cover Design:  Don Sellers
Assistant Art Director:  Bernard Vervin
Cover Photography:  George Dodson
Typesetter:  Alexander Typesetting, Inc., Indianapolis, IN
Printer:  Fairfield Graphics, Fairfield, PA
Typefaces:  Melior (text), Eurostyle Bold (display)

# INSIDE the IBM PC
## ACCESS TO ADVANCED *FEATURES* AND PROGRAMMING

## PETER NORTON

Robert J. Brady Co., Bowie, Maryland 20715
A Prentice-Hall Publishing and Communications Company

Inside the IBM PC: Access to Advanced Features and Programming

Library of Congress Cataloging in Publication Data

Norton, Peter, 1943-
   Inside the IBM PC.

   Includes index.
   1. IBM Personal Computer—Programming.
I. Title. II. Title: Inside the I.B.M. personal computer.
QA76.8.I2594N67      1983      001.64'2      83-3775
ISBN 0-89303-556-4


Prentice-Hall International, Inc., London
Prentice-Hall Canada, Inc., Scarborough, Ontario
Prentice-Hall of Australia, Pty., Ltd., Sydney
Prentice-Hall of India Private Limited, New Delhi
Prentice-Hall of Japan, Inc., Tokyo
Prentice-Hall of Southeast Asia Pte. Ltd., Singapore
Whitehall Books, Limited, Petone, New Zealand
Editora Prentice-Hall Do Brasil LTDA., Rio de Janeiro

Printed in the United States of America

   84 85 86 87 88 89 90 91 92 93 10 9 8 7 6 5

## Note to Authors

Do you have a manuscript or a software program
related to personal computers? Do you have an idea for
developing such a project? If so, we would like to hear
from you. The Brady Co. produces a complete range of
books and applications software for the personal computer market. We invite you to write to David
Culverwell, Editor-in-Chief, Robert J. Brady Co., Bowie,
Maryland 20715.

# Contents

*Documentation*

## Apologies

Let my first words in this book be an apology for whatever errors do appear here, and for whatever overlooked topics don't. I have done my darnedest to make this the most useful book possible, the book that I would have wanted when I began digging past the IBM/PC's easy surface soil into its dark and fascinating subterranean reaches.

But it is inevitable that I have gotten some facts wrong, written some misleading passages, and left out some juicy topics. For this, you and every reader have my apologies. And my request that you bring them to my attention.

## Disclaimer

The author and publisher of this book have used their best efforts in preparing this book and the programs contained in it. These efforts include the development, research, and testing of the theories and programs to determine their effectiveness. The author and publisher make no warranty of any kind, expressed or implied, with regard to these programs or the documentation contained in this book. The author and publisher shall not be liable in any event for incidental or consequential damages in connection with, or arising out of, the furnishing, performance, or use of these programs.

## Trademarks

This book drops quite a few names, many of them trademarks. Here are their owners:

IBM, IBM Personal Computer, Displaywriter and PC-DOS are trademarks of International Business Machines Corporation.

Microsoft, MS, MS-DOS, XE-DOS and XENIX are trademarks of Microsoft Corporation.

Volkswriter is a trademark of Lifetree Software Inc.

VisiCalc is a trademark of Visicorp.

Supercalc is a trademark of Sorcim.

JFORMAT and JEL are trademarks of Tall Tree Systems.

Vedit is a trademark of Compuview Products.

EasyProof is a trademark of Norell Data Systems.

Proofreader and Grammatik are trademarks of Aspen Software.

CP/M and CP/M-86 are trademarks of Digital Research.

Peachtree is a trademark of Peachtree Software.

EasyWriter is a trademark of Information Unlimited Software.

Apple and Apple II are trademarks of Apple Computers.

Univac is a trademark of Sperry Univac.

Context MBA is a trademark of Context Management Systems.

Forth is a trademark of Forth Inc.

The Source is a trademark of Source Telecomputing.

TP-I and Smith Corona are trademarks of SCM Corp.

Ada is a trademark of the United States Department of Defense.

WordStar is a trademark of MicroPro International.

UCSD p-System is a trademark of the Regents of the University of California.

Amdek Color II is a trademark of Amdek Corp.

Atari is a trademark of Atari, Inc.

DiskLook, SecMod, UnErase, FileHide, The Norton Utilities, and Power Tools for the IBM PC are trademarks of Peter Norton.

## Acknowledgements

Quite a few people assisted in the preparation of this book, and general thanks is given to them all here. Due particular thanks are Dr. Larry Joel Goldstein, for initiating the project, and David Culverwell and Tracy Smith of the Brady Co for husbanding it. Several people at Microsoft provided assistance, particularly Alan Boyd and Chris Larson. Of the many people who contributed review effort and suggestions, particular thanks are due to Joseph Capps Jr., of IBM, and Mike Todd, president of the Washington D.C. user's group Capital P.C., while Stephen Rowe made the most valuable contribution of suggestions. Special assistance in the preparation of this book was given by Eileen Harris.

## Technical information

When photographers see books of photographs, they always want to know all about the f-stops and such, and I suppose that some readers of this book will want to know what hardware and software was used to produce it. Two IBM/PC's were used for the research of this book—like a couple of laboratory animals sacrificed on the altar of science.

My primary IBM/PC, on which this book was written, is a monochrome system with two 320 kilobyte diskette drives, and 576 kilobytes of memory—64 K of standard memory, and 512 K on a jumbo memory expansion board full of the 64 K chips made notorious by the many articles that have appeared in the press about the competition between Japanese and American chip manufacturers. The JEL/JFORMAT program, by John Henderson of Tall Tree Systems of Los Altos, California, is used to create a 320 K electronic diskette simulation, and a 64 K print spooler, out of part of the 512 K memory expansion. This jumbo memory was bought on a lark, but has proved very valuable both in speeding the mechanics of writing this book, and in providing astonishing improvement in my Pascal programs. Proof once again that, in computing, more is always better.

Two excellent programs assisted the mechanics of writing. Vedit, from CompuView of Anne Arbor Michigan, was the text editor program used—I personally prefer it to several word processors that I have bought and put aside. Work-a-day spelling checking was done by EasyProof, from Norell Data Systems of Los Angeles, California. These two programs had their performance substantially enhanced by the JEL electronic diskette.

More rigorous spelling checking, and some usage polishing was provided by ProofReader and Grammatik, by Aspen Software, of Tijeras, New Mexico. I have found these two programs to be annoying yet useful.

Color and graphics features were checked-out on my second IBM/PC system, using the Amdek Color II monitor. That system has 128 K of true-blue IBM memory, twin Tandon TM 100-2 diskette drives, and the standard color-graphics adapter.

For printing, one of these systems has an Epson MX-80 printer, which is the standard IBM/PC printer with its maker's name on it, instead of IBM's. The other has a Smith-Corona TP-I daisy-wheel printer; rock-bottom performance, at a rock-bottom price.

Like many IBM/PC system owners, I am torn between the safety of IBM-approved configurations, and the siren-call of exotic options. My own choices have drifted between them, with a bias towards the True Blue.

## About the Author

Peter Norton grew up in Seattle, Washington, and was educated at Reed College. He has labored in the various vineyards of computing for the last twenty years, with time out to teach medicine in the Army, to study for five years in a monastery, and to back-pack around the world. Mr Norton lives on the beach in Venice, California, and always wears his shirt sleeves rolled-up.

# 1

# Fitting Your Wizard's Cap

## 1.1 What this book is about—your wizard's cap

This book is about magic—the magic that can be done on the IBM Personal Computer.

When the IBM Personal Computer was introduced, it set a new and much higher standard for quality and performance in personal computers. People who already knew and understood personal computers saw in the IBM/PC capabilities beyond what they had seen before. And other people, who had always thought of personal computers as toys, began to recognize computers for what they really are—the premier tool for working minds.

There are many books that will introduce you to computers, but this is not one of them. This book is for those who want to go beyond the beginner's material, and discover the real capabilities of a personal computer—the IBM Personal Computer. This book is for those who want to learn the magic and discover the sorcery.

There are many wonderful tricks that the IBM/PC can do, and we are going to tell you about them all. Whether you are an experienced computer sophisticate, or a recent graduate of beginner's books on computing, if you are ready to take the step into a thorough understanding of how the IBM/PC works and what it can be made to do, this book is for you.

This is an understand-it book and partly a how-to book. For anyone who is ready for intermediate and advanced material on the IBM/PC, here it is. We'll help you understand how this machine ticks, and understand its full potential. And there will be many guides and clues about programming the PC.

But this in not a book of programming tricks for the PC—that belongs in a book on programming, and this book is mostly about the capabilities of the IBM/PC.

To many people, capable computer technicians have always formed an exotic brotherhood of wizards who knew how to make those marvelous machines dance and sing. With this book, you can fit yourself for a wizard's cap.

1

## 1.2  What we will cover—a preview of this book

This book is mostly about programs—software—for that is where most of the magic in a computer lies. But we also need to take a look at the hardware that makes up the IBM Personal Computer—Chapter 2 will do that.

In Chapter 3 we'll look at how the IBM/PC thinks, by going over the fundamentals of the micro-processor—the brains of the PC.

The operating system, PC-DOS, is outlined in Chapter 4, with some explanation of how DOS works. Program tools to provide access to the features of DOS accompany Chapter 4.

Next, in Chapter 5, we will explain the insides of diskettes and how data is stored on them. Programming examples will show how to decode the intimate information about diskettes.

Chapter 6 introduces the Read-Only-Memory programs that are built into the IBM/PC, and shows you how to explore and snoop in the ROM. This is in preparation for Chapters 7 through 11 which cover, topic by topic, the service routines provided in ROM. Each of these chapters has accompanying programs that let you gain control of that part of the computer.

Chapter 7 shows how to access the diskette control routines. Chapters 8 and 9 cover the display screen—in character mode and graphics mode. Chapter 10 covers the keyboard, and Chapter 11 rounds up all the odds and ends.

The appendixes to this book give a narrative glossary of computer terminology, an introduction to Pascal, and a discussion of how to successfully make the connection between assembly language programs and Pascal or other high-level language programs.

## 1.3  What you need to get the most out of this book

If you just want to learn a great deal about the IBM Personal Computer, then this book is all you need. However, to put this knowledge into practice, you will need some more, starting with an IBM/PC.

To use the programs presented in this book, you will need an IBM/PC with 64 K of memory and one diskette drive. The programs here may be used with either the monochrome display or the color graphics adapter. You will also need the DOS operating system, and the tools that come with it, such as the DEBUG program. Any version of DOS may be used: the original 1.00, the unofficial and temporary 1.05 version, the improved 1.10 version or DOS 2.00.

To make full use of all the features that the IBM/PC provides, you will need the separate diskette package which accompanies this book. Access tools to all of the PC's features were written for this book, but it is not practical to use many of them except from a diskette copy. Appendix five lists the contents of this package.

You will not need the IBM Macro Assembler to make use of the assembly language access routines that this book presents. All of those programs are included, as ready-to-use object modules, in this book's diskette package. However, if you want to make changes to the assembly programs to adapt them to your own needs, then you will also need the Macro Assembler, and knowledge of how to work with assembly language. Part of what this book will show you, is a simple introduction to using the Macro Assembler.

To use the Pascal programs that appear here, either by themselves or as part of your own programs, you will need the IBM Pascal Compiler.

Finally, you may wish to have a copy of The Norton Utilities. They include programs to repair damaged diskettes (FileFix), and recover erased files (UnErase); modify diskette sectors (SecMod), and control hidden files (FileHide and BatHide); arrange file entries (DiskOpt and FileSort), and control the display screen (Reverse, ScrAtr, and Clear); plus several other useful utilities.

## 1.4 Programs, programming languages and the diskette package

Plenty of programs will appear in this book, and we'll start off right away with a nice little toy program, which you will see in listing 1.1. This BASIC program displays each of the 256 character codes that can be shown on the display screen of the IBM/PC. It's surprising how many users of the PC have never seen all its characters, and this program will show them all to you. Having all these characters displayed together can be useful helping you choose among them for special effects. This program displays the characters in a grid, with sixteen characters in each row. If you need to know the index number of any character, what the BASIC language refers to by the CHR$ function, the first row shows CHR$(0) through CHR$(15), and the second row proceeds with CHR$(16) through CHR$(31). The hexadecimal code for each character is shown by the row and column markers.

This book will make use of three programming languages—BASIC, Pascal, and assembly language. Every IBM/PC comes equipped with BASIC, and so I have used it as often as was practical. But BASIC is not well-suited to serious programming, and so this book will focus mostly on Pascal.

In the world of personal computers, Pascal has become very popular, thanks to its power, compactness and safety features. There are rivals for Pascal—particularly the C language and Forth. But Pascal has two great advantages for us. It is simpler and easier to learn than either C or Forth, and most important of all, IBM has supported Pascal for the

PC from the very beginning. Since we need to speak in some language to communicate, most of the programming in this book will be expressed in Pascal.

You may not be familiar with Pascal. Don't despair. The easiest and most painless way to learn a little of the language is to read the examples given in this book. They have been carefully written to make them as understandable as possible, and to gradually teach a little Pascal on the side. In addition, the second appendix to this book gives a brief tutorial on Pascal, showing the flavor and style of Pascal, and explaining the most important parts of the language.

I highly recommend Pascal to anyone who is undecided about which language to use for programming the IBM/PC. If you plan to use another language to program the IBM/PC, the Pascal programming examples that appear here will still be very useful to you. They will show you how things are done on the IBM/PC, and their methods can be readily adapted to other languages.

Many of the most powerful and interesting features of the IBM/PC are only accessible through assembly language. In this book we will explain what these features are and how they work. To give you full use of them, there is a complete set of assembly language interface routines which will make all the features of the IBM/PC and its DOS operating system available to you.

The third appendix to this book explains how the connection is made to assembly language routines. The details concern Pascal, but they can be used with little or no change for any language which uses the standard calling mechanisms.

Quite a few programs have been written for this book. Illustrative programs—to show you how things are done. Exploratory programs—to help you discover information about your PC, such as the memory that is hidden inside it. And tool programs—to give you access and control over the many powerful features built into the PC. As much as possible, these programs have been included in listings that appear here in this book, particularly those programs that are useful to read and study. But some of the tool programs are not particularly interesting reading—they are valuable to use, but not to read. This book contains all the programs that are useful for you to read, and practical for you to key into your computer. The others appear in the separate diskette package which accompanies this book.

The diskette package contains all the programs that appear as listings in this book, and many other programs that are useful access tools. So that you will know what is available in the diskette package, this book will make reference to them, indicating how they can be used. The fifth appendix to this book outlines the entire contents of the diskette package.

The assembly language programs in the diskette package are presented in both source format, and as ready-to-use assembled object modules. If you want to make custom changes to the assembly language routines, the source code will make it practical for you to do so. But since the programs are already assembled, you will not need to know assembly language, or to have the IBM Macro Assembler, to get full use out of these powerful access tools. The Pascal programs in the diskette package also come in source format and as compiled modules, so that you can immediately make use of them.

One additional program is included in the diskette package, DiskLook. DiskLook is a utility which makes available to you complete information about everything on the diskettes that your IBM/PC uses. It will show you the list of files in order by name, date or size, and the names of all the files erased from the diskette. DiskLook will also map the diskette's complete space utilization, show the location of each file, and display the data from any part of the diskette.

## 1.5 Three overlapping circles

It hasn't been widely recognized, but the introduction of the IBM/PC began a series of three overlapping circles of interest. It has taken some time for these three circles to become apparent, but you ought to know about them and about their relationship to this book.

The introduction of the IBM Personal Computer was, silly as this may sound, the introduction of the first of the IBM/PC-like machines; the original, but not the only. It was also the introduction of the MicroSoft operating system, MS-DOS; the IBM/PC version of MS-DOS is called PC-DOS, or IBM-DOS or just DOS.

Out of this has arisen three circles of interest. First, there is interest in the IBM/PC itself. Then there is interest in the computers which imitate the IBM/PC to a greater or lesser extent. Finally, there is interest in the family of computers that use a version of the MS-DOS operating system.

There is a great deal of over-lap in these circles, and any book which is focused on one circle, will cover much material concerning the others. This book is devoted to the originator of all this interest, the IBM Personal Computer, but much of what we will have to say will be useful to those interested in PC-like computers, and those interested in the MS-DOS family of computers.

Occasionally in this book, when it is possible to make the distinctions, I will point out what does and doesn't apply to the other two circles.

## 1.6 Sources of information

Not every aspect and detail of the IBM/PC can be covered in a book like this. Here is a list of the most important and useful reference sources for you to use when you need more details.

Almost everything that appears in this book has been gathered from these sources, together with some experimentation and a little savvy. Compared to many other personal computers, the IBM/PC was introduced with very open sources of information, thanks to IBM's desire that the machine be as accessible as possible to developers of software and hardware add-ons. As the author of this book, I didn't have access to very many secrets that aren't also available to you. All that I have done, is to digest what is publicly available, make sense of it, and separate the most widely useful information, from what is of limited interest.

When you need more than this book provides, here is where you should turn: The richest source of information is IBM's own Technical Reference manual for the Personal Computer. In the technical reference manual you will find all this, and more:

- general descriptions of how the PC is organized on a hardware level. Even if you are not a computer hardware expert, you can gain an understanding of the behind-the-scenes workings of the IBM/PC by browsing through this information.

- detailed specifications of much of the electronics of the IBM/PC; this is mostly for knowledgeable hardware experts, but it will also provide very useful clues about how parts of the system are directed under software control. As an example, if you really want to understand the full potential of the color graphics adapter, you should study the discussion of the Motorola 6845 CRT controller.

- general descriptions of the use of the read-only-memory (ROM) programs that are built into the PC.

- a detailed listing (with comprehensive notes) of the ROM-BIOS, or Read-Only-Memory Basic-Input-Output-System; these programs provide the most fundamental control and service programming for the IBM/PC. This listing is in assembly language, which means that you will not be able to fully comprehend it unless you can understand 8086 assembly code. Nevertheless, this ROM-BIOS listing is a gold-mine of information about the services that are available to programs. Even if you do not understand the assembly language, the descriptions of the services that are available, and how they are organized, are a key to understanding this computer. (While a listing of the BIOS services routines is included, a listing of the built-in BASIC language, ROM-BASIC, is not given. You can get a listing of that with the DOS command DEBUG, but the listing will not have any explanatory comments, and will be useless to anyone but a compulsive puzzle-solver.)

- two very nice tables explaining the complete 256 character codes used by the IBM/PC, and the function of the "attribute characters," which control the color of text displayed on the IBM/PC's screen.

The next most useful source of information is the manual which comes with the DOS operating system. The appendixes to the DOS manual are rich in useful information about diskette formats, the conventions for DOS service routines, file control blocks, program segment prefixes, and so forth. The DOS manual is generally poorer than most of our reference sources, for it does not provide comprehensive technical information about DOS. What this manual does cover provides very useful information and clues.

To understand the actual computer within the IBM/PC, you can turn to several reference books on the Intel 8086/8088 micro-processor. I have found two books particularly useful. For an understandable presentation of the philosophy behind the 8086 micro-processor and how it works, read The 8086/8088 Primer by Stephen P. Morse (Hayden, 1980). For more in-depth details about this micro-processor, turn to The 8086 Book, by Russell Rector and George Alexy (Osborne/McGraw-Hill, 1980).

For Pascal programming the reference book to use is the IBM Pascal Compiler manual. This is not a good introductory book on Pascal programming, but it is the only reference book for the particular features of IBM Pascal for the IBM/PC. To learn Pascal, choose one of the many beginner's Pascal books (computer stores are full of them). Or, if you learn things without any hand-holding, read the IBM Pascal Compiler manual cover to cover. For almost any technical detail that you need to know about using IBM Pascal, the information is either fully explained, or implied by the examples given. The authors of the IBM Pascal manual did a very good job, I think, of providing all the necessary clues to subjects that they could not explain in detail. (You can also learn a lot of Pascal by studying the Pascal examples that appear in this book, and by reading the short tutorial on Pascal in appendix 2.)

For assembly language programming, as with Pascal, use the IBM Macro Assembler manual for detailed reference. But don't expect to learn the machine language instruction set from the IBM manual. For that, turn to the two 8086 books mentioned above. The IBM Macro Assembler manual is especially bad about explaining things, and about providing necessary related information; but the manual is necessary to use the Macro Assembler. (Appendix 3 to this book covers the techniques of making the connection between Pascal and assembly language, and will give you many helpful clues towards getting started in assembly language.)

## 1.7 Some notes on notation

There are many ways to say things, and in the world of computers there are many confusing notations. In this book we'll try to be as simple, clear, and consistent as possible. If you find a term used that you don't understand, look for it in the narrative glossary in the first appendix to this book.

Here are some notes to clarify how we will refer to things here, in this book. First, let's consider numbers.

Numbers will always be given in the usual decimal digits that we all learned as children. Where it is useful, hexadecimal numbers will also be given, identified with the word "hex." Hexadecimal numbers are based on the number 16, and are very useful when discussing computers, since they are a convenient shorthand for the binary numbers that are so fundamental to computers. While there are ten decimal digits, 0 through 9, there are sixteen hexadecimal digits, 0 through 9 followed by A (with a value of ten), B, C, D, E, and finally F (with a value of fifteen). This book has 11 chapters (hex B); the Declaration of Independence was signed in 1776 (hex 6F0).

You may be puzzled why it is useful for this book to give numbers in both decimal and hex notation, particularly since nothing in the programming languages BASIC, Pascal, and Assembler require the use of hex. There are three reasons. One is that some numbers, particularly memory address locations, make more sense in hex notation. Another is that the DOS tool program DEBUG uses only hex notation. Finally, some of the literature on the IBM/PC, particularly the Technical Reference manual, makes extensive use of hex notation, often without warning. To help you relate the information here to information in other sources, we'll often give both decimal and hex versions of a number.

Another bit of computer jargon concerning numbers is the letter "K." "K" means exactly 1,024, so that 64 K is 64 times 1,024, or 65,536. The term K is used extensively because it is a handy abbreviation for a number that is roughly one thousand—so it's easy to understand that 64 K is approximately sixty-four thousand. The value of K, 1,024, is a round number in binary notation—two to the tenth power.

Occasionally we'll need to refer to characters by their index numbers, which range from 0 through 255. For this we'll use the BASIC language notation, for example CHR$(65), which is a capital "A." The Pascal way of saying the same thing is chr(65).

Next, let's consider bits. There is no end of confusion in referring to the individual bits which make up bytes and words. Different sources use different ways of referring to them, which makes life more difficult for us all. Three schemes are used most often, and I'll explain them here; it is hard to say which is best— we'll use the simplest. If you want to read much technical literature on computers you will need to be familiar with all three methods.

If you lay out the eight bits which make up a byte, with the "most significant" bit first, and the "least significant" bit last, then you can number them as 1st through 8th; you might call this notation "bit order." This is the notation that we will use—it is the simplest and clearest, but it has the disadvantage that it doesn't particularly mean anything. The other two methods pay attention to the numerical significance of the bit locations. The next method numbers the bits from right to left, the opposite from bit order, starting with zero. This is "bit power" notation, and it indicates the power of two to which each bit corresponds. This bit power notation is probably the most commonly used in technical literature. The final method, which we'll call "bit value", identifies each bit with the value of the power of two for its position.

Here is a table which outlines the three notations:

| Bit Order | Bit Power | Bit Value | Bit in an eight-bit byte |
|-----------|-----------|-----------|--------------------------|
| 1st | 7 | 128 | 10000000 |
| 2nd | 6 | 64 | 01000000 |
| 3rd | 5 | 32 | 00100000 |
| 4th | 4 | 16 | 00010000 |
| 5th | 3 | 8 | 00001000 |
| 6th | 2 | 4 | 00000100 |
| 7th | 1 | 2 | 00000010 |
| 8th | 0 | 1 | 00000001 |

As mentioned, we'll use the "bit order" notation in this book. The other two, particularly "bit power" notation, you'll run into elsewhere. The main use of "bit value" notation is to make clear how to relate the numeric value of a byte, and its bits. For example, in a program, you can set the 1st and 8th bits by setting a byte to the value 128 + 1. Each of these three notations can be extended from an eight-bit byte to a 16-bit word, and you may occasionally encounter them used that way.

```
1000 REM   Listing 1.1 -- A program to display all screen characters
1010 REM                    (C) Copyright 1983, Peter Norton
1020 REM
1030 GOSUB 2000   '  TITLE
1040 GOSUB 3000   '  GET WHICH DISPLAY TYPE, AND SET ADDRESS
1050 GOSUB 2000   '  SET THE TITLE AGAIN
1060 GOSUB 4000   '  BUILD THE SURROUNDING COMMENTS
1070 GOSUB 5000   '  BUILD THE DISPLAY ARRAY
1080 GOSUB 6000   '  FINISH UP AND RETURN TO DOS


2000 REM   Title subroutine
2010 KEY OFF : CLS : WIDTH 80
2020 REM
2030 PRINT "               Programs for INSIDE THE IBM PERSONAL COMPUTER"
2040 PRINT "                  (C) Copyright 1983 Peter Norton"
2050 PRINT
2060 PRINT "             Program 1-1: Demonstrate all screen characters"
2999 RETURN


3000 REM   Subroutine to inquire about display type
3010 PRINT
3020 PRINT "Before we go any further, is this a color-graphics display? ";
3030 GOTO 3060
3040 PRINT
3050 PRINT "  (answer Y or N)  ";
3060 ANSWER$ = INKEY$
3070 IF LEN(ANSWER$) < 1 THEN 3060
3080 IF LEN(ANSWER$) > 1 THEN 3040
3090 SEGVAL! = 0
3100 IF MID$(ANSWER$,1,1) = "Y" THEN SEGVAL! = &HB800   ' Color segment
3110 IF MID$(ANSWER$,1,1) = "y" THEN SEGVAL! = &HB800   ' Color segment
3120 IF MID$(ANSWER$,1,1) = "N" THEN SEGVAL! = &HB000   ' Monochrome segment
3130 IF MID$(ANSWER$,1,1) = "n" THEN SEGVAL! = &HB000   ' Monochrome segment
3140 IF SEGVAL! = 0 THEN 3040
3150 DEF SEG = SEGVAL!
3999 RETURN


4000 REM      subroutine to build the surrounding messages
4010 FOR HEX.DIGIT% = 0 TO 15
4020    LOCATE 6,HEX.DIGIT%  * 3 + 14
4030    PRINT HEX$(HEX.DIGIT%)
4040    LOCATE HEX.DIGIT%+8,8
4050    PRINT HEX$(HEX.DIGIT%)
4060 NEXT HEX.DIGIT%
4070 LOCATE ,,0
4999 RETURN


5000 REM      subroutine to set the display array
5010 FOR ROW% = 0 TO 15
5020    FOR COL% = 0 TO 15
5030       POKE (ROW% + 7) * 160 + COL% * 6+ 26, COL% + ROW% * 16
5040    NEXT COL%
5050 NEXT ROW%
5999 RETURN


6000 LOCATE 25,1,1
6010 PRINT "Press any key to return to DOS... ";
```

LISTING 1-1     11

```
6020 IF LEN(INKEY$) = O THEN 6020   '  wait for a keystroke
6030 CLS
6999 SYSTEM

9999 REM    End of program Listing 1-1
```

# 2

# The Hardware Story

In this chapter we'll take a look at the material side of the IBM Personal Computer, the equipment and circuitry, and the "chips" that make it work. The physical "hardware," as opposed to the program "software." This isn't a computer hardware book, so we won't go into very much detail. But we will cover enough to help you understand the key points of how the IBM/PC works, what optional equipment can be attached to the PC, and how those attachments relate and interact with the rest of the PC system.

A computer is very much like an automobile, in being made up of many component parts. And, like a car, you don't need to understand the parts to use the complete machine. Yet, if you want to understand the whole system, you have to have at least a rough understanding of how the parts work, and that is what we will cover in this chapter.

## 2.1 The brains behind the operation

The center of a computer system is its processor, the "brain" of a computer. It is the processor that has the ability to perform the instructions that make up a computer program. Personal computers use micro-processors, which have shrunk in size until they fit into a single plug-in circuit element, or "chip." The micro-processor used in the IBM/PC was designed and built by the Intel Corporation, which pioneered micro-processing years ago.

Our particular micro-processor is the Intel 8088, which is a little brother to a slightly different micro-processor, the 8086. The 8086 and our 8088 perform the same instructions, and from the point of view of a programmer they are identical (their differences appear only to a circuit designer, and we'll explain that shortly). Anything that you see written about programming the 8086 applies to the 8088 that our IBM/PC contains.

One principal thing that sets the IBM/PC apart from the previous generation of personal computers, is that its micro-processor is what is called a 16-bit processor. Before the IBM/PC, the most popular personal computers had used 8-bit processors, such as the the 6502, used in the Apple II, the 8080 and the Z80. The difference between 8- and 16-bit processors is somewhat fuzzy. The least important difference is what gives them their names: 8-bit processors generally can only manipulate data 8 bits at a time, while 16-bit processors can also perform operations on 16 bits at a time. Both kinds of processors can achieve the same results, and so that part of the distinction between them isn't very significant.

What really sets 16-bit processors apart from their 8-bit predecessors is a large number of improvements in their speed, the power and usefulness of their instruction sets (which 16-bit operations are a part of), and, most important of all, their memory addressing capacity. Many 8-bit processors were limited to using no more than 64 K of memory, an amount that falls short of what is really needed to make effective use of a personal computer. The 8088 processor used by the IBM/PC has the ability to address 1,024 K, or over one million bytes of memory. There is no limit to how much memory capacity you might want, but one million bytes is certainly enough to satisfy your needs.

So the biggest difference between our 8088 micro-processor and the 8-bit processors that went before it, is this: memory addressing capacity is no longer a severe limitation on what can be accomplished with a personal computer.

What is the difference between our 8088 micro-processor, and its big brother, the 8086? Inside, they are functionally the same—both perform the same instructions, use the same data, execute the same programs. But when they talk to the world around them, they differ. The 8086, as a 16-bit computer, communicates with the circuitry that supports it 16 bits at a time, while the 8088 passes data back and forth with the world around it 8 bits at a time. The key difference between the 8086 and the 8088 is the size of their external data path— the 8086 transfers data 16 bits at a time, and our 8088 transfers data 8 bits at a time. This has lead some people to say that the 8088 is not a true 16-bit computer—a claim that is partly true, but only partly. The 8088 uses true 16-bit architecture internally, but it doesn't use a 16-bit external data path.

The external data path that is used to pass data around the system is called a data bus, and we'll learn a little more about the bus in section 2.3. The 8088 uses an 8-bit data bus.

The practical difference between the 8086 and our 8088 is two-fold. First, when passing around more than one byte of data, the 8086 passes it twice as fast. This doesn't mean that the 8086 gets work done twice as fast, since only part of the time is the micro-processor waiting for data to pass to or from the world outside it—and some times it only wants one 8-bit byte anyway. But when the processor does spend time waiting for large amounts of data to pass, the 8086 will spend less time waiting, and get its work done faster.

The second practical difference is circuit design and the selection of components. It is easier to design 8-bit circuitry, and there are many inexpensive and very reliable 8-bit components available. So by using the 8088, IBM was able to simplify the PC, and reduce its cost, at a small sacrifice in computing speed.

## 2.2 A quick outline of the rest of the parts

To make the micro-processor work takes many supporting parts. Just as it takes more than an engine to make a car run, there is much more to a computer than its processor.

Many parts of a car are interchangeable with other models, and that is even more true with personal computers. Very few of the working parts of the IBM/PC were custom made for it—in fact most of the PC is made up of quite standard, off-the-shelf components, beginning with the Intel 8088 micro-processor. What makes the IBM/PC distinct is the particular way that the parts were designed into a complete functioning system. The electronics industry provides computer designers with a tool box full of standard parts, and the designer's task is to put them together in a useful way.

Describing computer design that way may make it sound as though there is little to the job of designing, and little difference between computers. That would be like saying that great writing consists of using words found in the dictionary. Personal computers, including the IBM/PC, do consist largely of standard parts; but the key ingredient is the way the parts fit together.

There are three ways to look at all the parts of the IBM/PC—by where they are located, by what they do, and by how they talk to each other. Let's look at location first.

Physically the parts of the IBM/PC are divided into the system-board components, and the expansion-board components. All the major circuit parts that come with each and every IBM/PC are located on a large board called the system board. (Apple computers use the more colorful term mother board.) On the system board is everything necessary to make the computer work without any added options. It includes the micro-processor, the first 64 K of memory, and built-in programs, such as the core of BASIC, in read-only-memory chips. Most of the components that we'll cover in the next section, "What those other chips do," are located on the system board. Figure 2.1 shows a simplified drawing of the system board, with the more interesting parts pointed out.

The system board lies flat at the bottom of the PC's enclosing cabinet. It occupies the full length of the cabinet, front to back, and about two-thirds of the width. If you open the cabinet of your PC and look inside, you will see the system board lying at the bottom. If you look towards the center rear of the board, you will see the largest of all the circuit components in the IBM/PC—the 8088 micro-processor itself.

The right-hand side of the system board fits underneath the left-hand diskette drive, but the space above the left-hand side of the system board is open—to accommodate the expansion boards. The left rear corner of the system board has five open connectors, called expansion slots, which are used to connect any optional equipment that is

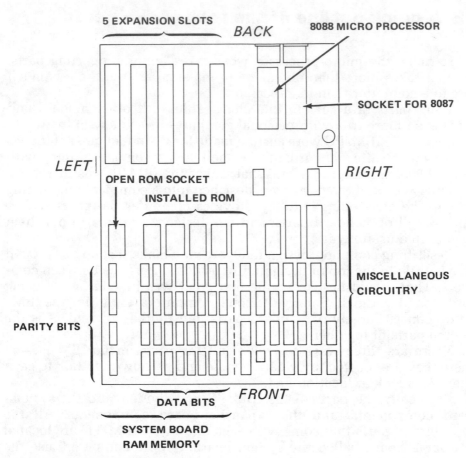

Figure 2.1—IBM PC System Board.

attached to the PC. Expansion boards plug vertically into these slots, and extend forward above the system board.

The expansion boards—or cards, as they are sometimes called—can be used to support anything that can be attached to the IBM/PC. Their use falls into two main categories: memory additions and equipment additions. If any add-on equipment fits into a circuit board then it sits right inside the cabinet of the PC. If the equipment doesn't fit inside—such as a display screen—then the circuitry to support the equipment is placed on the expansion card, and a connection is made outside the back of the PC's cabinet to the external equipment. Each expansion slot has its own covered opening in the rear of the cabinet, to allow external connections.

The system board belongs to IBM, and the expansion boards belong to the world. Everything on the system board is placed there by IBM design, while almost anything can be designed into an expansion board, provided that it follows IBM's ground rules concerning size, electrical connections, heat and so forth. A look at the products advertised as additions to the IBM/PC will show you an astonishing variety of things that can be stuffed into a single expansion board.

## 2.3 What those other chips do

It may not be of much use to you, but it is interesting to know what the main circuit components of the IBM/PC do for a living, and so we'll take a look at them in this section. When one of these parts has some significance that we will touch on in the rest of the book, I'll specifically mention it—otherwise you can assume that the facts and specifications in this section can be quietly forgotten.

Basic timing signals are provided to the system by an 8284A clock generator chip. These signals are used by the entire computer system to control the length of operations. Related to the clock is a timer chip, the 8255A-5, which is used in support of both the cassette interface and the built-in speaker. In Chapter 11, when we cover how to control the speaker, we'll see how to "program" the 8255A-5 to produce sounds on the speaker.

Interrupts are a fundamental part of the operation of a computer system, and we'll explain how they work in the next chapter. The 8259A interrupt controller chip is used to supervise the operation of interrupts.

Whenever data is passed around inside the PC system, it travels on a common data path that all the system components have access to—the data bus. The concept of a bus is one of the cleverest unifying techniques in computer design. Instead of trying to make all the special-purpose connections that might be needed among all the system components, the designers of computers put all data traffic onto a common bus. Data travels on the bus, together with signals indicating its purpose. This idea introduces a tremendous simplicity into computer design, and a great deal of flexibility. To add a new component, you don't need to make a lot of special connections, you just hook the component up to the bus. As you might imagine, traffic on the bus could get quite chaotic, so the 8288 bus controller chip keeps order on the bus.

All the components mentioned so far are on the system board. When we look at the main expansion boards, we find some other interesting parts. There are two types of display adapters for the IBM/PC. One is made to control the IBM monochrome display, and the other is made to control color-graphics displays (or simple monochrome displays that can be connected to the color-graphics adapter). Although the two types of displays operate differently, and have very different capabilities, the same main circuit chip controls them. The 6845 CRT controller is the main part of both display adapters.

On the diskette adapter board, a diskette controller chip is used to supervise the diskette drives. This chip is the NEC PD765 floppy disk controller, or its equivalent. (If you study the ROM listings for diskette control that appear in the IBM Technical Reference manual, and run across some cryptic references to "the NEC," they are talking about this controller chip.) Although this book will not go into that level of detail, it is possible to gain direct control of the diskette drives by issuing commands to this controller, and the Technical Reference manual gives the specifics of the NEC commands.

## 2.4 How the expansion slots work

Each add-on option for the IBM/PC plugs into one of the expansion slots, where there are 62 connecting wires. These 62 lines provide all the signals that are needed for any equipment that might be attached to the PC. The 62 lines operate in parallel, so that any expansion board can be plugged into any of the five expansion slots. Any signal sent to one expansion board will be seen by them all, since they are all connected to common signal lines. This is an extension of the idea of a common data bus; all the expansion boards use a common 62-line connection, called the I/O channel.

The specific uses of the 62 lines break down into four categories. First, eight of the lines are used to provide electrical power to the expansion cards, at various voltage levels.

Next, another eight of the lines are used to pass the eight bits of the data bus. All data passes through this bus, whether it is going to or from memory or input/output devices, such as the display screen.

The next 20 lines are dedicated to addressing. When data is passed to and from memory or an input/output device, an address must be specified, indicating the memory address location or the device number. For memory use, all 20 lines are used to indicate which of the 1,024 K memory locations is being addressed. For input/output devices, nine of the address lines are used, allowing up to 512 different devices to be addressed.

The remainder of the channel lines are used to pass basic control signals. An example of these signals are the memory-read-command, the memory-write-command, and the read and write commands for input/output devices.

Each piece of equipment attached to the expansion slots is constantly looking at the I/O channel signals. For example, suppose that an I/O read command is given, indicated by the appearance of a signal on the I/O read command line. When that happens, all the I/O devices pay attention to the address lines, while the memory circuitry ignores them (since no memory command was given). If a memory command had been issued, the reverse would happen—the I/O devices would ignore the address lines, and the memory circuits would take a look at the address given. Since an I/O command was requested, each I/O device takes a look at the address lines. If its address comes up, then the device springs into action—otherwise, it cools its heels.

And that is how the expansion slots, and expansion boards, work.

## 2.5  Other things that you need to know about your hardware

There are several interesting odds and ends to know about the system board on the IBM/PC.

First, there are two sets of switches buried inside the PC. These are known as the system configuration DIP switches. ("DIP" refers to the way they are mounted on the circuit board.) These switches are set to indicate what equipment is attached to the PC, such as the number of diskette drives, how much memory is available, and so forth. These switches do not actually control anything—their use is strictly conventional. When the IBM/PC is turned on, the start-up programs in the PC read the settings of the switches, and then, in turn, set some standard memory locations to reflect what the switches were set to. Later, when any program needs to know how much memory is installed, or how many diskette drives there are, the information in those memory locations is checked. (Using the memory to hold the information from the switch settings is a clever idea that makes it possible for the information to be changed, when appropriate, by a program. In effect, a program can change the switch settings, and seemingly change the list of equipment attached, by changing the record in memory.)

As you can see, the use of these system configuration switches is "logical" rather than "physical." Changing the switch settings doesn't actually connect or disconnect any equipment—it simply changes the program's knowledge about what equipment is attached.

Next, let's consider the co-processor. When the 8088 micro-processor was designed, it included the ability to do ordinary integer arithmetic, but not what is called floating-point, or "real", arithmetic—what in BASIC is called single and double precision arithmetic. Floating-point arithmetic was left to be done either of two ways. The first and most common way was by programming—with subroutines which use logical operations and integer arithmetic to produce floating-point results. The other way was to use a specialized co-processor.

The 8088 micro-processor was designed to use a companion processor, the Intel 8087 co-processor. The 8087 has a specialty—fast work with floating point numbers. It has the ability to do ordinary addition, subtraction, multiplication and division, and also more exotic operations, such as calculating trigonometric functions. Special signals were incorporated into the design, to allow the 8088 to pass work over to the 8087, and receive results back. To make use of the 8087 a computer must have both processors, and it must have programs which make use of the special codes needed to activate the 8087. While IBM did not provide the 8087 with the original PC, it did allow for its use by providing a socket in the system board to accommodate it. If you look inside your PC or at figure 2.1, in the center rear next to the 8088 chip, you will find an open socket for the 8087.

The design of the 8086/8088 actually allows for two main ways to add more computing horsepower. One is the 8087 co-processor, which IBM has provided for, with an open socket in the system board. The other is multi-processing, where two or more regular micro-processors co-operate, sharing the computing work load. IBM did not make provision for this kind of multi-processing in the design of the PC. Another auxiliary chip, the 8089 input/output processor, can increase the overall work capacity of an 8086/8088-based computer, but like multi-processing, it was not included in the design of the IBM/PC.

Finally, let's consider one more open socket on the IBM/PC system board. The programs that are built into the PC are stored in Read-Only-Memory (ROM) chips, located about midway from front to back on the system board, towards the left-hand side. There are five of them, as you will see in figure 2.1 or inside your own PC. Next to them, on the left, is an open socket. This ROM memory socket has been left available for the addition of more built-in programs. The purpose of this socket is a matter for speculation. I can see three intelligent guesses about what IBM intended it for. First, it can be a safety net—if errors were found in any of the ROM routines which required an expansion beyond the current size, this socket (and the memory address locations which implicitly go with it), could accommodate corrections. Second, if IBM wished to add support for new devices, such as high-capacity disk storage, then this socket could hold the related ROM programs. However, the expansion circuit board for any new devices could also contain any needed ROM programs, so this socket isn't really necessary for that purpose. The third, and perhaps most likely possibility is 8087 support. With an open socket to accommodate the 8087 arithmetic co-processor, it is reasonable to expect a ROM socket to accomodate programs that support the 8087. It is likely that such programs would give the PC's built-in ROM BASIC access to the 8087's power, and they might also provide support for the use of the 8087 by other languages, such as Pascal, Fortran, and compiled BASIC.

## 2.6 Three circles again

Everything we have said so far in this chapter applies strictly to the original IBM/PC, our first circle of interest. For IBM/PC-like computers, only some of the information above will apply, and it will vary from computer to computer. The one thing most likely to be the same among all PC-like computers is the form of the expansion slot connections. This is the area where PC-like computers will closely mimic the IBM/PC.

In the world of large computers, there long ago emerged a world of so-called plug compatible components. Plug compatible components could replace some part of the whole system, by unplugging the original, and plugging in the replacement. This happened on both sides of the plugs—either the computer peripheral equipment, or the computer processor could be replaced.

The same thing is happening with the IBM/PC. Wherever there is a plug, you will find competing replacement parts on both sides of the plug. The one thing that is stable is the format of the plug—it's the only thing that doesn't get replaced. And so, for PC-like computers, the expansion slot format will be the one thing that they all have most in common with the IBM/PC.

For our third circle of interest, the circle of computers which, like the IBM/PC, use some form of the MS-DOS operating system, nothing that we have said so far in this chapter necessarily applies. However, when we look at the significance of the optional equipment attached to a personal computer in the next section, what we have to say about the IBM/PC is equally true for all personal computers.

## 2.7 The significance of your equipment—several different IBM/PC's

In this section, we'll take a short look at what it means to have different combinations of optional equipment attached to an IBM/PC. There is more significance to the equipment that you attach to your IBM/PC than most people realize. An IBM/PC is an IBM/PC, and equipping it with one set of options or another doesn't change that. But in practice, the kind of equipment that you attach to your PC makes a significant change in the focus of how it can best be used.

This is an idea that hasn't gotten very much attention, and so I would like to put forth an idea that, from the very beginning, there have been three or four distinctly different IBM Personal Computers.

The three or four different IBM/PC's that I am referring to, are simply the familiar IBM/PC, with different equipment attached; equipment that leads the machine in different directions. The different versions of the PC are:

● THE TOY. This is the IBM/PC with no disk storage, the "cassette system." This configuration, I think, was never taken seriously by anyone, and probably never should have existed. I'm convinced that it was set up only to create a stripped-down, rock-bottom price for the machine, so that advertised prices wouldn't scare off the timid. The toy cassette version could hardly be used for anything, and crippled this powerful machine so it was something comparable to the game computers of Atari and Mattel. The proof of the silliness of this toy system is the lack of cassette programs for it on the market. The only virtue of this toy system is that it was a place to start, before upgrading to serious equipment.

The next two versions of the PC have been the mainstream of the IBM/PC in its early days. These two form the heart of my argument that, in some degree, there isn't one IBM/PC with various equipment, but several fairly different IBM/PC's.

- THE BUSINESS MACHINE. This is an IBM/PC with a monochrome display screen, preferably IBM's own display screen. Naturally this machine will have appropriate equipment attached—two diskette drives, a printer, and maybe some other gear. But what sets this machine apart is its display screen. There are no graphics, just characters; and, if the IBM monochrome display is used, very easy to read characters. The focus of this machine is office work. The screen can be looked at all day without eyestrain. The uses of this machine are typically business accounting (for example, using the Peachtree accounting packages) or financial planning (for example, using VisiCalc) or writing, using a word processing program.

- THE GRAPHICS MACHINE. This is an IBM/PC with a color graphics display screen, and again appropriate equipment, including diskettes. The focus of this machine is access to graphics, with a sacrifice of the legibility of the display of characters. The uses of this machine are harder to put into simple categories, but they include engineering and architectural drawings, business charts and graphs, animation and graphics games.

I am claiming that "the business machine" and "the graphics machine" are separate IBM Personal Computers, because they will tend to be used for very different purposes. And, more important, the software products for them also tend to be separately focused. Now, it is true that business programs, which have character displays, will run on color-graphics machines, with the cost of a little eye-strain. But that misses this point: users of these two versions of the PC are often distinctly different in what they use a computer for. Certainly any programs developed for the graphics capabilities of the color-graphics system cannot be used on a business system.

This partial split between the intended uses of business-system IBM/PC's and graphics-system IBM/PC's make them, in effect, quite different machines, with their own market place for products, and their own community of users. Now, for all IBM/PC systems, there is a great deal of common ground in equipment, software products and user interest, so the differences shouldn't be belabored. Yet there is also more of a split between graphics and business IBM/PC's than most people realize. My point in discussing this split is to help you be aware of a dividing line that is too little understood.

To finish off this theory, let's take a look at one more distinct IBM/PC computer—a version that IBM didn't create, but one that is very important to the future of this computer system:

- THE WINCHESTER MACHINE. This is an IBM/PC with a high-capacity, fast-access disk storage system attached. These disk storage systems are commonly called "hard disk" (to distinguish them from "floppy" diskettes) or "winchester disks" (after the code name, years ago, of the IBM project that developed the technology that they use). The distinctive feature of a winchester-equipped IBM/PC is that it has plenty of storage capacity: enough capacity to hold the complete business information of a small company; enough to hold the patient records of a doctor's or dentist's office; enough to hold a research data base. In short, a winchester-equipped PC has enough storage capacity to put a great deal of data immediately on tap to the computer.

It doesn't take very much use of an IBM/PC to realize that the main limiting factor in the speed, power and usefulness of this machine is disk data storage. The computing speed of the 8088 micro-processor used in the IBM/PC is, for most purposes, quite fast. (If you have any programs that you consider slow running, it is most likely due to an inefficient implementation. The most common examples of this are any programs which use the interpretive BASIC.)

The memory capacity of the IBM/PC is very good as well, and certainly much higher than previous personal computers. Most former personal computers were limited to 64 K of memory total, while the IBM/PC easily provides 256 K or more for you to use, plus a lot of free memory. (I say "free" because special memory is dedicated for the use of the display screens, the BASIC interpreter, and the "BIOS" control programs; the memory used by these parts of the system doesn't come out of PC's main complement of memory. In the next chapter we'll see where this memory is, and learn how to explore it.)

The limits of the power of the IBM/PC are found in the speed and capacity of the diskette storage attached to it. The solution to that limitation is winchester-type hard disk systems. Typically, a winchester disk will provide from 2 to 25 million bytes of storage; the equivalent of from 12 to 150 single-sided diskettes. Plus, winchester access speed is much faster than floppy diskette access speed.

So it is with winchester hard disks that the fourth and probably most important IBM/PC emerges. We can legitimately consider a winchester IBM/PC a separate version of the computer, because what it can do is really a dimension apart from the other systems. Only with the capacity of a winchester disk (or its equivalent) can a computer hold a data base of serious content, or encompass the entire business records of a company. Winchesters turn personal computers into either complete business machines, or real data access tools. Winchesters greatly magnify the potential of the IBM/PC.

When the IBM/PC was first introduced, IBM did not provide, or support, the attachment of winchesters to the IBM/PC, but disk manufacturers quickly provided both the disk equipment and the program support to set up winchester IBM/PC's. This is why, initially, the winchester system did and didn't exist: it was in a kind of limbo without IBM's official blessing. But if the IBM/PC is going to realize its full potential, then winchester disks (or some equivalent high-capacity, fast-access storage medium) will become a component in a significant proportion of IBM/PC's.

While I don't want to make too much of the idea that differently equipped PC's are, in effect, quite different computers, you should realize that there is a degree of truth in the theory. Recognizing the significance of the differences among various equipment configurations can be very useful in any planning concerning the IBM/PC and its uses.

Before we end this discussion of the significance of equipment attached to IBM/PCs, we ought to give some recognition to the humble asynchronous communications adapter. The communications adapter is such an ordinary, and unrevolutionary, piece of equipment, that no one makes much fuss over it. Yet, the most exciting prospects for personal computers lie with network connections. And the path to a network connection is the communications adapter—so it may well be the most significant optional attachment of all.

# 3

# How the IBM/PC Thinks and Remembers

In this chapter we'll take a look at the brains of the IBM/PC, the 8088 micro-processor—how it thinks, how it uses its memory, and how it relates to the world around it. If you have heard of, and been puzzled by, such computer terms as interrupt, stack, and port, here you'll learn what they are all about.

Just about everything in this chapter applies fully to our three circles of interest. That's because what we are talking about is the inner workings of the 8086/8088 micro-processor, which is common to the IBM/PC, PC-like computers, and the MS-DOS family of computers.

## 3.1   Memory, part 1: what it is and how it's read

A key ingredient in a computer's ability to operate is memory. The memory inside a computer is a place to store information while it is being worked on. The internal memory of a computer is a temporary work-space; in contrast, external storage, such as a diskette file, is a place for keeping data from day to day. The internal memory is transient—anything placed in memory will be forgotten when the computer is turned off, and none of your own information is kept in memory permanently.

By analogy to office work, the micro-processor is an office worker, and the computer memory is the worker's desk-top: the work space used, temporarily, to get things done. To complete the analogy, a diskette is the computer's filing cabinet, where information is kept when it's not being worked on.

Computer memory is organized as many storage locations where values can be kept; each location is identified by an address. How big the locations are, and what kind of values can be stored in them, varies from computer to computer. Some older computers have very large-sized memory locations, some even as large as 64 bits to each location.

On this kind of computer, the large locations are called "words" (but this type of computer shouldn't be confused with word-processing computers, which are something else entirely). The Cray super-computers and Univac computers are all word-oriented.

The difficulty with a large word-size is that often the programs running on computers need to work with much less than a full word of information, and this can be clumsy on a word-oriented computer. So most modern computers, including all personal computers, use a much smaller sized storage location—one made up of only 8 bits, and called a "byte." A byte is a very handy-sized unit of information, partly because it is just the right size to hold a single letter of the alphabet, or character. Since a byte is the right size to store a character, the terms "byte" and "character" are sometimes used interchangeably.

Since our IBM/PC uses storage locations that are eight bits, or one byte, in size, they can hold any value that can be expressed in eight bits. This allows for two to the eighth power of possible values, 256 in all. The significance, or meaning, of the value stored in a byte depends upon what use is being made of it: for one use a particular value means one thing, and for another use the same value can mean something else entirely. By itself, a byte could be considered to hold the coding for an alphabetic character—what is called an ASCII code. Or it could be considered to be a number; and as a number, the 256 possible values could be taken as positive numbers, ranging from 0 to 255, or as a signed range of numbers from -128 through +127. On the other hand, a single byte could be used as a part of a larger amount of data, such as a string of characters, or a two-byte number.

To manipulate character data in a sensible way, a computer needs to have the characters translated into byte values in a well-organized code. Most computers, including the IBM/PC, use ASCII, the American Standard Code for Information Interchange. (Most of IBM's computers use another character coding scheme, known as EBCDIC; ASCII and EBCDIC are organized differently, but it is not difficult to translate from one to the other.)

ASCII assigns numeric values to all the conventionally used characters, such as letters of the alphabet, both upper and lower case, numeric digits, and punctuation symbols. ASCII also reserves a small number of codes for control purposes, such as indicating the end of a string of characters; these special control codes mostly appear in the character codes CHR$(0) through CHR$(31). There are some peculiarities in how the IBM/PC treats these special control codes; the fourth appendix to this book discusses them.

Properly speaking, ASCII is only a 7-bit code, with 128 possible code values. Standard ASCII normally uses the first 128 of the 256 possible byte values. Various other purposes are assigned to the remaining 128 code values, to make up an "extended ASCII" character set. There are no standards for what the extended codes should be used for, and different computer devices use them differently. For the PC display screen, IBM used the extended ASCII codes to represent symbols used in languages other than English, plus various mathematical symbols, and shapes that can be used for drawing. The program given in listing 1.1 will show all the IBM's special display symbols, and Chapter 8 will discuss more about how they are organized.

The matrix printer that is standard for the IBM/PC, the Epson MX-80 printer, translates the extended ASCII character codes into printed shapes that are different than the display characters the IBM/PC display screen shows. If you run program 1.1, and then use the Print-Screen operation to copy the screen to an Epson printer, you will be able to compare the screen and printer versions of the same extended ASCII codes.

You can find tables of the standard ASCII codes and the IBM/PC extended ASCII codes in many places. One appears in the back of the BASIC manual. A very useful form of the table is given in the IBM Technical Reference manual, appendix C.

So far we have considered the uses of the IBM/PC's memory one byte at a time, but often several bytes are used together to represent more complex values than one byte can accommodate. When strings of characters are needed, they are stored one character per byte, in adjacent memory locations; the first, or left-most, character of a string is stored in the first byte, the one with the lowest address location.

When integer numbers larger than a single byte are needed, they are stored in several bytes, also in adjacent locations. The most common format uses two bytes, or 16 bits, which is a very convenient size for a 16-bit micro-processor like the IBM/PC's 8088. In the terminology of the 8088, a two-byte integer is called a word. Many of the instructions in the 8088 are tailor-made for manipulating 16-bit numbers. Longer formats can be used—three, four or more bytes—but this is not as common as two-byte numbers, and requires some special programming to handle.

When numbers of two bytes or more are stored in the 8088's memory, they are placed with the least significant byte first, which is the opposite from what many computer-experienced people are accustomed to. If any of your programs operate on individual bytes in memory, then you should be aware of this storage convention.

The 8087 arithmetic co-processor uses several special formats, including four byte integers, floating-point numbers in three sizes—two bytes, four bytes and a huge ten-byte format—and also a twenty-digit decimal format. The 8088 doesn't use these formats directly, but when the 8087 co-processor is added to the PC, these formats become an extended part of the 8088's repertoire of data formats.

## 3.2 Memory, part 2: what's your address

Every memory location has an address that is used to locate it. Addresses are numbers, beginning with zero for the first address location, and extending onward to the highest address location. Since addresses are numbers, the computer uses its ability to do arithmetic to calculate and manipulate memory addresses.

Each computer design has its own limitations on how big addresses can be. The highest possible number for an address determines the size of the address space of the computer, or how much memory it could use. Normally a particular computer has less actual memory attached than the address space allows. If a computer design has a small address space, it can be a severe limit on the problem-solving capacity of the computer.

The IBM/PC makes use of the full address space of its microprocessor's design. In the 8088 addresses are twenty bits long, and so the processor has an address space of two to the twentieth power, 1,024 K, or over one million bytes.

Having that big an address space allowed IBM to be liberal in its use of memory, and to dedicate some portions of memory to special purposes, which we will see in the next section. Before we go into that, though, we'll look at how a 16-bit computer is able to work with 20-bit addresses, and what effect it has in placing limits on your programs.

Most of the arithmetic that the 8088 can do is limited to manipulating 16 bit words, which have a range from 0 to 65,535, or 64 K. Since complete addresses are 20 bits long, some practical method had to be devised to control 20 bits, working 16 bits at a time. The solution was found in an idea known as segmented addressing.

If you take a 16-bit number, and add four binary zeros after it, you have a 20-bit number, which could be used as a 20-bit address. By adding four zeros, or shifting the number four binary places, you have effectively multiplied the number by 16, and its value can now range as high as 1,024 K. Unfortunately, with those four zeros, such a 20-bit number can only specify one out of every 16 memory locations—the one whose 20-bit address ends in four zeros. All the other locations which have addresses that end in any of the other 15 possible combinations of four bits can't be specified by that kind of addressing method.

To complete the solution to the problem of 20-bit addressing, two 16-bit numbers are used. The first is considered to have four binary zeros tacked onto its end, so that it is 20 bits long; this number is called the segment part of the address. The second 16-bit number isn't shifted four binary places—it is used as is; this number is called the relative part of the address. Added together, the two numbers make up a complete 20-bit address, that can locate any of the 1,024 K bytes in the IBM/PC's address space. The segment value specifies a location that is a multiple of 16, a location that is called a paragraph boundary. The relative value specifies an exact location some relative distance from the paragraph. Figure 3.1 diagrams how this is done.

To make things clearer, let's go over that again. A complete 20-bit address is specified in two parts, both made up of 16-bit words. The segment part of the address specification is treated as if it had four binary zeroes (or one hex zero) after it, making it 20 bits long. This segment part can refer to any part of the entire one million byte address

Ordinary 16-bit Address Register;

| 1 | 2 | 3 | 4 | 16-bits (4 hex digits)
4 bits per hex digit

Offset Segment Register

| 5 | 6 | 7 | 8 | 0

Segment Register and Address Register Combined

| 5 | 6 | 7 | 8 | 0 | Implied hex-0

| 1 | 2 | 3 | 4 |

| 5 | 7 | 9 | B | 4 | Result - a 20-bit Address

**Figure 3.1—Memory Addressing.**

space—but it can only point to a sixteen byte boundary, that is, to an address that ends in four zero bits. The relative part of the address specification is added to the segmented part, so that a complete address is made. The relative part of the address can specify any memory location that follows where the segment part points to—any location, that is, up to 64 K away from the segment location.

While the relative part of the address is only needed to specify the last four bits of the 20-bit address, the relative part of the address can have any value from 0 to one less than 64 K. And most manipulation of memory addresses is done with the relative part, not with the segment part. In effect the segment part of an address becomes a base location for a 64 K working area, which the relative part can address.

There is a conventional way of expressing a segmented address, which you will see in use by the DEBUG program (which we will show you in Chapter 6), and in assembler listings, such as the one that appears in the IBM Technical Reference manual, appendix A. The segment part of the address is written first, followed by a colon, and then the relative part of the address. As an example, if we had a segment part that was, in hex, 2222, and a relative part that was 3333, then the segmented address would be written 2222:3333. The actual 20-bit address value, in hex, would be 25553 by this simple addition:

$$
\begin{array}{r}
22220 \\
+\ \ 3333 \\
\hline
25553. \\
\end{array}
$$

(At the end of this section, we'll give you some examples of manipulating segmented addresses, in BASIC and Pascal.)

To make use of these segmented addresses, the 8088 micro-processor has special segment registers dedicated to holding the segment part of addresses. With some value loaded in a segment register, it is possible to address any of the 64 K memory locations that follow. Without changing the segment register, the computer has temporary working address space of 64 K, located within its complete 1024 K address space. By changing the segment register, any location can be addressed.

To make it possible to work with more than 64 K at a time, the 8088 has four different segment registers—each of them with a special use. A computer uses its memory for several different purposes—some of it is used to hold a program, and some of it is used to hold the data that the program is working on. So two of the segment registers are dedicated to program code and to data. To locate the program, or code segment, the CS register is used. For the data segment, the DS register is used. For a special use of memory known as the stack (which we'll cover in section 3.6 below), there is a stack segment register, SS. Finally, to provide some extra addressing capacity, there is an extra segment register, ES.

When a program is prepared to be run, the operating system, such as DOS, decides which paragraph locations will be used for the programs code, data and stack. The segment registers CS, DS and SS are set to point to those locations. When it is running, the program makes use of the segment register values to find its way through memory.

Understand that these four segment registers don't have to be referring to memory that is located far apart. They can point anywhere, to locations that are near or far, or even at the same paragraphs. If there are only a few thousand bytes of program and data needed, the code and data segments will be placed close together. And although the working portions of the code and data segments are distinct, the 64 K spaces addressed by their segment registers can overlap. Figure 3.2 illustrates how the three segments—code, data, and stack—might be used, and how segment spaces can overlap.

If a program doesn't change its segment registers, then it is limited to using only 64 K of data, and having only 64 K of program code. On the other hand, if a program manipulates the segment registers, then it could work on data of any size, up to 1024 K. Either style of operation could be used, but in practice the data segment register is left fixed, and the code segment register is changed as needed. This particular way of doing things is encouraged by the 8088 instruction set, which provides particularly convenient mechanisms for loading the CS code segment register, through using the FAR CALL and FAR RETurn instructions.

The practical result of this is that DOS and the programming language processors use coding conventions that allow programs to grow

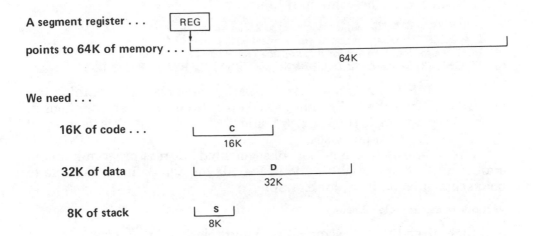

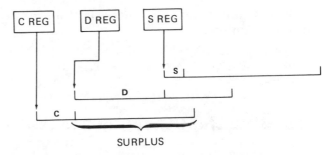

**Figure 3.2—Code, Data, and Stack Segments.**

to any size, while their addressable data space is limited to 64 K. If you use either Pascal or compiled BASIC, you will find this the case. For the interpreter BASIC that is built into the IBM/PC, the interpreter is the actual program that is running, and what you think of as your BASIC program is actually part of the interpreter's data. So, for interpreter BASIC, the size of your program and its data, combined, are limited to the 64 K that the DS data segment register covers at one time.

Both BASIC and Pascal give you the ability to manipulate segmented addresses, to a limited degree. You can't directly play around with the segment registers, CS, DS, SS and ES—the programming language has to maintain control over them, or things would become a complete mess. But our programs are allowed to work with segmented addressing somewhat.

In BASIC, here is how it is done. A segment paragraph can be specified with the DEF SEG statement. Some of the BASIC features, for

example PEEK and POKE, work relative to whatever segment paragraph has been set with DEF SEG.

For example, if we take the address shown above as 2222:3333,
BASIC can access the value in it this way:

```
10   DEF SEG = &H2222 ' set the segment to 2222 in hex
20   X = PEEK (&H3333) ' grab the value offset 3333 in hex
30   REM just for fun, let's test for a lower case letter, and capitalize it
40   IF (CHR$(X) >= "a") AND (CHR$(X) <= "z") THEN POKE &H3333, (X-32)
```

So in BASIC you can access any part of memory by a combination
of DEF SEG and the PEEK and POKE operations. You can see them in
action in program listings 1.1, 3.1 and 8.1, which use this feature of
BASIC for different purposes.

Pascal allows the same sort of segmented address programming, in
a more unified and flexible way. In Pascal, you can define a variable to
be a segmented address, for example

```
VAR address_example : adsmem;
```

and then directly set its segment ('.s') and relative ('.r') parts:

```
address_example.s := #2222;
address_example.r := #3333;
```

With that done, you can access or store memory, using the segmented
address pointer:

```
x := address_example^;
if (chr(x) >= "a") and (chr(x) <= "z") then
   address_example^ := x - 32;
```

## 3.3 How the PC organizes its memory

With over a million bytes of address space, the IBM/PC has a gen-
erous supply of space, which gives it much more flexibility concerning
memory use than smaller personal computers. This million-byte potential is organized in an interesting way. On the one hand, it is very useful
to be able to reserve parts of it for special purposes. On the other hand,
reserving memory locations can put restrictions on what can be done
with the computer. What was done for the IBM/PC was to reserve several ranges of the highest memory locations for special purposes, and
keep all the low memory locations free for open use. This achieved the
benefits of reserved blocks of memory, while keeping as much of the
address space as possible open for ordinary use.

Figure 3.3 is a simple outline of the allocation of memory. The top
quarter of memory, from segment paragraph, in hex, C000 up to the end,
is informally reserved for use by read-only-memory, or ROM. (All our
reference to paragraph addresses in this section will be in hexadecimal,
which we won't keep mentioning.) Only the highest part is actually
occupied by information stored in ROM. The top 8 K, from paragraph
FE00, is used by the ROM-BIOS, which we will cover in detail begin-

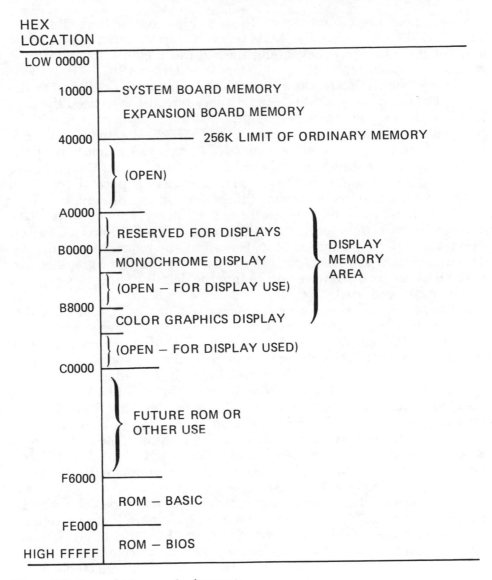

HEX
LOCATION

LOW 00000

10000 —— SYSTEM BOARD MEMORY

EXPANSION BOARD MEMORY

40000 ——————— 256K LIMIT OF ORDINARY MEMORY

} (OPEN)

A0000

RESERVED FOR DISPLAYS

B0000

MONOCHROME DISPLAY                    DISPLAY
                                      MEMORY
} (OPEN — FOR DISPLAY USE)            AREA

B8000

COLOR GRAPHICS DISPLAY

} (OPEN — FOR DISPLAY USED)

C0000

} FUTURE ROM OR
   OTHER USE

F6000

ROM — BASIC

FE000

ROM — BIOS

HIGH FFFFF

**Figure 3.3—General Memory Assignments.**

ning in Chapter 6. The ROM-BIOS contains all the fundamental service routines that are built into the IBM/PC, including the test programs that are executed when the computer is first turned on.

The next lower 32 K is used to hold the ROM-BASIC, the version of BASIC that is built into the PC. ROM-BASIC starts at paragraph F600 and ends where ROM-BIOS begins. In Chapter 6 we will snoop around a bit inside the ROM-BASIC.

Any of the rest of memory could be used for additional ROM data, but to follow the general ground-rules for IBM/PC memory usage, any ROM should be located above paragraph C000. You'll recall from Chapter 2 that there are 5 ROM chips plugged into the IBM/PC's system board, and one open ROM socket. These 5 chips contain the ROM-BIOS and ROM-BASIC, with 8 K of ROM on each chip. Another 8 K could be plugged into the open socket, and the natural memory location for it would be at paragraph F400, just before the ROM-BASIC.

Below the ROM area, is a large block of memory dedicated to the support of the display screens. Any display screen has to keep the data that it is displaying somewhere; either inside the screen, or inside the computer to which it is connected. In the IBM/PC, the display memory is part of the computer's address space (although this memory is physically located on the expansion board for the display). In Chapter 8 we will see more about why this display memory is part of the main address space, and the interesting things that we can do with it.

The display memory block begins at paragraph address B000, extends for 64 K up to paragraph C000, and is divided into two halves. The lower half, at paragraph B000, is used by the monochrome display. The upper half, at paragraph B800, is used by the color-graphics display. In Chapters 8 and 9 we will go into the details of how this memory is structured and used.

Neither of the two display adapters need, or use, the full 32 K that is allotted to them. The monochrome display only uses 4 K, and the color-graphics uses 16 K. The left-over amounts may remain unused, or they may be used in the future for enhanced display formats.

Actually more memory is reserved for display adapters than just the 64 K block from paragraph B000 to C000. The 64 K block below it, is also reserved. According to IBM documentation, the A000 block is reserved in two ways. The first 16 K, from A000 to A400, is mysteriously reserved, with no indication of its intended purpose. The remaining 48 K of the A000 block, from A400 up to B000 is part of a full 112 K area marked as reserved for display memory. So the complete display memory area goes from A400 to C000.

It is reasonable to speculate that this large area, especially the 48 K in the A000 block, is intended to be used by a new higher-resolution display, which would need more memory than the original monochrome display and color-graphics display. The intriguing part of this memory area is the 16 K set aside at the bottom of the A000 block, but not marked at part of the display memory area.

The entire amount of memory located below paragraph A000, a whopping 640 K, is available for conventional memory usage. The first 64 K, up to paragraph 1000, is located on the original format of the system board, and any additional memory is located on expansion boards. As announced by IBM, the PC only supported a maximum of 256 K of memory, but that limit was only the amount of memory that the ROM-BIOS start-up test programs would inspect and test for errors. It has always been possible to attach much more than 256 K of memory.

All of the ordinary RAM memory that is installed in your computer is located in the low address locations of the memory address space. You can have as little or as much installed as you want, up to the limits set by the reserved memory locations. Whether you have only 48 K, or a jumbo 576 K (in the case of the machine this was written on), the RAM on your computer occupies the low memory locations, from the beginning at zero (paragraph 0000) up to the size of your RAM.

So the working read-write memory, or RAM, is in the low memory locations, and the permanent storage, in ROM, is in the highest memory locations. In between is the special-purpose display memory. There are gaps, of course. A gap between the end of your RAM and the display memory, and a gap between the display memory and the ROM area. This is an inactive part of the PC's address space, which just sits there, ready to be used whenever memory is installed in its locations. (In a minute, we'll explore these gaps.)

The RAM memory is there to be used by working programs and data, on a temporary basis. Some of this memory, at the beginning of the address space, gets taken over by the needs of the micro-processor itself, while other small parts are used by DOS and BASIC. The rest is fair game for any program to use.

The very lowest part of memory, starting from the memory location zero and extending for about 1500 bytes, is dedicated to holding fundamental operating information for the computer. The first part of this area holds interrupt vectors, which we will explain in section 3.5. Following the interrupt vectors is data for the BIOS control routines, the DOS operating system, and BASIC to use as their working storage. After these reserved parts of low memory, the ordinary part of memory begins, where programs are loaded, and where the programs' working storage is placed.

It is possible to explore the memory that is connected to your PC, and discover how much is working and where it is located in the address space. Programs can attempt to read or write anywhere in memory. You might think that trying to use memory that wasn't there would result in an error signal, but in fact that doesn't happen. The reason for this is simple—when the 8088 micro-processor talks to its memory, it just shouts down the I/O channel described in the Chapter 2, and listens for the result. If no memory is there, the 8088 doesn't know the difference.

However, it is possible to detect memory that is present or absent by some simple tests. One technique is to try to read from each area of memory, and then check the results. A little experimenting will disclose that when this is done by most methods, such as with DEBUG, or Pascal programs, the result usually has all its bits set, giving a value of hex FF, or CHR$(255).

This isn't too surprising—the most likely guesses for what would result from reading missing memory are all bits off, or all bits on. For some reason that I haven't figured out, the interpreter BASIC usually returns the value CHR$(233). The results aren't completely consistent, but most of the time BASIC returns this odd value, CHR$(233), when reading from missing memory.

We can take advantage of this quirk to check the entire address space for memory that is active. Listing 3.1 shows a simple BASIC program which will read a few bytes from each 1 K of memory, and check them for the CHR$(233) value. If you run this program on your system, it will show you the memory you have. Figure 3.4 shows the results from running this program on the IBM/PC on which this book was written. Let's see what it has to tell us.

First, notice that three blocks of memory were detected—which is exactly what a normal IBM/PC has. The first block begins at paragraph 0, the very beginning of memory. This is the ordinary, usable read-write memory for the system. On this particular PC, the first block is 576 K bytes in size. It consists of the standard 64 K of memory on the system board, and an expansion board containing 512 K.

The second block of active memory begins at paragraph B000, which is where the monochrome display memory is located. So we know that this particular system has the monochrome display, and not the color-graphics adapter. Notice that our exploration program thinks that this memory extends for 32 K, even though there really is only 4 K included in the monochrome adapter. The extra 28 K that was detected is probably just an odd side effect of the circuitry that supports the 4 K of real memory. Running this same experimental program on a color-graphics system also detects 32 K of memory, although there is only 16 K on the color-graphics adapter.

After the display adapter memory, the program detects the ROM memory at the high end of the address space. For this last block, like the first one, the program detected exactly what was there, without any phantom accompaniment.

While this program is interesting in its own right, in exploring your system's memory, it is also a good example of what you can do to gain mastery of your IBM/PC system. IBM didn't advertise the fact that BASIC finds the 233 value in missing memory, and no one told me how to examine memory. But with a little curiosity and a little exploration, I was able to produce the program shown in listing 3.1. This is the sort of thing that I would urge you to do on your own. Explore your system, poke around in its dustier corners—and you will gain a world of insight into how the PC works.

By the way, you should be forewarned that some non-IBM memory boards give curious results when this program is run. That's another way that you can learn more about your system.

## 3.4 A scratch pad: the registers

Besides a memory as a working place, the 8088 micro-processor uses registers as a scratch pad to speed up its work. Here we'll take a quick look at the registers.

For a full discussion of the registers, turn to a guide to the 8086 instruction set and its assembly language. We'll cover just enough here so that you will not be lost when registers are mentioned by name, in this book or elsewhere.

```
         Programs for INSIDE THE IBM PERSONAL COMPUTER
              (C) Copyright 1982 Peter Norton

          Program 3-1: Find and Display Active Memory

          Be patient-- this program takes 65 seconds
       (Addresses given as segment paragraphs in hexadecimal)

Active memory begins at        0
              ends at       8FFF 576 K-bytes ( 589824 bytes )

Active memory begins at      B000
              ends at       B7FF 32 K-bytes ( 32768 bytes )

Active memory begins at      F000
              ends at       FFFF 64 K-bytes ( 65536 bytes )
Finished.
```

**Figure 3.4—Results of Program 3-1.**

For general use, there are four 16-bit registers known as AX, BX, CX, and DX. Each of them can be divided into two 8-bit registers, using the high (H) or low (L) part of the complete (X) register. The 8-bit registers are named AH, AL, BH, BL, CH, CL, DH, and DL. Because of the relationship of the 8-bit registers to the 16-bit registers, loading the hex value ABCD into the AX register is the same thing as loading hex AB into the AH register, and hex CD into the AL register.

While these four 16-bit registers are for general use, each of them also has some specialized use. For example, when an operation is to be repeated for some number of times, the CX register is used to contain the count of how many times.

We have already mentioned the four segment addressing registers: CS, for the code segment; DS, for the data segment; SS, for the stack segment; and ES, for the supplementary extra segment. Various registers can provide the relative part of a segmented address, to be used with the segment part that is given in a segment register. For the current address of the program being executed, the instruction pointer, IP, is used with the CS segment register. For the current stack location, the stack pointer, SP, is used with the SS segment register.

For addressing data, several registers can be used to provide a relative address to go with the DS data segment value. The DX register often serves that purpose. Two specialty registers, named SI and DI are also used with the DS segment. When a string of bytes is being operated on, the SI and DI registers are used to provide a source index and a destination index, relative to the DS segment. The base pointer register, BP, can be used as a relative base location, to the SS segment.

## 3.5 Getting your attention: interrupts

A computer has to be able to respond to things that happen outside its microprocessor—for example, to acknowledge your typing on the keyboard. There are two ways that it could do this. One is to be looking constantly for anything that needs the computer's attention. This method is called "polling," and polling can take up much of the computer's time, just checking for possible work to do. The other method is for the computer to quietly go about its business, until something in the world outside it grabs its attention; this approach is called "interrupting." Using interrupts is a major factor in efficient computer operation, because the processor doesn't waste its time looking for work—when there is something to be done, the work comes looking for the processor.

What are some examples of interrupts? One is you, pressing a key on the keyboard. Another is a tick of the clock that is built into the IBM/PC; eighteen times a second, the PC's clock interrupts the 8088 micro-processor, to tell it that it is time for another tick of the clock. The DOS operating system keeps track of the time of day simply by counting the ticks of the internal clock; the time of day can be calculated based on the number of ticks since last midnight. Another example of an interrupt is the diskette drive generating an interrupt to inform the processor that some diskette operation has finally been completed. Since diskette operations are slow compared to the working speed of the processor, the processor doesn't wait for diskette operations. Instead, the 8088 gives orders to the diskette drive, and then goes on computing until the diskette drive issues an interrupt to indicate that the operation is complete.

The main idea of interrupts is that anything that needs the processor's attention should come to it in the form of an interrupt. Using interrupts has tremendous advantages. If there is nothing that needs attention—which is true almost all the time—then the processor wastes no time at all looking for things that need to be taken care of. On the other hand, when there is something that needs attention, it gets that attention immediately, since interrupts normally are serviced the instant that they are requested.

Sometimes it is important that the processor not be disturbed in its work, because it is doing something very critical which would be disrupted if an interrupt took place. To allow for this, the 8088 micro-processor has an instruction that permits it to temporarily suspend interrupts, putting them on hold, and a companion instruction that turns interrupts back on. When interruptions are suspended, a request for an interrupt isn't lost—it's held ready for when interruption is activated again.

Normally interrupts aren't suspended for any length of time. The custom is to only suspend interrupts for very short bits of computer housekeeping, usually just a small handful of instructions long. A typical example of such housekeeping, is anything that would leave the computer in a confused state if it was interrupted midway through, such as loading a new set of values in the segment address registers. Since these registers are needed for any program to operate properly, having a mixed-up set of addresses in them can cause havoc—so interruptions are briefly suspended while new addresses are loaded into them.

To give you a small but dramatic example of the effect of suspending interrupts, consider two programs we'll call BEEP and WARBLE. If you have the diskette package that accompanies this book, you will find both programs ready to use. If you have the macro-assembler you can produce these programs from the assembler code given in listing 3.2. Both BEEP and WARBLE are short programs to generate a tone on the IBM/PC's speaker. (You'll have to wait until Chapter 11 before we explain how sounds are generated.) The code in each of them will produce a pure steady sound. But WARBLE doesn't suspend interrupts. So, 18 times a second, it is interrupted by the clock ticking; the interruption is very brief, but it is just long enough to produce a striking warbling sound. BEEP, on the other hand, suspends interrupts, and its tone stays solid and pure. Run BEEP and WARBLE, and you can experience the effect of suspending interrupts.

The mechanism of interrupts works like this: Each basic kind of interrupt has a number assigned to it. For example, the clock tick is interrupt number 8; the diskette drive uses interrupt number 14. Stored at the very beginning of the PC's memory is a table of the addresses of the programs which are to be activated when the various kinds of interrupts occur. These addresses must be complete segmented addresses, so they occupy two words, or four bytes, each. These addresses are sometimes called the interrupt vectors. Interrupt number 0 has its vector stored at memory location 0, interrupt 1 has its vector at location 4, and so on. When interrupt number "X" occurs, the vector at location 4 times X is loaded into the 8088's program address registers, registers CS and IP, and the computer begins running the interrupt handling program that is located at that address.

When the interrupt handler is done, it returns control to the program that was running when the interrupt occurred, using a special "interrupt return" instruction, IRET. To make that possible, before the interrupt vector address is loaded into the program address registers CS and IP, the current program address is saved using the stack—which we'll discuss in the next section.

The concept of an interrupt was created as a practical way for a computer to deal with the needs of the world outside its processor. But once the idea was developed, it quickly became apparent that interrupts were just as useful internally. This lead to the development of three kinds of interrupts which we'll call hardware, logical, and software. There is nothing fundamentally different about or between them, but their uses put them into three separate categories.

Hardware interrupts we've already discussed—they are generated by some equipment demanding attention. There are surprisingly few of them in the IBM/PC. First, there is the so-called Non-Maskable-Interrupt, used to signal things like a power failure; this is interrupt number 2. Next comes interrupt 8 for the timer, 9 for the keyboard and 14 for the diskette drives, for a grand total of four hardware interrupts. There are seven reserved interrupt numbers, 6 and 7, 10 through 13, and 15, that can be used for any future needs for additional hardware interrupts. Two of those seven already have their subject matter assigned: interrupt 12 is reserved for use by a communications adapter, and interrupt 15 is reserved for use by a printer interface.

Logical interrupts are generated by the 8088 micro-processor itself, when it encounters some unusual condition. There are four of them. Interrupt 0 is generated when the 8088 encounters an attempt to divide by zero. Interrupt 1 is used to operate the 8088 in single-step mode, executing one instruction at a time; this interrupt is set up by program testing routines to deliberately march through a program one step at a time. Interrupt 3 is generated by the 'break-point' instruction, which is also used for program testing. Interrupt 4 is generated by an overflow condition, for example when an arithmetic operation produces a result too large to fit into a register. So these four logical interrupts come to us as two pairs: two for arithmetic (zero-divide and overflow) and two for program testing (single-step and break-point).

Software interrupts are the most interesting kind. When a program needs to make use of another program, or subroutine, it has to pass control of the computer to that routine. Traditionally this has been done with an instruction known as a CALL. To CALL a routine your program had to know its address; but the called routine didn't need to know your address, since the calling mechanism automatically generated the return address for the called routine to use when it was done. To go to a subroutine and return, you only had to provide a one-way ticket—the return ticket was free. The idea of a software interrupt is to be able to go both ways for free—that is, to be able to invoke a subroutine, and have it return control when it is done—without either party needing any knowledge of where the other is.

A software interrupt accomplishes this by letting a program do what the outside world can do—generate an interrupt. So, if your programs need to have the time of day calculated, for example, they don't need to know the address of the time-of-day program—they just need to know that the time-of-day routine is invoked with interrupt 26.

Software interrupts are used for all the services that are made available to the general public. These services include all the ones that are built into the IBM/PC in its ROM-BIOS, and those services that are provided by the operating system, DOS. There are two reasons why interrupts are used instead of using addresses directly. The most important is that it allows the service routines that interrupts invoke to be changed, when necessary. Changing a routine usually alters its size and location. But if the routine is invoked by an interrupt, then any programs that use it don't have to be revised when the routine is changed.

The other reason why software interrupts are used to invoke service routines is to make it practical to over-ride them. Let's create an example. As you will see in Chapter 8, the service routines for the display screen cause the IBM/PC's speaker to beep whenever the character CHR$(7) is written. Suppose you wanted to keep the beep from sounding. To do this, you could write a small program that would check the characters that were being written to the screen, and whenever a CHR$(7) appeared, you could change it to a blank; after doing its check, your new program could pass control onto the regular display screen routine to complete the work. In effect, you are tacking a small addition onto the front of the regular display screen program. To put your program into service, you would replace the interrupt vector for display screen services, interrupt 16, with the address of your new program.

Software interrupts are very important to the operation of the IBM/PC. In fact much of the rest of this book will be devoted to describing them in detail. Chapter 4 will go over the interrupts used by DOS, and Chapters 7 through 11 will cover the ROM-BIOS interrupts. To make those services fully accessible to you, the separate diskette package which accompanies this book contains a complete set of interface routines—first, assembly language routines to make the interrupt service routines accessible to any language that you are using (including BASIC and Pascal), and then Pascal support programs to make it particularly easy to get full use of the assembler routines.

Before we finish discussing interrupts, there is one unusual use of the interrupt vector table that we need to mention. The interrupt vector table at the beginning of memory is intended to be used to hold the complete segmented addresses of programs that will service their corresponding interrupts. But IBM extended the use of the vector table in an interesting way. While the table is supposed to contain the segmented addresses of interrupt service programs, IBM has used it as a convenient place to store the addresses of three items that aren't programs at all, but data— important system data. The idea was to use the interrupt vector table as a unified place to store important segmented addresses; normally, of course, addresses of programs—but when necessary, also the addresses of data. So three interrupt numbers, 29, 30, and 31, have their vector locations pre-empted to hold the addresses of three important data tables. Naturally these interrupts can't be used: if a program requested interrupt number 29, or 30, or 31, then the computer would jump to one of these data tables, and try to execute it as a program.

In Chapter 6, where we discuss the ROM in more detail, we'll see what these three tables are. Then we'll cover them one by one, in Chapters 7, 8, and 9.

## 3.6 Your holding file: the stack

Stacks are one of the most interesting and important features of modern computers. Together with interrupts, stacks are the heart of what makes it possible for a computer to be efficient and effective.

What is a stack? A stack is a place for the computer to place its working notes in a way that one set of notes doesn't interfere with another set.

Stacks take their name from a metaphor used to explain how a stack works: consider a stack of plates, particularly the kind of plate stack that you'll find in a cafeteria, where the dishes are supported by a spring-loaded platform that moves up and down. When the cafeteria needs to store some clean plates, it puts them on to the top of the stack, and the older plates are pushed down. When someone takes a plate off the top, the rest of the stack pops up. The plates are used in a Last-In-First-Out basis, so stacks are sometimes also called LIFO stacks.

When a computer is busy working away, and it receives an interrupt, it needs some place to hold a record of what it was doing. If it receives another interrupt while it was processing the first one, it needs a place to keep a record of that. And when the second interrupt is done, the computer must go back to the most recent thing that it was doing, which in this case was the first interrupt. For handling interrupts, and for many other operations that must be dealt with on a most-recent basis, a LIFO stack is a natural mechanism for the computer to keep its records.

The way a stack works in the IBM/PC is that a portion of memory is given for the use of stack storage, and the special stack segment register, the SS register, points to the area in memory where the stack is located. The top of the stack is indicated by a register called the stack pointer, or SP. While a stack of plates on a spring physically moves when plates are pushed on and popped off, the computer stack doesn't move. Instead the location of the top of the stack moves, as indicated by the SP stack pointer.

Data is placed onto the computer's stack by an operation called a PUSH, and removed by a POP operation. These colorful terms come from the way the spring-loaded cafeteria stacks work.

When an interrupt occurs, the current program address, which is kept in the CS and IP registers, is pushed onto the stack; then the address of the interrupt's service routine is loaded into the CS and IP, so that the service routine is executed. Behind the SP stack pointer is all the previous work that has been suspended, awaiting re-activation. Ahead of the stack pointer is open space, which the interrupt service routine can use, if it needs any working memory while it is carrying out its duties. If another interrupt comes along, the new interrupt routine finds its working area further along the stack.

When each routine is finished in turn, it pops the stack. First any working storage is popped off the stack, and then the previous routine's program address, the CS and IP values, are popped off, and into the CS and IP registers. All the while, the stack mechanism automatically keeps order, making sure than every thing is done in the proper sequence.

Stacks are used for more than handling interrupts—they are also used whenever one program calls another. For both calls and interrupts, the principle is the same: old work must be set aside, temporarily and safely, so that new work can be begun. And when the new work is done, the old work is returned to, in the order that it was suspended.

In the process of calling a subroutine, parameters often must be passed to it, and the stack serves as a place to pass them as well. In the third appendix to this book, when we discuss how to make the connection between Pascal and assembly language, you will see how the stack is used to pass parameters.

Stacks are so fundamental to the operation of computers that it is remarkable that they are a relatively recent addition to computer design. The 360-series of computers, which has been the mainstay of IBM since the 1960's, do not have the concept of stacks built into them, and 360 and its successors have suffered greatly from the lack of stack support. There is a fascinating legend that the manager who was responsible for killing stack architecture at IBM was later exiled to IBM's equivalent of Siberia.

Stacks can be used for more than what I have described here. Our 8088 micro-processor only uses stacks as a holding place for suspended work, which is how most computers use stacks. However, it is possible to completely re-orient the way a computer works with its instructions and its data, so that a stack is at the core of everything that is done. Burroughs computers have used this complete stack orientation, and anyone who would like to understand one way that computers can be radically different from ordinary machines like the IBM/PC, can look to descriptions of the Burroughs computers.

There is one detail about the stacks used in the IBM/PC's 8088 processor that you should know, if you will ever be making use of the contents of the stack or inspecting a working stack. Stacks are used from high memory locations to low. This means that old stack contents are at higher locations than the position of the SP stack pointer. So, for example, to access subroutine parameters that have been pushed onto the stack—as explained in the 3rd appendix of this book—positive displacements are used. On the other hand, the open space on the stack, which normally is never accessed directly by memory address but only by pushing and popping, is located at negative displacements from the stack pointer.

## 3.7 Looking out the port hole

Ports are a mechanism that the 8088 micro-processor uses to simplify and unify the way it communicates with the world outside it. The 8088 only knows three things outside itself. One is being hit over the head with an external interrupt, which grabs its attention. Another is its memory, which it talks to by referring to memory addresses. The third is ports. Ports are the only way that the 8088 has of passing data to or from anything other than its memory.

Anything that the micro-processor needs to talk to, such as the keyboard, the diskette drives, and the speaker, is given a port to use. A port is a hypothetical data path, that has a port number assigned to it, and that can accept or send data at the command of the processor. When the 8088 needs to send data out to a port, it uses the OUT instruction, specifying the port number, and the data being sent—which is always either one or two bytes. In effect, the OUT instruction shouts down the data bus, "Hey, port number X, take this data." The IN instruction works the same way, shouting into the data bus, "Hey, port number X, send me some data." The 8088 micro-processor has no idea which ports are in use, and all its IN and OUT requests are blind operations.

BASIC, by the way, gives us direct access to the ports. While the 8088 machine language has the IN and OUT instructions mentioned above, BASIC provides the same capabilities with INP and OUT. Just to show you how it is done, here's an example of reading and writing ports in BASIC, playing with the speaker:

```
10  X = INP (97) '   read the port which controls the speaker (and other
                     things)
20  REM              X is probably 76—see what value you get
30  OUT 97,X + 3 '   turn on the speaker bits—a sound begins
40  OUT 97,X '       turn the speaker bits back off—the sound ends
```

Ports can be used in conjunction with interrupts. For example, when you press a key on the IBM/PC's keyboard, no data is sent to the computer. Instead, an interrupt number 9 is generated, indicating that there is keyboard data available. In response to the interrupt, the ROM-BIOS routines issue an IN instruction for the keyboard's port; only then does data indicating what key was struck pass into the computer.

As we saw with memory, there are 1024 K different possible memory locations, and the micro-processor is unaware of which ones actually have memory installed. Ports act the same way, and the 8088 can attempt to talk to any possible port, whether it is working or not.

Port addresses are specified with 16 bits, so there are potentially 64 K ports that can be used. Only a very few port numbers are actually assigned, so there is an over-abundance of room for growth.

On the IBM/PC ports are used several ways. The first way is as an ordinary data path. For example, the key-codes that indicate which keys on the keyboard have been struck, pass through one port; data going out to the printer passes through another port.

Another way that ports are used is to pass control conformation to devices, and receive back status information. For example, initialization of the monochrome display adapter is done through port 952. Yet another use of ports is reading the switch settings on the system board that indicate what equipment is installed.

For your interest, we'll list some of the more important port assignments here. Like some of the hardware details given in Chapter 2, these port numbers aren't likely to be of much actual use to you, and I'm naming them here simply for their interest.

Port 96, hex 60, is used to pass data, in scan-code format, from the keyboard. When we cover the keyboard in detail in Chapter 10, we'll see more about the scan codes and how they are used, but we won't monkey with the port.

Port 97, hex 61, is used to control the speaker, and also the cassette motor. It also activates a hardware timer, which we'll see more about when we cover the speaker in Chapter 11. Ports 64 through 67, hex 40 to 43, are used to control the programmable timer, used by the speaker and cassette interface. In Chapter 11 we will show you how to use these ports.

The monochrome display uses a series of ports beginning with 944, hex 3B0, and the color-graphics display uses a series at 976, hex 3D0. The diskette controller uses a series of ports from 1008, hex 3F0, and the actual data passing to and from the diskette drives goes through the particular port 1013, hex 3F5.

As a companion to the program given in listing 3.1, which explores memory, listing 3.3 and 3.4 show a program, written in a combination of Pascal and assembly language, which will read all the ports and report on the ones which seem to be active. A ready-to-run version of this program appears on the diskette package which accompanies this book. Unlike the memory-search program, this port-search program doesn't produce much of a practical result, but it can be rather interesting.

Since BASIC gives access to the ports, this program could have been coded in BASIC, but that wouldn't show you anything new. Instead, we've given it to you in assembler and Pascal, as a good introduction to how assembly programming is done, how Pascal programming is done, and how the two are connected.

```
1000 REM   Listing 3.1 -- A program to scan for and report active memory
1010 REM                          (C) Copyright 1983, Peter Norton
1020 REM
1030 GOSUB 2000  '   TITLE
1040 GOSUB 3000  '   SEARCH AND DISPLAY
1050 GOSUB 4000  '   RETURN TO DOS

2000 REM   Title subroutine
2010 KEY OFF : CLS : WIDTH 80
2020 REM
2030 PRINT "            Programs for INSIDE THE IBM PERSONAL COMPUTER"
2040 PRINT "                (C) Copyright 1983 Peter Norton"
2050 PRINT
2060 PRINT "            Program 3-1: Find and Display Active Memory"
2070 PRINT
2080 PRINT "            Be patient-- this program takes 65 seconds"
2090 PRINT "    (Addresses given as segment paragraphs in hexadecimal)"
2100 PRINT
2999 RETURN

3000 REM    Subroutine for the main search and display
3010 TRUE.%  = -1
3020 FALSE.% =  0
3030 IN.MEMORY.% = FALSE.%
3040 FOR PARAGRAPH.! = 0 TO 65535! STEP 64   ' CHECK EACH 1K OF MEMORY
3050   GOSUB 5000 ' CHECK FOR ACTIVE MEMORY
3060   IF (IN.MEMORY.%=FALSE.%) AND (MEMORY.HERE.%=TRUE.%)  THEN GOSUB 6000
3070   IF (IN.MEMORY.%=TRUE.%)  AND (MEMORY.HERE.%=FALSE.%) THEN GOSUB 7000
3080   IN.MEMORY.% = FALSE.%
3090   IF MEMORY.HERE.% THEN IN.MEMORY.% = TRUE.%
3100 NEXT PARAGRAPH.!
3110 IF IN.MEMORY.% THEN PARAGRAPH.! = 65536 : GOSUB 7000
3999 RETURN

4000 REM    Subroutine to finish up
4010 PRINT
4020 PRINT "Finished."
4999 SYSTEM

5000 REM  Check for memory present -- sample the first four bytes
5010 DEF SEG = PARAGRAPH.!
5020 BYTE0.% = PEEK (0)
5030 BYTE1.% = PEEK (1)
5040 BYTE2.% = PEEK (2)
5050 BYTE3.% = PEEK (3)
5060 CHECK.COUNT.% = 0
5070 IF BYTE0.% = 233 THEN CHECK.COUNT.% = CHECK.COUNT.% + 1
5080 IF BYTE1.% = 233 THEN CHECK.COUNT.% = CHECK.COUNT.% + 1
5090 IF BYTE2.% = 233 THEN CHECK.COUNT.% = CHECK.COUNT.% + 1
5100 IF BYTE3.% = 233 THEN CHECK.COUNT.% = CHECK.COUNT.% + 1
5110 MEMORY.HERE.% = FALSE.%
5120 IF CHECK.COUNT.% <= 3 THEN MEMORY.HERE.% = TRUE.%
5999 RETURN

6000 REM  Subroutine to start an active block of memory
6010 IN.MEMORY.% = TRUE.%
6020 START.! = PARAGRAPH.!
6999 RETURN
```

LISTING 3-1    47

```
7000 REM   Subroutine to end a block of active memory
7010 SIZE.! = (PARAGRAPH.!-START.!) * 16
7020 IF SIZE.! < 8 * 1024 THEN 7999  ' SUPPRESS SMALL-BLOCK FALSE REPORTS
7030 PRINT "Active memory begins at ",
7040 PRINT HEX$(START.!)
7050 PRINT "                    ends at ",
7060 PRINT HEX$(PARAGRAPH.!-1);
7070 PRINT SIZE.! / 1024;"K-bytes"; (";SIZE.!;"bytes )"
7080 IN.MEMORY.% = FALSE.%
7090 PRINT
7999 RETURN

9999 REM     End of program listing 3.1
```

```
;   Listing 3.2 - Beep and Warble programs
;   (C) Copyright 1983 Peter Norton

;   This program, run in two versions, will demonstrate the effects of
;   clock interrupts on a program which generates a pure tone on the speaker

;   The BEEP version, with interrupts disabled, will produce a pure tone
;   The WARBLE version, with 18 clock interrupts each second, will warble

;   The listing here includes the CLI and STI instructions which disable
;   interrupts, for the BEEP version.  For WARBLE, remove these instructions

;   If you are new to preparing assembler programs for execution, here is a
;   quick guide.  After entering the program into a text file named BEEP.ASM
;   do these three steps:

;   1) assemble the program, with    MASM    B:BEEP    B:BEEP    CON;
;   2) link the program with         LINK    B:BEEP    B:BEEP    CON;
;   3) convert to "COM" format with  EXE2BIN B:BEEP.EXE B:BEEP.COM

;   This program operates by sending a series of on and off pulses to the
;   speaker; the speed of the pulses is controlled by a loop which just
;   kills time for 50 loop cycles.  The length of the tone is controlled
;   by the number of speaker-pulse cycles, 3000, in this program.

beepseg segment 'code'

        assume   cs:beepseg

beep    proc    far

        cli                ;   clear-interrupts -- remove this for WARBLE

        mov     bx,3000    ;   count of speaker cycles
        in      al,61h     ;   input control info from keyboard/speaker port
        push    ax         ;   save on stack
more:   and     al,0fch    ;   turn off bits 0 and 1  (speaker off pulse)
        out     61h,al     ;   send command to speaker port
        mov     cx,50      ;   time for tone half-cycle
11:     loop    11         ;   kill time
        or      al,2       ;   turn on bit 1 (speaker on pulse)
        out     61h,al     ;   send command to speaker port
        mov     cx,50      ;   time for tone half-cycle
12:     loop    12         ;   kill time
        dec     bx         ;   count down of speaker cycles
        jnz     more       ;   continue cycling speaker
        pop     ax         ;   restore speaker/keyboard port value
        out     61h,al     ;   send port value out

        sti                ;   start interrupts  -- remove this for WARBLE

        int     20h        ;   return to system
beep    endp

beepseg ends

end

;   End of listing 3.2
```

LISTING 3-3    49

```
{  Listing 3.3 -- PORTTEST program to access every port    }
{  (C) Copyright 1983, Peter Norton                        }

{  This program accesses every possible port value, through an   }
{  assembly language routine, called INPORT, which appears in    }
{  listing 3.4.  Based on practical experience, this program     }
{  filters-out the most common false input values returned:      }
{        0, 78, 110, 188, 202, 203, 207, 254, 255               }

{  If you are new to compiling Pascal, and especially to linking  }
{  Pascal with assembler routines, here is a brief outline of     }
{  how it is done.  Assuming you have entered this source program }
{  as a text file named PORTTEST.PAS, on a diskette in drive B    }
{  and have already assembled the INPORT routine, here is what    }
{  you do:                                                        }

{  To compile this program, in two steps, do this:                }
{        B:                                                       }
{        A:PAS1 PORTTEST,PORTTEST,CON;                            }
{        A:PAS2                                                   }
{        A:                                                       }

{  To link the Pascal and assembly module, do this:              }
{        LINK B:PORTTEST+B:INPORT,B:PORTTEST,CON;                }

{$debug-,$line-,$ocode-}

program porttest (output);

function inport (x : word) : byte;
  external;

var
  count : word;
  b     : byte;
  w     : word;
  c     : array [wrd(0)..255] of word;  { used to hold the value profile }
  headc : word;

procedure header1;
  var [static]
    i : integer;
  begin
    writeln;
    for i := 1 to 8 do
      write ('  Port Val');
    writeln;
  end;

procedure header2;
  var [static]
    i : integer;
  begin
    writeln;
```

```
      for i := 1 to 8 do
        write (' Val Count');
      writeln;
    end;


procedure initialize;
    begin
      count := 0;
      headc := 0;
      for b := 0 to 255 do      { clear profile counts }
        c [b] := 0;
      for w := 1 to 25 do       { roll the screen   }
        writeln;
      writeln ('Program for INSIDE THE IBM PERSONAL COMPUTER');
      writeln ('(C) Copyright Peter Norton, 1983');
      writeln ('Listing 3.3: PORTTEST - read all ports');
      writeln;
      writeln ('The following may be active ports:');
      header1;
    end;


procedure scan_all_ports;
    begin
      for w := 0 to maxword do      { loop through every possible port }
        begin
          b := inport (w);          { get the value   }
          c [b] := c[b] + 1;        { add to profile }
          if not (b in [wrd(0),78,110,188,202,203,207,254,255]) then
            begin
              write (w:6,b:4);   { show the port number, and the value }
              count := count + 1;
              headc := headc + 1;
              if headc > 159 then
                begin
                  headc := 0;
                  header1;
                end;
            end;
        end;
      header1;
    end;


procedure finish_up;
    begin
      writeln;
      writeln ('Here is a profile of the values returned for all of the ',
               'possible ports:');
      header2;
      for b := 0 to 255 do
        write (b:4,c[b]:6);
      header2;
      writeln (count,' ports may possibly be active');
      writeln;
      writeln ('Finished.')
    end;
```

LISTING 3-3    51

```
begin
  initialize;
  scan_all_ports;
  finish_up
end.
```

{ End of listing 3.3 }

```
;  Listing 3.4 -- INPORT assembly language subroutine
;  (C) Copyright 1983 Peter Norton

;  This program, when called from Pascal, reads a requested port, and
;  returns the value found in the port


;  INPORT -- read port and return to Pascal

;  Pascal declaration of this routine:

;  function inport (port : word) : byte;
;     external;

inport_code segment 'code'

public inport

inport proc far          ;  Pascal 'external' routines are far calls
       push bp           ;  save the base-pointer
       mov  bp,sp         ;  get the stack pointer
       mov  dx,[bp+6]     ;  grab the port number from the stack
       in   al,dx         ;  get the port's input value
       pop  bp            ;  restore the base-pointer
       ret  2             ;  return to the Pascal routine

       db   '(C) Copyright Peter Norton, 1983'

inport endp

inport_code ends

       end

;  End of listing 3.4
```

# 4

# Fundamental DOS

In this chapter we're going to take a quick look at DOS, the primary operating system for the IBM/PC. We won't go into very much depth—partly because DOS is subject enough for several books by itself, and partly because this book is mostly about the inner workings of the IBM/PC, and not about the inner workings of DOS.

But since DOS is used so much on the PC, you need to have some basic understanding of it. And since the main focus of this book is access to the PC's advanced features, we'll give you ways to access the features and services of the DOS operating system.

Our three circles of interest closely coincide here. Virtually everything in this chapter applies equally to the IBM/PC, to PC-like computers, and to the family of computers that use MS-DOS.

## 4.1 What does an operating system do for a living?

To be the intellectual master of you computer, you need to understand its operating system. In this chapter we will give you a quick tour so that you know what DOS is about. You won't be able to take DOS apart and put it back together again, but you will know a little about how to tinker with it.

The purpose of an operating system is to run a computer, smoothly. An operating system, in the full sense of the term, is the first and most important program on a computer system. It is also usually the most complex. There is both irony and magnificence in the fact that the most sophisticated computer programs are used simply to supervise computers. The irony is that computers and their programs are supposed to be doing their work for you, not chasing their own tails. The magnificence is that the most powerful tool man ever built—the computer—is powerful enough to be used on itself; you can't use a saw to cut itself in half, but you can use a computer to operate a computer, thanks to operating systems.

Most of the work that an operating system does is to hide some very messy and tedious details from you. By way of illustration, let's look at the DOS command COPY. Suppose we are using it to copy from one diskette to another. That seems like no big deal, doesn't it? Well here are just a few of the things that the operating system has to worry about to do a copy for you. You may be amazed at how much work an operating system has to do, to accomplish such a simple task as copying.

- Is there a file with the given name on the source diskette?
- Is the copy target something other than a diskette file (such as the printer)?
- Is there already a file by that name on the target diskette?
- Is there room for the file on the target diskette (taking into account any available free space on the diskette, and, if a copy of the file is already there, all the space used by the old copy)?
- If the file is new to the target diskette, is there room for a new directory entry, or is the directory full?
- Is the source diskette single or double sided, or another format?
- Is the target diskette single or double sided, or another format?
- Is the file being copied to itself (which is not allowed)?
- Do the source and target diskette drives actually exist, or is this a single-diskette system, that has to fake a drive B?
- Should we find the end of the source file from its directory size or by a logical end-of-file marker (e.g. for an ASCII text file)?
- Is the File Allocation Table for the source in memory?
- Is the File Allocation Table for the target in memory?
- Does the source file trace correctly through its File Allocation Table?
- Is the directory file-size compatible with the allocated file size?
- How much room is there in memory to buffer the file copy?
- Is the buffer space over or under 64 K?
- Do we need to wipe out the command interpreter to get more buffer space?

Are you getting tired of this list, so far? We've hardly begun! That was just the logical side of the problem, and even then I glossed over many details. Here is the physical side, with even more of the real details skipped:

- Is the motor running on the diskette drive?
- Is the seek arm located on the right track?
- How many sectors of data do we want to read/write on this track?
- Is the drive ready for a command?
- Is the diskette acting up? Do we need to re-start, re-try, re-calibrate?

- If we are retrying, have we done it enough times to complain?

- What was the response to our complaint? Retry, ignore or abort?

- Are we waiting for the drive?

- Did the read/write/seek complete successfully? Is the target write-protected?

What you have seen here is just a crude outline of some of the messy details that are involved in copying a file. And that is a relatively simple DOS operation (although one that does a little of nearly everything). By the way, the distinction that we made here between the logical and the physical is a very important one in an operating system, and we'll see more about it, later in this chapter.

The principal job of an operating system, such as DOS, is to remove all these details from your concern. The greatest part of that task involves the nitty-gritty of input-output devices such as the diskette drives, printers, or asynchronous communications links through the telephone.

After that, DOS provides higher level services such as diskette directory searches, file copying, and program loading.

One of the keys to making an operating system design successful is modularity. An operating system is simplified, and made more effective, when its designers break down the work to be done into cleanly distinct parts. Then the parts need to be organized into a carefully defined hierarchy, where each level works with its assigned details, and saves the levels above it from having to concern themselves with those details (and, in turn, saved from worrying about the details of levels below). So next, we'll look at the modular parts of DOS.

## 4.2  Outlining the job in six parts

There are essentially six modular parts to DOS, and we'll outline what they do here. The first of the six parts is the ROM-BIOS. The ROM-BIOS comes built into the IBM/PC, and can be used as part of any operating system. The job of the ROM-BIOS is to provide most of the basic and fundamental services needed by the computer. Since the IBM/PC's ROM-BIOS is built into it, the ROM-BIOS isn't a distinctive part of DOS—it is a part of every IBM/PC operating system.

Next is the diskette "boot record." The boot record is a very short and simple program that is located on the first sector of every diskette. The job of the boot record is to start the process of loading the operating system when the PC is first turned on, or restarted (with the Ctrl-Alt-Del keys). The boot record reads the next two parts of the operating system into memory, so that they can finish the task of loading DOS.

The next two parts are two diskette files, IBMBIO.COM and IBMDOS.COM. Both are loaded by the boot record, and both stay loaded in memory while DOS is working, so the distinction between them isn't obvious.

IBMBIO.COM serves as a changeable extension to the ROM-BIOS. Beginning with DOS release 2.00, IBMBIO.COM can be extended with other parts, known as independent device drivers, which we'll see more about later. Taken together, the ROM-BIOS, IBMBIO.COM and the device drivers make up the "physical" part of the operating system.

IBMDOS.COM provides the core DOS services. It is the "logical" part of the operating system's input-output.

Both of these files are "hidden" "system" files (which we'll tell you more about in Chapter 5). As hidden files, they are not seen if you use the DIR directory command to list the files on a diskette. However the CHKDSK command (for DOS versions 1.10 and later) will tell you that they are there, but doesn't give you their names. If you use the utility DiskLook to inspect your diskettes, you will see IBMBIO.COM and IBMDOS.COM listed by name, and you can browse through these two files to see what's in them. One of the jobs of IBMBIO.COM is to load the next part of the operating system.

The fifth part is a diskette file named COMMAND.COM. The primary job of COMMAND.COM is to process the commands that you type into DOS. The DOS commands that are classified as internal—such as TYPE, COPY, and DIR—are actually located inside COMMAND.COM. COMMAND.COM itself breaks down into two parts: one becomes an extension of IBMDOS.COM, and the other becomes the transient command processor. More on that in section 4.7.

The sixth and last part of DOS consists of all the external commands, such as FORMAT and DISKCOPY. The jobs of these commands vary, and the programs to carry them out are loaded into memory as they are needed. Unlike the other five parts that we have covered, the external command programs strictly speaking aren't an integral part of the DOS operating system, though they are provided with DOS. And some of these external commands, such as FORMAT, are so important, that you couldn't do much without them.

The external commands are the non-resident parts of DOS, since they do not stay in memory all the time. The two system files IBMBIO.COM and IBMDOS.COM, together with any device handlers, are the resident parts of DOS. COMMAND.COM is in a special category of its own, since it is semi-resident, which we'll see more about later. The boot record, of course, is only used temporarily, so it isn't a resident part of DOS. In the next six sections, we'll take a closer look at each part of DOS.

## 4.3 The inner-most part: ROM-BIOS

The first part of DOS is the ROM-BIOS, or the Basic Input / Output System, located in Read-Only-Memory. The ROM-BIOS provides some of the most fundamental and primitive services of the operating system.

The ROM-BIOS is located in the ROM storage at the hex paragraph locations FE00 through FFFF, just above the ROM-BASIC. The memory outline shown in Chapter 3 diagrams the location of the ROM-BIOS.

Since the ROM-BIOS is built into the IBM/PC, and can only be changed by modifying the system's hardware, it is very fundamental to the PC. As a built-in part of the IBM/PC, the ROM-BIOS isn't a part of DOS per se; it's a part of any operating system that runs on the IBM/PC.

The ROM-BIOS consists of several parts, most of which are programs (the rest are some important tables of data, which we'll look at in later chapters). The first ROM-BIOS program to be executed is the power-on self-test routine.

This is a program that tests the memory and equipment attached to the IBM/PC, when the power switch is turned on. One of the reasons that it takes the IBM/PC so long to start operating when you turn it on, is that it is performing this self-test program. The more memory you have attached to your system, the longer the test takes to run—since one of its most time-consuming tasks is to test the memory.

The next part of the ROM-BIOS to be executed is a program to start the operating system—to pull the operating system up by its bootstraps. This program checks to see if a diskette drive is installed, and then reads the 'boot record' from the diskette. After reading the boot record, the start-up program gives control to the boot record, so that it can read the rest of the operating system.

If there is not a diskette drive in the system, or if there was an error in reading the boot record, then the ROM-BIOS start up program turns control over to the cassette BASIC system. Whenever you have turned on your IBM/PC without a diskette inserted into the drive, you've seen the cassette BASIC program come into action. This is why that happens.

Besides the two parts we've mentioned—the power-on self-test, and the start-up boot loader—the ROM-BIOS is full of other programs, and they are the part that is most interesting to us. They include support programs for all the standard peripheral equipment on the IBM/PC. These are programs that perform the main operating functions for the keyboard, the display screen, the diskettes, the asynchronous communications adapter, the printer, and the cassette interface. These are the programs that we need to get our hands on to do most of the really interesting tricks with the IBM/PC. We'll discuss them in detail in Chapters 6 through 11.

## 4.4 Starting to load: The Boot Record

The boot record is used to start up DOS. The idea of a boot record is used in almost all computers. A boot record contains the minimal amount of program needed to read and start the main parts of the operating system. It is used, as the saying goes, to pull the system up by its bootstraps, and that is how it got its name. It is the "boot strap loader," or just "boot," for short.

When you start your IBM/PC, either by turning on the power or by pressing Ctrl-Alt-Del, the ROM-BIOS start-up routine reads the first record of the diskette in the A diskette drive and puts it into a standard location in memory, at address 31744, hex 7C00. After the boot record has been read, the ROM-BIOS passes control to the boot program by branching to location 31744. The boot record must then continue the job of loading the operating system.

The main task of the boot record for DOS is simply to load the IBMBIO.COM and IBMDOS.COM files. The boot-record is the size of a standard diskette sector, 512 bytes, which is not big enough for a very complicated program. To simplify the job of the boot program, the two files IBMBIO.COM and IBMDOS.COM are placed at a predefined location on the diskette. This saves the boot program from having to be smart enough to search for them, as all other files are searched for.

This, by the way, is why a "system formatted" diskette is different from an ordinary diskette—it contains the two system files IBMBIO.COM and IBMDOS.COM, and it has them stored at a standard, pre-defined location. This is also why you can't ordinarily change a regular diskette into a system diskette—the reserved locations for the two special system files may be in use by other files.

While the boot record program is not smart enough to search for the location of the files, it is smart enough to check the directory to see if the two system files are properly listed. Since the two system files do appear in the diskette directory, they are protected from being erased, or otherwise tampered with, by being marked as both hidden and system. (In the next chapter, on diskettes, we'll explain hidden and system files.)

Because of the simplicity of its task, the boot record is a relatively stable part of the DOS operating system. It would have to be changed if the system files were changed in size or location, and that did occur when support was added for double sided diskettes, with DOS version 1.10.

You will find differences in the boot records in different versions of DOS. (If you have the utility DiskLook, which is part of the diskette package which accompanies this book, you can easily inspect the boot record: start DiskLook, press function key f7, type in the boot records location, side 0, track 00 and sector 1, and then press function key f6— and the boot record will be displayed.)

There is one unimportant difference in the DOS boot records which you can easily see—the original 1.00 version boot record contained the name of Robert O'Rear, while the later versions contain the name of Microsoft. The boot record in the diskette package which accompanies this book has some special changes.

## 4.5 Finishing the devices: IBMBIO.COM

The first of the two system files, IBMBIO.COM, has the task of providing extensions to the ROM-BIOS. Both the ROM-BIOS and IBMBIO.COM deal with input-output handling, or device handling, as it is also called. This job involves taking care of all the rather tedious details of operating the I/O devices, such as the diskettes. Included in that task is error detection and correction, which is even trickier and more tedious to program.

What makes the program in the IBMBIO.COM file distinct, though, is that it can be easily changed, unlike ROM-BIOS. It is the task of IBMBIO.COM to do three things that ROM-BIOS can't. The first is to be tailored to the specific needs of the particular operating system, DOS. Any operating system, including CP/M-86 and the UCSD p-System, can use the general BIOS in ROM; but where operating systems differ, they must provide their own parts of BIOS.

The second task of IBMBIO.COM is to fix any errors in ROM-BIOS, whenever it becomes necessary. A program like ROM-BIOS is tested with great care, since putting it into ROM makes it essentially unchangeable. If any errors are later found in the ROM-BIOS, corrections can usually be made, through changes to IBMBIO.COM. This is done by having IBMBIO.COM reset the interrupt vectors, so that BIOS operations go first to IBMBIO.COM and then to ROM-BIOS. The calling convention for programs in ROM-BIOS, as we will see in Chapter 6, always involves using an interrupt, rather than jumping to the program locations in ROM. One very important reason for using interrupts is to allow ROM-BIOS programs to be superseded by programs in IBMBIO.COM; otherwise, we would have no way to over-ride the ROM-BIOS programs. When we get to Chapter 7, and cover the diskette control program known as the "disk base," you'll see one change that was made, over-riding part of the ROM-BIOS.

The third thing which ROM-BIOS can't do, and that IBMBIO.COM must do for it, is handle new peripheral devices, such as high-capacity hard disks, or 8 inch diskettes, or plotters, or any of the hundreds of computer devices that could possibly be added to a PC. As new input-output devices are added to the IBM/PC, support for them can be added in IBMBIO.COM, or its auxiliaries, without having to replace the ROM memory chips that hold ROM-BIOS.

In the earliest versions of DOS, the task of adding a new device involved making changes within IBMBIO.COM, and possibly within the other basic DOS programs as well. While this might not matter greatly to either Microsoft or IBM, it creates a real mess for anyone else who wants to add support for equipment to DOS. For you or I to add device support to DOS this way would mean doing some very intimate tinkering—a difficult and hazardous task.

Since the freedom to add new devices is a very important part of the success of a computer, DOS has been changed to make it more practical, starting with DOS version 2.00. When IBMBIO.COM first goes into operation, it checks for a configuration file in the diskette. If the configuration file is found, then it is read for instructions, part of which can set various system parameters.

The instructions in the configuration file include the names of any device-handler programs that need to be included into the BIOS. In turn, each device handler is loaded as an appendage to IBMBIO.COM. This scheme makes it practical to add new devices in a modular way, without disturbing the DOS system files.

Normally any programs run on an IBM/PC will want to use the conventional DOS versions of the BIOS. But occasionally a program requires special handling of I/O operations. Since IBMBIO.COM is a diskette file, which can be changed, it is practical to have custom versions of IBMBIO.COM, if it is needed. You will find an example of this in the diagnostic programs.

The diagnostic programs, which come with the IBM/PC's Guide to Operations, make use of this possibility; the IBMBIO.COM program file on the diagnostic diskette is different than the one used for DOS. Diagnostics routines have their own special and rigorous needs for how I/O is done—for one thing, they want to know about any errors, rather than having errors hidden from them. So if you compare the copies of IBMBIO.COM on your diagnostic diskette and your DOS diskette, you will find them different.

## 4.6 The heart of DOS: IBMDOS.COM

The second of the two system files is IBMDOS.COM. This file contains DOS service routines that are separate from immediate support of input and output. Although it is not essential to separate the functions of IBMBIO.COM and IBMDOS.COM, having these two distinct program files makes DOS more modular, and separates the parts that are most likely to be specific to one computer, from those parts that are common to all DOS computers.

The DOS service routines are divided, somewhat arbitrarily, into those which are invoked through their own special interrupts, and those which share one interrupt code (number 33, hex 21). In DOS terminology, the first group is called DOS interrupts, and the second DOS function calls. In both cases software interrupts are used to invoke them, for the same reason that BIOS programs use interrupts: modularity.

The range of interrupts 32 through 63 (hex 20 through 3F) are reserved for use by DOS. Only a few of these are in use, and the rest are provided for future needs. The DOS interrupt services include reading and writing of diskette sectors (which is very valuable to some of the service programs given in this book and its diskette), access to control over DOS errors, and over the Ctrl-Break keyboard operation.

The DOS function services provide mostly input-output services, on an intermediate level. Examples are reading keyboard input, ordinary output to the display screen, input and output to the asynchronous communications line, and printer output. Logical operations for the diskettes are provided—opening and closing a file, file directory searches, file erasure and creation, and reading and writing data. These routines provide almost all the elemental operations that a program would need to manipulate files and data in files, without the program having to do its own decoding of the directory, file allocation table, and so forth. If your programs need more control over the manipulation of files and data than your programming language allows, but you don't want to get lost in the morass of diskette data format, then DOS file service functions are what you need.

Most of these DOS service routines are used heavily by the higher level of DOS programs. For example, the directory search service is used by the DIR and COPY commands. It is also used by the command interpreter to find program files. In section 4.9 below, we will go over the complete list of DOS service routines.

## 4.7  At your command: COMMAND.COM, and the Internal Commands

The next part of DOS is COMMAND.COM and it is one of the most interesting, both in terms of what it does for us, and how it operates. COMMAND.COM has several functions. Foremost, it is the "command processor," which means that it is responsible for reading the commands which we enter on the keyboard, and determining what to do with them.

If we enter an internal command, such as DIR, COPY, TYPE, REM, or PAUSE, then we are requesting a service that is built into COMMAND.COM, and it can be performed right away.

To be able to recognize internal commands, COMMAND.COM contains a table of command names. If you browse inside the diskette file that holds COMMAND.COM, you will find the names of the commands. You can use either DEBUG, or DiskLook to inspect COMMAND.COM. In it you will also find the starting messages that DOS displays when it begins operation. If you wish, you can change these messages with DEBUG or a utility like SecMod, so that DOS begins by greeting you by name, or displaying your company logo. It is also possible to change the names of the internal commands, which is easy if you do not change the length of the names.

If a command is not in the table of internal commands, then we have an external command, one that COMMAND.COM expects to find residing in a diskette file. In response to our request, COMMAND.COM searches the appropriate diskette for a command processing file, and starts its execution.

There are three kinds of command processing files, and COMMAND.COM searches for them all, in a strict order. No distinction is made in the command name, which is the same as the filename of the file which contains the command processor. The three kinds of command processing files are distinguished by their filename extension. The three extensions, in order of priority, are: ".COM," which indicates a program file in one of the two program formats; ".EXE," which indicates a program file in the other format; and ".BAT," which indicates a batch processing file. (The formats of these files, and a great deal of other information concerning diskette files, are covered in the next chapter.)

When COMMAND.COM finds a program file, in either format, it does the work of loading the program into memory, and doing any conversion that might be necessary. After loading the program and building its program segment prefix, COMMAND.COM turns control over to the program, so that it can do its job.

If the command processing file is a ".BAT" batch file then it contains, in ASCII text file format, a series of commands which are to be carried out just as if they had been entered at the keyboard. One of the many tasks of COMMAND.COM is to keep track of its place in a batch processing file, so that when one command in the file is finished, the file can be read for the next command. If one of the commands in a batch processing file starts up the processing of another batch processing file, the first one is not returned to: batch files cannot be nested, but they can be chained from one to another.

On some computer systems, all command input can be re-directed to a file, and this applies equally to programs which get their input from the keyboard, as well as to the command interpreter—but this is not the case for DOS. Only the COMMAND.COM command interpreter automatically reads from batch processing files.

By the way, it is possible for a program to write changes to a batch processing file, and thereby control which commands or programs are executed next. This is commonly done in sophisticated applications, and it can act as a crude substitute for program chaining.

There is much more to COMMAND.COM than we've seen so far. COMMAND.COM actually breaks into three parts. The first part is placed in memory next to the programs from IBMBIO.COM and IBMDOS.COM, and like them, becomes part of the resident portion of DOS. In effect, this part of COMMAND.COM is no different than IBMDOS.COM.

The second part of COMMAND.COM is used only temporarily; at start-up time, it is used to check for, and execute, an AUTOEXEC.BAT batch file. Once this is done, this part of COMMAND.COM is discarded.

The third, and most interesting part of COMMAND.COM is semi-resident, one of the more clever features of DOS. This part contains the command interpreter, including the programs to carry out the internal commands. Now a program as sophisticated as a command interpreter isn't tiny. On the one hand, we would like the command interpreter to be in memory all the time. On the other hand we don't want it taking up memory space all the time, especially if we don't have very much (for example, on a 64 K system).

The interesting solution to this problem is to place this part of COMMAND.COM in the high end of memory (usually the last part to be used), and allow it to be overwritten by other programs. When the time comes for the command interpreter to be used, the resident portion of COMMAND.COM first checks to see if the command interpreter is still there, unchanged. If it isn't, then it is re-loaded from diskette. (This, by the way, is why copies of COMMAND.COM are needed on most of your diskettes, even ones which aren't system formatted. If you ever get the message "Insert DOS disk...", it is because COM-MAND.COM is missing from the diskette you are using.)

In order to test if the transient portion is in memory or not, the resident part of COMMAND.COM calculates a check-sum on the locations where the transient portion is supposed to be; if the sum does not match what is expected, then COMMAND.COM is reloaded. Incidentally, a check-sum calculation is performed when COMMAND.COM is reloaded, and if there is any difference, DOS complains. This happens even if the only difference is in the DOS start-up message ('The IBM Personal Computer DOS...'), which I mentioned that you could change. If you do make this, or any other change to COMMAND.COM, you should use it consistently in all your diskettes.

One of the reasons why COMMAND.COM is a separate file by itself, and not combined with the two IBM system files, is to make it more practical for custom versions to be written. This is one of the main ways that the IBM/PC can be tailored to special needs. If it is necessary to make some user commands internal, or if changes are needed in the way that the command interpreter operates, then a special COMMAND.COM can be written.

One example of a custom version of COMMAND.COM is the original 1.00 version of the EasyWriter word processor. It had its own special COMMAND.COM, and that is part of the reason why switching from DOS to EasyWriter and back to DOS required rebooting the system.

As the IBM manual points out, the operating system can be re-booted by pressing the keys Ctrl-Alt-Del. This does a complete restart of the system, from reading the boot record. However, there is a less radical way of restarting. If you enter the command COMMAND, then COMMAND.COM will be reloaded, and the system will be restarted without re-loading IBMBIO.COM and IBMDOS.COM. This can be done to get a refreshed copy of the command interpreter, and to execute any AUTOEXEC batch file.

# 4.8  All the other parts: the external commands

The last part of the DOS operating system consists of the external commands. These are called external commands because they are not included in the parts of DOS that are kept resident in the IBM/PC's memory. Instead, the external commands reside in program files kept on your diskettes.

As with all program files, the external commands have file name extensions of either ".COM' or ".EXE," which indicates which of the two program formats they are in. We'll discuss these formats when we cover diskettes and diskette files in the next chapter.

Examples of external commands are DISKCOPY, COMP, FORMAT, and EDLIN. BASIC and BASICA, in a sense are also external commands, although it's more reasonable to think of them as language processors, in the same category as the Macro Assembler or the Pascal Compiler.

External commands are no different from any program files that you create or buy. From one point of view the external commands are truly a part of the operating system, especially the ones that you couldn't use your system without—such as FORMAT. But from another point of view, the external commands are just auxiliary programs—just utilities, which are handy, but not actually the operating system itself. The difference between an external DOS command and an ordinary program is a matter of how you think of it—as a part of DOS or not—and not anything fundamental.

## 4.9 The DOS services—gaining access

In this section we'll discuss all the service routines that are available from DOS. This is the first of several lists of service routines that appear in this book. This section covers the DOS services, and sections in later chapters will cover, topic by topic, the service routines that are provided by the ROM-BIOS programs.

Before we get into the details of these services, let's set the stage for what will appear here and in the later chapters. One by one, we will list the services, giving their identifying code numbers, and we will describe what each service does. We won't describe every detail of how the services are invoked, because that isn't of very much interest. Another reason for not poring over the details of how each service is invoked, is that we will provide for you, in the diskette package, interface routines which will save you from much of the bothersome details of registers loaded and flags set.

Whenever there is something interesting to say, about the service, its subject matter, or its relation to other parts of the IBM/PC system, we will pause to cover it. Even if you do not intend to write programs which make use of these services, you may want to read these discussions carefully. They will show you a great deal about how the IBM/PC works, what its facilities are, and how it can be made to perform some wonderful tricks.

If you are writing programs for the IBM/PC, it can be very useful for you to have access to the full power of all the service routines that are available. To make it as easy as possible to use these services, I have written a complete set of interface routines which appear in the diskette package which accompanies this book.

All the DOS services, and the ROM-BIOS services, are set up in a format intended to be used only by assembly language programs. For each of the services, I have provided an assembler interface program which makes the services accessible from Pascal and other high-level languages. For the DOS services covered in this section, the assembly interface programs appear in listing 4.101.

In many cases, it is very helpful to have more than just an interface routine. Some supporting program code can be helpful as well. For this purpose, numerous Pascal routines are provided to make it as easy as possible to get the full use of the services being invoked. For the DOS services covered in this section, the Pascal support programs appear in listing 4.102.

Together, the assembly language interface routines and the supporting Pascal code, will make it possible for your programs to gain access to all the advanced features of the IBM/PC.

With that out of the way, let's look over the DOS services in detail. Some of these services will touch on areas which we will cover in detail in later chapters, where their meaning can be made more clear. When this happens, we'll refer you to the later discussion. Unfortunately that leaves some of the following explanations incomplete, but it is better to point you to a full treatment of each subject than to try to summarize everything here.

There are seven DOS interrupt services, plus an eighth, used to invoke all the DOS functions. We will cover the separate interrupt services first.

Interrupt 32, hex 20, is used to terminate the operation of a program. It is the normal way for a program to indicate that it is done, and request that DOS do any clean-up work that is necessary.

The clean-up work that DOS does is two-fold. First, there are three service interrupts that a program is permitted to change, for its use, and DOS resets the three interrupt vectors to their default values. (See the discussion of the three interrupts 34, 35, and 36.) Second, if the program has changed any diskette data, there may be system buffers holding data which has not been written, and DOS writes them. However, DOS does not close any open files, and a program should take care of this duty before requesting interrupt 32.

Interrupt 33, hex 21, is used by the function calls, which we will cover as a group, below. The next three interrupts, 34, 35 and 36, are not used in the same way as the others. While the other DOS interrupts are invoked by our programs to activate parts of DOS, these three are just the opposite: DOS invokes these interrupts to activate routines in our programs. Each of the three interrupts is generated, by DOS, at the appropriate time for each one, which we'll describe below. If we set the interrupt vectors for these three interrupts to point to interrupt handlers in our programs, then our programs will be able to take action when the interrupt occurs. The three interrupts are intended to let us take charge when DOS detects any of three conditions.

Interrupt 34, hex 22, is activated when a program ends. This interrupt allows our programs to have some finish-up routines that will be invoked when DOS terminates our programs. This can be a safe and useful way to make sure that no matter how our programs end, the clean-up work gets done.

Interrupt 35, hex 23, is activated when the Ctrl-Break key combination is pressed. This allows our programs to intercept the break signal, which otherwise would be a signal to DOS to terminate the program. You can see an example of this service in action by using the EDLIN editor which comes with DOS. Be aware that DOS does not act on the Ctrl-Break key at just any time. It only checks for it when a program is reading keyboard input, or sending out display screen data. See the discussion below, under the DOS functions, particularly at function service 8.

Interrupt 36, hex 24, is activated when DOS runs into trouble. DOS has a catch-all trouble condition called a "critical error," and this interrupt allows our programs to get control when this occurs. There are currently two kinds of critical errors, although we can expect to see some expansion here in the future. The first, and most common kind, is a 'hard disk error' (don't be confused: that's a hard error on the diskette, not an error on a hard disk).

Hard disk error occurs when the diskette drive fails to work properly, even after DOS has given it three tries to get things right. The other critical error is caused by some error in the memory copy of a diskette file allocation table (which we'll cover in the next chapter); this is most likely to happen if a program has inadvertently been changing low-memory locations.

After those three, come some more ordinary interrupt services. Interrupt 37, hex 25, is used to read diskette sectors. While data can be read within a file using the DOS function calls, this service makes it possible to read diskette sectors anywhere in a diskette, whether or not they are part of a file. A data area must be provided to read the sectors into, and three things must be specified: the diskette drive (with an index number, where 0 is drive A, and 1, 2, and 3 specify drives B, C, and D), the number of sectors to be read together, and the identifying number of the first sector being read.

For this service, and the next, sectors are identified by a consecutive number that is used only for this purpose. The numbering begins with 0 for the first sector on the diskette, which, by the usual way of specifying sectors, is sector 1 of track 0 of side 0. (For background material on sectors, tracks and sides of diskettes, see Chapter 5). Sectors are numbered consecutively across the first side of a diskette, side number 0. The numbers proceed from 0 through 319, hex 13F, on the first side, and then, for double-sided diskettes, continue with the first sector on the second side, using numbers 320, hex 140, through 639, hex 27F.

Another way to understand this numbering scheme, is by using a formula. If the sides are numbered 0 and 1, the tracks 0 through 39, and the sectors 1 through 8, then the id number used by this service is figured by:

INDEX   = (SECTOR - 1) + (TRACK * 8) + (SIDE * 320)

A one-byte error signal is returned by this service, with each bit indicating a separate possible error condition. The bits, their numeric equivalent, and the meaning of the error is given by this table:

| Bit | Number | Meaning |
| --- | --- | --- |
| 1st | 128 | No response from the diskette drive |
| 2nd | 64 | Seek failure (read/write head did not move to the track) |
| 3rd | 32 | Control failure (see the NEC controller, in Chapter 2) |
| 4th | 16 | CRC error (cyclical-redundancy-check, used to detect data errors) |
| 5th | 8 | DMA over-run (an error in direct memory addressing) |
| 6th | 4 | Sector not found (invalid sector, or formatting error) |
| 7th | 2 | Diskette write protected (for the write operation) |
| 8th | 1 | (not used) |

This service can be very useful for reading the parts of the diskette that are dedicated to system usage, such as the boot record, and the file directory. (See Chapter 5 for more details about these parts of a diskette.)

Interrupt 38, hex 26, is used to write diskette sectors, just as 37 is used to read them. The details of these two services are the same.

Similar services to these last two are provided by the ROM-BIOS. There are some advantages in using these DOS services though—DOS provides automatic retry and error recovery, and a greater degree of flexibility in what kind of diskette is used.

These DOS services allow you to read or write more than one sector at a time. For a discussion of the relative advantages and disadvantages of reading sectors one at a time, or several at a time, see Chapter 7.

Interrupt 39, hex 27, is called terminate-but-stay-resident. This service is used by programs which are to stay in memory after they have been loaded and run. The main purpose of this service is to make it possible to load a program which will act as an interrupt handler for later programs to use.

DOS keeps track of how much of the low memory area is in use for various things such as interrupt vectors, and the DOS programs themselves. Any programs that are loaded, are loaded after the reserved areas. When this service is invoked, that address is changed to follow the program which is to stay resident.

When this service is being used by a program which is setting up business as an interrupt handler, the following happens. The program is executed once, which causes DOS to load the program, and pass control to it. Then that program will begin by doing little more than moving its own address into the interrupt vector table, and request this stay-resident service. Later, whenever the particular interrupt occurs, control will be transferred to the resident program.

Besides these seven DOS interrupt services, there are 41 DOS function services. Each is invoked using interrupt 33, hex 21. Here is a list of all of the services.

Service number 0 is exactly the same as interrupt 32—it ends the execution of a program. There is no reason to favor one way of doing this over another.

Service number 1 is used to get a single character of input from the keyboard, and echo it to the display screen. This service waits for a key to be struck. If a special key, such as one of the function keys, is used, the keystroke is translated as if it were two separate characters, which are returned by two separate uses of this service. When this happens, the first of the two characters is CHR$(0), and the second is a special code. For more discussion of these keys and their codes, see the discussion of the keyboard in Chapter 10. This service will check for the special key combination Ctrl-Break, which is used to interrupt program operations.

Service number 2 is used to send a single character to the display screen. For ordinary characters, like letters of the alphabet, this happens in a straightforward way. For some special characters, other things happen. See appendix 4 for a discussion of the peculiarities, and Chapter 8 for more details of output to the display screens.

Service number 3 is used to receive a single byte of input from the asynchronous communications adapter. This service waits for input, and it provides for no error signals. This is one instance where the DOS services are more spartan than the services provided by the ROM-BIOS. For more discussion, see Chapter 11.

Service number 4 sends a single byte of data out through the asynchronous communications adapter, the reverse of service 3.

Service number 5 is used to send a single byte of data to the printer. Unlike the ROM-BIOS services, you cannot specify which printer—DOS works with just one printer. If there is more than one printer adapter attached this service only sends data to the first one. For the related ROM-BIOS services, see Chapter 11.

Service number 6 is a curious one, for it is used both for keyboard input and display screen output. Any character, except for CHR$(255), may be sent out to the screen. If this service is invoked as if to send CHR$(255) to the screen, then a keyboard input operation is performed. Like service number 1, two-byte codes are used for special keystrokes. But, unlike service number 1, this service does not wait for a keystroke—if none is available, then the service returns with an indication of no input. For this service, there is no special handling of the Ctrl-Break keystroke.

Service number 7 is like service 1, but the input character is not echoed to the display screen. Also, as with service 6, Ctrl-Break is not checked for.

Service number 8 is like service 1, without the echo to the display screen. Like service number 1, and unlike service number 7, Ctrl-Break is checked for.

You will notice that services 1, 6, 7, and 8 provide four keyboard input services with some of the eight possible combinations of waiting or not, echoing or not, and Ctrl-Break checking or not. To reduce any confusion, here is a summary table:

| Service | Wait | Echo | Ctrl-Break test |
|---------|------|------|-----------------|
| 1 | Yes | Yes | Yes |
| 6 | No | No | No |
| 7 | Yes | No | No |
| 8 | Yes | No | Yes |

In addition, service 6 doubles for display screen output. Apparently these services were set up on an ad-hoc basis, to satisfy the standard needs of DOS command programs, rather than as a complete logical set of keyboard services.

Service number 9 is used to send a string of characters to the display screen, with each character treated in the same way that service 2 does. The peculiarity of this service, which reduces its usefulness, is that instead of accepting a count of the length of the string, the service uses a dollar sign, "$" to indicate the end of the string. This is another indication that some of the DOS facilities were not developed in a general way, but just took care of some particular needs.

Service number 10, hex A, provides buffered keyboard input. While the previous keyboard input services passed their results immediately to your program, this service accumulates a complete logical unit of input, which is ended by the enter key. The other keyboard services have the advantage of letting a program respond immediately to keystrokes. But they have the disadvantage of making the program perform any editing operations, such as interpreting a backspace to mean rubbing-out the previous character. This service puts the standard DOS editing operations at the command of your programs, which can be a great convenience. Using this service when appropriate, and the other services when appropriate lets your programs get the best of both worlds. To use this service, your program must provide an input buffer, which may vary in size. The first byte of the buffer is used to tell DOS how big the buffer is, and the second byte is used by DOS to tell you how many characters of input there are.

Service number 11, hex B, is used to test if keyboard input is available—without reading it, if it is. Like service 6, this service does not wait for input. But, unlike service 6, the character is not taken if it is available, and a test for Ctrl-Break is done.

Service number 12, hex C, clears the keyboard buffer of any characters which have been typed. It is always possible that the person at the keyboard has typed ahead of what is being taken in. If a program detects an error and sends an error message to the user, it needs to be sure that any keyboard input is in response to the error message, and isn't something that was typed before. This service fills that need by clearing the keyboard buffer. (For an explanation of how the keyboard buffers work, see Chapter 10.) This service also goes on to perform one of services 1, 6, 7, 8, or 10. The buffer referred to here is an internal buffer, and not the program's buffer used in service number 10.

Next come the diskette service functions. For information about diskette files, in order to make more sense of what is said here, see Chapter 5. To make use of most of these services, you must be able to correctly use a DOS file control block, which we won't go into here.

Service number 13, hex D, is used to reset the diskette system. If the default drive has been changed, it is set back to drive A. Also see service 25.

Service number 14, hex E, is used to set the default diskette drive. The drive is specified by number 0 through 3, for drives A through D. Also see service 25.

Service number 15, hex F, is used to open a diskette file. Your program must provide a standard DOS-format file control block, which includes the file name. If the file is not found on the diskette, then an error signal is returned. If you wish to open-old-or-create-new, then use service 22. The actual opening of a file makes a logical connection between a diskette file directory entry and a program's file control block.

Service number 16, hex 10, is used to close a diskette file, which was opened with service 15. The actual practical function of closing a file is to update the file directory entry on the diskette.

Service number 17, hex 11, is used to start a search of a diskette's file directory. This service is used when generic file names are used, such as "B:*.BAK", or "???QQ.INC". If a matching file is found, then DOS constructs a complete file control block for the specific file, which makes it possible for your programs to then open the file. Allowing for the use of generic file names can add a great deal of power and flexibility to your programs.

Service number 18, hex 12, is used to continue a generic file name search that was begun with service 17. Service 17 starts the search, and returns the first matching file found. Service 18 continues the search, and returns any subsequent matching files.

Service number 19, hex 13, is used to delete a file from the diskette. The file name given may be generic, so it is not necessary to use services 17 and 18 to delete a group of files.

Service number 20, hex 14, is used to read a file sequentially. The next record in order is read from the file. Error signals are set if the read was not successful.

Service number 21, hex 15, is used to write a file sequentially. The next record in order is written to the file. Error signals are set if the write was not successful.

These sequential read and write services, and the random service numbers 33 and 34 described below, are used for fixed length records—DOS does not provide the services necessary to work with variable length records, such as the lines of a text file. To work with variable length records, your programs must do the logical record handling. Often the best way to do that is to describe the file to DOS as a sequential file of one byte records, which you can then read and write one character at a time.

Service number 22, hex 16, is used to "create" a file. If there is an existing file with the given name, it is re-used; if not, a new file directory entry is created, with a data length of zero. This service also opens the file, so it may be used in place of service 15 when your intention is to open a file without regard to whether or not it already exists. Service number 23, hex 17, is used to rename one or more files. For this service generic file names may be used.

There is no service 24. Service number 25, hex 19, is used to find out the current default diskette, by its numeric code; 0 through 3 are drives A through D. See also services 13 and 14.

Service number 26, hex 1A, is used to set the address of the disk transfer area, or DTA, where actual diskette operations will take place. Unless your programs replace the DOS default DTA, there will be only 128 bytes in the DTA, and no larger records can be transferred. The DTA is not the sector read-write buffer used by DOS.

Service number 27, hex 1B, is used to get the memory address of the current diskette drive's file allocation table (see Chapter 5 for more details on that), along with other diskette information. This service can be used to snoop around inside the current FAT—for example, to discover if you are about to run out of space on a diskette. This is a relatively advanced service to use. Starting with DOS 2.00, this service only provides access to the first part of the FAT, which identifies the type of diskette.

There are no services 28 through 32. Service number 33, hex 21, is used to read a "random" record, that is, one specified by logical record number. DOS computes the location of random records from the fixed record size and the record number.

Service number 34, hex 22, is used to write a random record.

Service number 35, hex 23, is used to determine the size of a file. There are a number of oddities about this service. A generic file name may be used. The file must be unopened. The size is determined in terms of the file's record size, as specified in the unopened file control block. To get the size in bytes, set the record size to one byte.

Service number 36, hex 24, is used when switching between sequential and random modes. It sets the random record field to the same position as the current sequential location.

The next two services depart from diskette handling.

Service number 37, hex 25, is used to set an interrupt vector. Since it is very easy to set interrupt vectors directly, it is unclear why this service exists—perhaps it is to add an extra measure of safety.

Service number 38, hex 26, is used to create a new program segment, in preparation for running a dependent program. This is a relatively advanced service to use.

Now we return to diskette file services. Service number 39, hex 27, is used to read a number of records, from a random file position. This can be used in place of separate uses of service 33, which reads one random record, if you have memory enough to read blocks of your files.

Service number 40, hex 28, is used to write a number of records, from a random file position.

Service number 41, hex 29, is used to parse a file name, from the form that people use, such as "B:CHAPTER.4" into the file control block format that DOS uses. This is obviously a very valuable service, since it lets your programs take in file names in the ordinary form that people write them, and leave the work of interpretation and conversion to DOS. If you wish, this service will allow you to set a default drive id, filename, and filename extension, which will be used if they are not specified in the string being parsed. This can be very useful. This service also takes care of converting generic file names that include an asterisk, as in "B:*.BAK", into the form of generic file names with question marks, which is the format required in file control locks.

Service number 42, hex 2A, is used to read the system date. The date is returned in the form of three binary numbers, corresponding to the year, month, and day of the month. As we will see in Chapter 11, the date will automatically be updated the first time that the DOS date or time service is requested after each midnight. This happens when the time is required for any purpose, including updating the time-stamp on a diskette file directory entry. If the time is not requested even once between two midnights, then the date will be incorrect.

Service number 43, hex 2B, is used to set the system date.

Service number 44, hex 2C, is used to read the system time. The time is reported in hours, minutes, seconds, and hundredths of seconds. The clock count, which is the basis of the system time, is only changed about 18 times a second, so the hundredths of a second figure is only approximate. Since the clock is updated roughly each .0546 second, it cannot be used to time very short intervals. The calculation of hundredths of seconds, however, is done accurately from what the clock count shows, and over a period of time the hundredths of a second value will be evenly distributed from 0 to 99. This means that your programs can safely use the system time to generate a pseudo-random number.

Service number 45, hex 2D, is used to set the system time.

Service number 46, hex 2E, is used to control diskette write verification. If verification is turned on, then each write operation to the diskette will be verified for errors, by re-reading the data, and comparing it with the original data. It is unlikely that you will need this service, since diskettes are quite reliable, and since quite a bit of error checking is done automatically. But if you want verification, here it is.

This is the end of the list of DOS services available. Later, when we cover the services provided by the ROM-BIOS, you will see some overlap between them and these DOS services. But for the most part, DOS and the ROM-BIOS cover very different kinds of service needs.

In the next chapter we will move on to a big topic—diskettes, and how their data is formatted.

# 5

# Laps Around the Track—
# Inside Diskettes

Diskettes have become the standard, and most widely used, medium for storing personal computer programs and data. In this chapter we'll discuss everything you need to know about diskettes, how data is stored on them, and how diskette data is structured. As a bonus, you'll learn a little about copy protection.

We are nicely in the middle of our three circles of interest. Everything covered here generally applies to the IBM/PC, to PC-compatible computers, and to the family of computers that uses MS-DOS. Some of the other computers will, however, use other diskette sizes and formats.

As we mentioned in the last chapter, starting with DOS version 2.00, new types of diskettes can easily be added to DOS. The scheme for doing this requires that new types of disks are used in the same manner as the diskettes that were originally available for the IBM/PC. So what we cover in this chapter should apply to any new disk devices that are added, except that the detailed numbers, which specify specific capacity, will be changed.

## 5.1 Diskette mechanics

Floppy diskettes, as they are known, are ideal for use as a storage medium for personal computers like the IBM/PC. Their size is convenient, their cost is low, and they are fairly reliable. With reasonable care, diskettes are rarely damaged. All in all, it is easy to see why they became the most widely used storage media for personal computers, long before the IBM/PC appeared. It was only natural that IBM would use diskettes when choosing a storage medium for the IBM/PC.

Let's take a quick look at what a diskette is. (See figure 5.1 for a simple diagram.) The diskette itself is a circular piece of soft plastic covered with the familiar brown oxide coating common to all magnetic media, such as recording tape. While the storage disks used on large computers have been made of rigid metal platters, the plastic used for diskettes is flexible, which lead to the popular name "floppy diskettes,"

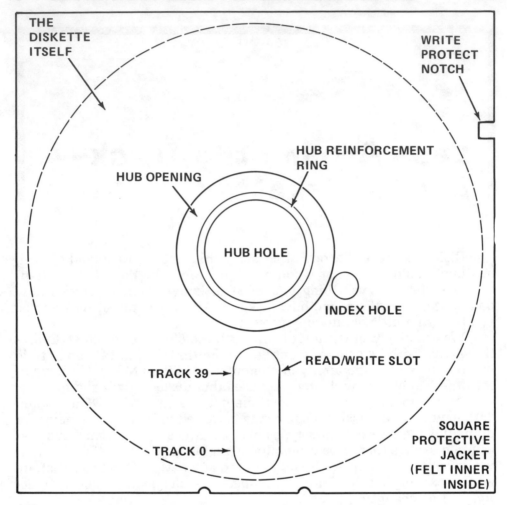

**Figure 5.1—A Diskette Revealed.**

or floppies. The flexibility of floppy diskettes made them much less likely to be damaged when people handle them, and that is a large part of their success.

The circular, magnetically coated disk is always enclosed in a square protective jacket. On the inside of this jacket, unseen until you peek inside, is a white felt-like layer which helps protect the diskette. It acts as a cushion and as a dust catcher.

The square protective jacket—which for some reason seems always to be black—has openings in it for four different purposes. The first is the hub opening in the center. Through this hub opening the diskette drive reaches in and grabs the flexible disk, in order to spin it around.

The second opening in the protective jacket is an oblong slot through which the diskette drive's reading and writing mechanism, the magnetic recording heads, approach the brown recording surface. All the actual reading and writing of data goes on through this slot.

The third opening is a small hole near the hub. This hole in the case is used to reveal a small index hole punched in the diskette. The index hole is used to indicate the starting and ending of a circular recording track on the diskette. This index hole is a reference point for identifying what is recorded on the diskette. If you have never seen the index hole, gently turn a diskette in its case until the hole appears in the opening. For the sort of diskette used on the IBM/PC, there is one hole in the full circle of plastic.

The fourth opening, a square cut on the side of the protective case, is the write-protect notch. Almost all magnetic storage media have some variation of write-protection. If this notch is open, the diskette drive has permission to write data onto the diskette; if the notch is covered, the diskette is protected from writing. Some diskettes don't have this notch cut into their jackets at all, to completely prevent you from accidentally changing the data recorded on them. Many of the diskettes that come with IBM software, such as the DOS diskette itself, don't have the write-protection notch. Diskettes like these are recorded on specially modified diskette drives that ignore the write-protection.

Don't be fooled into thinking that by covering the write-protection notch, you have absolutely protected your diskettes from being erased or over-written. A covered notch only means that a diskette drive that is working correctly won't try to write on the diskette. A defective drive could do anything, notch or no notch. It is unlikely that you will ever lose data this way, but it could happen.

## 5.2 Storage format

Data is stored on a diskette in "tracks." A track is a full circle around the diskette, some distance away from the hub. Different tracks are different distances away from the hub. The format used for the IBM/PC has forty tracks on a diskette.

Each track is divided into parts called "sectors," or "records." Sectors are the fundamental unit of diskette storage. Whenever the computer reads or writes on a diskette, it always reads and writes full sectors, no matter how much or how little data is wanted. Although you, or your programs, may organize your data into units of whatever size you want, the computer and the diskette always work with sectors as units of storage—behind the scenes and generally hidden from you. For the IBM/PC, with DOS, there are eight sectors on a track. Each sector holds 512 bytes, or characters, of data. (To understand how your data is shoe-horned into 512-byte sectors, see sections 5.9 and 5.10 below.)

The term "record" is sometimes used to mean the same thing as "sector." We'll be better off to save the word "record" for our programs' logical units of data, and use "sector" for the diskette's physical unit of data.

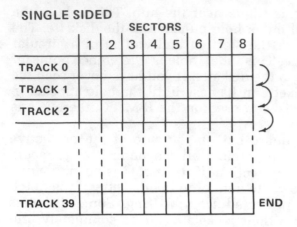

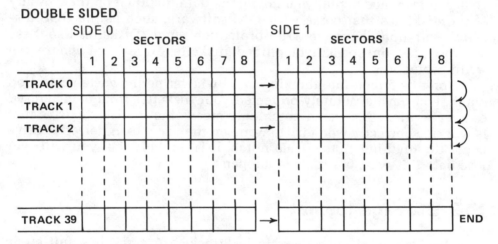

**Figure 5.2—Diskette Sector Diagram.**

Diskettes can have data stored on one or both sides. The IBM/PC uses both single and double sided formats. Initially the IBM/PC could only use single-sided diskettes; but later, beginning with DOS version 1.10, IBM added double sided diskettes. See figure 5.2 for a diagram of the sectors on a diskette.

At this point, we had better pause to get our notation straight. There are one or two sides to a diskette; forty tracks of data per side; eight sectors per track; and 512 bytes of data per sector. How are we going to refer to them? In this book, we will use the numbering convention that IBM has adopted in its reference books, even though it is a little inconsistent. The sides are numbered 0 and 1; a single-sided diskette has only the first side, side number 0. The tracks are numbered 0 through 39; track 0 is on the outside of the diskette, and is the beginning part of the diskette, while track 39 is closest to the hub. The sectors, just to be inconsistent, are numbered 1 through 8. Thus the first sector on the diskette, is side 0, track 0, sector 1.

For the data within a sector there isn't any particular convention to follow. If we refer to data offsets, then the offsets begin with 0; the first byte (character) in a sector is at offset 0, the 2nd is at offset 1, and so forth. As appropriate, we'll refer to bytes either by offset (beginning with 0) or by order (beginning with 1).

The sectors on a diskette have a consecutive order and, as much as possible, they are used in this order. The order begins with the very first sector on a diskette, the one at side 0, track 0, sector 1. It is followed by sectors 2 through 8, on the same track. For a double-sided diskette, the 8th sector on side 0 is followed by the 1st sector on side 1, at the same track location. For either single or double sided format, the last sector at one track location is followed by the first sector of the next higher track number.

You've probably noticed that, when following the consecutive sector order on double-sided diskettes, the side changes before the track does, so that both sides are used at one track location before the system moves on to another track. It would make most sense to refer to sector locations in the order track-side-sector, instead of side-track-sector—since that is the logical order in which they are used. But the IBM manuals usually refer to sectors by giving the side, then the track, then the sector number, and we'll follow their convention.

## 5.3 Various kinds of diskettes, and the secret of copy protection

In the world of diskettes there are many more varieties than are used by the IBM/PC. Let's take a look at them, to get a better understanding of what the IBM/PC uses.

The customary floppy diskettes come in two sizes. The larger format is 8 inches in diameter, and the smaller is 5 1/4 inches. (A newly-arrived format, about 3 inches in diameter, comes in a rigid case and isn't floppy to the handler.)

The IBM/PC, like most personal computers, uses the smaller 5 1/4 format, while the IBM Displaywriter (a close cousin to the IBM/PC), uses the larger format. To make a distinction between the two, the computer trade sometimes calls our 5 1/4 format a "mini-diskette", so don't be surprised if you see that term used in catalogues of computer supplies. Mini-diskettes are what the IBM/PC uses.

Recording density—that is, how much information is squeezed into the recording space—is another variable factor in diskettes. There are various densities used, and the terminology used is a little confusing. The standard diskettes used by the IBM/PC have a recording density that is usually called double-density, and they provide 40 tracks of data on the recording surface. Another format is called quad-density, and provides 80 tracks in the same space. You may occasionally see recording density specified in tracks per inch. Double density—the normal density for the PC—is 48 tracks per inch, or 48 TPI, while quad density is 96 TPI.

There are two ways that sectors can be placed on a diskette. They are known as hard sectoring and soft sectoring. If the size of the sectors is strictly predefined, mechanically, then the sectoring is hard. A hard sectored diskette has an index hole for each sector in the circle around the tracks, since the sectors are exactly placed in pre-defined locations. The alternative to hard sectoring is soft sectoring.

On a soft sectored diskette, the sectors can be of more or less any size and the size is determined by the control programs, working intimately with the diskette drive. A soft sectored diskette needs only one index hole, to indicate the location of the beginning and end of the tracks. The soft sectoring used on the IBM/PC allows sectors to be any of four sizes, all round numbers in binary notation: 128 bytes, 256 bytes, 512 bytes (the DOS standard), and 1,024 bytes.

Diskette data can't be written and read arbitrarily. It needs to have a framework of electronic signals around it, stored on the diskette. This framework is called formatting, and it is analogous to the lines ruled on a tablet of writing paper. It is for this reason that new diskettes must be formatted with the DOS command FORMAT, before they can be used.

A key part of the formatting process is the writing of address marks, which identify each sector and indicate its size. When you get into the details of diskette data access, and the errors that can occur when reading and writing to diskettes, you will see missing address marks as one of the error conditions.

The diskette FORMAT command not only creates diskette sectors, complete with their address marks, but also sets the data sectors on the diskette to a particular value (hex F6), or character code CHR$(246). Looking for this value is one way of telling if a sector has ever been used or not.

Our IBM/PC uses soft-sectored diskettes, even though officially, under DOS, only the 512-byte sector size is used. There are several advantages to soft sectoring, even when a fixed sector size is actually used. One advantage is simply to keep all possible options open. Another is to allow operating systems, other than the IBM-standard DOS operating system, to set their own conventional sector size.

But probably the strongest reason for soft sectoring is copy protection. The DOS operating system is designed to only read and write standard 512-byte sectors, yet the diskette drives can read and write other sector sizes. So a smart program can bypass DOS, and have some or all its data in unconventional sector sizes that DOS, and normal DOS programs, can't read. This is the heart of copy protection on the IBM/PC. Although there are several ways to copy protect diskettes, the most common is simply to make use of sectors of a size different than DOS's standard size. Usually only a small part of a copy-protected diskette has odd-sized sectors, while the bulk of the data will be in the conventional 512-byte DOS sector format.

As you might imagine, the various varieties of diskettes, 8 inch or 5 1/4 inch, double or quad density, soft or hard sectored, and so forth, are almost completely incompatible with each other. The one exception, is that single and double sided diskettes can be used together. There is more to diskette compatibility than the physical differences, however. To be used together, diskettes must have compatible logical formatting (such as how the file directory is stored). This is why you can't just merrily pass data from an Apple computer diskette to your IBM/PC, or from the DOS operating system to the CP/M-86 operating system, unless you have conversion programs designed to perform that specific task.

## 5.4 Our diskette drives—the standard Tandon

It happens occasionally that one company designs a product so well that it becomes an industry standard—capturing most of the market through a combination of its own sales and sales of close imitations. This has been the case with Tandon's TM-100 series of diskette drives. IBM seems to have adopted the Tandon as its quality standard for diskette drives and, as much as anyone can determine in this area of closely guarded secrets, only the Tandon TM-100's have been sold as the official diskette drive for the IBM/PC.

There are four popular variations on the Tandon TM-100. By looking at them we can see what IBM chose to give us, and what it didn't.

The Tandon TM 100-1 is a double-density (that is, 40-track) single sided drive. This was the standard for the original release of the IBM/PC. Later, beginning with DOS release 1.10, IBM began using the TM 100-2, still double density, but now double-sided, for twice the data capacity. (We'll cover how the DOS operating system handles two different kinds of diskettes below.) The other two popular Tandon TM-100's are the quad-density drives, the 100-3 and the 100-4, with eighty tracks per surface, single- or double-sided.

Why IBM did not choose to use the quad density drives is a matter of speculation. My best guess is that they considered the gain in data capacity to not be worth the risk of increased vulnerability to diskette damage and data error that usually accompanies increased density.

More mysterious is the original decision to use single-sided diskette drives, rather than only double-sided drives. From the long perspective on this machine it seems rather foolish to have used single-sided drives at all. The most likely reason is that IBM was concerned with the PC being priced too high above the range of the traditional home computer, and adopted single-sided drives to hold down the cost of the system.

There are several signs that IBM wanted to keep the price of entry-level machines as low as possible. This is the only reason, that I can see, to account for the almost completely unused cassette version of the machine, and also for the original use of single-sided diskettes. The idea appears to have been that serious users of the IBM/PC, with their eyes on the future, would get machines with appropriately high-powered disk equipment. But to keep from scaring off the hesitant beginner, IBM chose the most modestly priced diskette drive available, the single-sided drive.

## 5.5  File storage strategy

Many different schemes can be used to organize, store, and keep track of the data on a diskette. Each possible scheme has its strengths and weaknesses in terms of the efficient use of space, speed of access, safety and robustness. (How likely are things to go wrong? And when things do go wrong, how big is the mess? This is the measure of robustness.) The design of a data storage scheme is mostly an exercise in the art of balancing these different needs, which partially conflict.

In this section we'll explain the strategy that DOS uses for storing diskette data. Here is an outline of how it is done, before we get into the details: First, all file data is stored in standard-sized, 512-byte sectors. Second, these data-storage sectors are taken from an open pool of available sectors—no sectors or areas of the diskette are reserved (with one partial exception, the area reserved for the two system files IBMBIO.COM and IBMDOS.COM; we'll explain more about that, below).

Third, the allocation of these data-storage sectors, and the logical connection between the sectors that make up a file's data, is handled apart from the data sectors, in a mechanism known as the File Allocation Table (FAT). Finally, each diskette has a directory, or table of contents, used to keep track of the files on the diskette. This data storage scheme leads to four different categories of diskette sectors, one for data storage, and three others for special purposes.

As we saw in the the last chapter, any diskette which will be used to start-up the operating system must have a "boot" record program stored in its very first sector. For consistency, every formatted diskette contains the boot record, whether or not it will ever be used to start-up the system. This boot record is the first special category of diskette.

The next special category is the file allocation table, or FAT. The FAT occupies the two sectors which follow the boot record. The file allocation table is used to keep track of the data storage sectors, indicating which are in use and which are not.

The third and last of the special sector categories is the diskette file directory. The directory occupies the sectors immediately following the FAT. There are two sizes of directory: single-sided diskettes have four directory sectors, and double-sided diskettes have seven.

These special categories of sectors occupy the first seven sectors on a single-sided diskette, and ten sectors on a double-sided diskette. All the sectors that follow these seven, or ten, are used to store the data contents of files on the diskette. Figure 5.3 diagrams the location of these four categories of sectors.

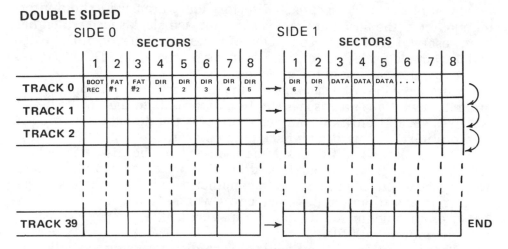

Figure 5.3—Diskette Diagram: 4 Types of Sectors ('Boot', 'FAT', 'DIR', and 'Data').

The directory and the file allocation table are placed at the beginning of a diskette, which seems to be a very sensible place to put them. But, when a file is accessed, DOS must find its entry in the diskette's directory and then go looking for the diskette data. On the average, data sectors are about 20 tracks away, half of the diskette's 40 tracks. Moving the diskette drives read-write head from one track to another is one of the slowest operations in running the computer. So the distance that the head must move, from the directory to the data, can matter.

If the directory were located in the middle of the diskette, the average distance to a data sector would be cut in half, to about 10 tracks. On the other hand, managing a data space that is in two parts, on either side of the directory, is more complicated. For a personal computer system, the benefit of placing the directory in the middle of a diskette is too small to justify the extra problems that it would create. But on large main-frame computer systems, this is a common practice.

Next we'll take a detailed look at the diskette directory and the file allocation table. With that covered, we will be able to discuss how space is allocated to files.

## 5.6 Details of the directory

The diskette directory contains a list of all the files on the diskette. The directory entries contain all the information available about a file, except for the file's space allocation (which is in the FAT).

Each directory entry is 32 bytes long, and so there is room for exactly 16 of them to fit into a 512-byte sector. On a single-sided diskette, there are four directory sectors, which makes room for 64 directory entries. On a double-sided diskette, seven sectors are used for the directory, making room for 112 entries.

Most of the 32 bytes of each directory entry are used to hold information about the files, but there is some unused slack space which has been reserved for future needs. One of the changes between DOS 1.00 and 1.10 made use of some of that expansion room, and DOS 2.00 has also expanded the use of the directory.

Here we'll describe each part of the directory entries in detail. Program listing 5.1 gives a Pascal definition of the data format, while listing 5.3 gives several program routines to process the directory—reading it, interpreting it, and writing it back to the diskette.

DiskLook, one of the programs included in the diskette package which accompanies this book, is designed to display complete directory information. You can use it, in conjunction with this chapter, to get a clearer idea of how a directory entry works. If you are using Disk-Look, press function key f4 to get a display of the complete directory information for each file.

There are eight parts, or fields to each directory entry, as follows:
FILENAME: This field is eight bytes long, located at offsets 0 through 7 in the directory. It contains the name portion of the file name. If the name is less than eight characters long, it is filled on the right with blank spaces.

By the ordinary rules for DOS file names, a file can't have a blank space in the middle of its name. Yet it is possible for files like that to be created. BASIC makes it easy to do since, in BASIC, filenames are enclosed in quotation marks. For example, this BASIC statment will create a file with a blank in its name:

OPEN  "AA BB.FIL"

The IBM Typing Tutor program, which is written in BASIC, uses files with blanks in their names. Because of this, if you write any programs which look at the filename in the diskette directory, you should not assume that the name ends with the first blank character that you encounter—there may be more to the name.

If the first byte of the file name field is hex E5, CHR$(229), then the directory entry is not in use to hold the information for a file. This could mean that the directory entry has never been used, or that the file which formerly used this entry is now erased. Testing the second character for a character code value higher than 'Z' distinguishes unused entries from erased ones.

When a file is erased, only two things happen to it: its space is de-allocated (which we'll cover in the next section on the FAT) and the first character of the filename in the directory is set to hex E5, CHR$(229). None of the directory information is lost, except for that first character of the filename. This is what makes it possible for Disk-Look to display the names of erased files, and what makes it practical for utility programs like UnErase to recover files.

EXTENSION: This field is three bytes long, located at offsets 8 through 10, within the directory entry. It contains the extension portion of the file name. As with the main part of the file name, a short extension is padded with space characters. If the file has no extension, this field contains three spaces.

ATTRIBUTE: This field is one byte long, located at offset 11 within the directory entry. The attribute field is used to control whether or not a file is "hidden," that is, not seen by ordinary directory searches. There are eight bits in the attribute byte, and two of them have been defined to control the "hidden" and "system" attributes. The other six bits were originally undefined, and some of them are being used by DOS release 2.00. For earlier versions of DOS, these six bits are undefined and are set to zero.

The 7th bit of the attribute byte, with a numeric value of 2, controls the hidden attribute. The 6th bit, with a value of 4, controls the system attribute. Thus a normal, visible file has an attribute value of 0, a hidden file 2, a system file 4, and a file that is both hidden and system, 6.

Although the system attribute is controlled independently from the hidden attribute, the two attributes are functionally the same. Each independently causes a file to be invisible to ordinary directory searches. Although it is tempting to speculate that the system attribute was defined for some future use, Microsoft indicates that it was set up simply to create more compatibility with other operating systems.

RESERVED: This field is used to hold the part of the directory entry that is not yet in use. For the original release of DOS, version 1.00, this field was 12 bytes long, located at offsets 12 through 23; for DOS 1.10, it is ten bytes long, located at offsets 12 through 21.

Any future additions to the function of the file directory will make use of this space. The unused bytes in this field are set to hex 00 when a directory entry is used. Before an entry is used for the first time, the FORMAT operation leaves this field set to hex F6, CHR$(246). Any other value in this field is an indication of expanded use.

TIME: This field is two bytes long, in the format of a 16-bit unsigned integer, located at offsets 22 through 23. Starting with DOS release 1.10, this field holds the time of day of the creation, or updating, of a file. In the original DOS release, only the date was kept, and this field was part of the reserved field.

Most of the operations which will display a file's time stamp, such as the DIR directory listing, only show the time to the minute. But the format that the time is stored in allows an accuracy to within two seconds.

The format of the time stamp is as a 16-bit unsigned integer, with its value given by this formula:

TIME    = HOURS * 2048 + MINUTES * 32 + SECONDS / 2

DATE: This field is two bytes long, located at offsets 24 through 25. Like the time, it is formatted as a 16-bit unsigned integer, with its value given by this formula:

DATE    = (YEAR - 1980) * 512 + MONTH * 32 + DAY

The year may range from 1980 through 2099, kept as the relative values 0 through 119. Although the format for storing the date can accommodate a relative year up to 127 (which is 2107), DOS programs only handle years through 2099. No one expects DOS to be in use anywhere near that long.

Both the format and the location of the date and time fields are carefully set up so that the date and time marks can be treated as one four-byte integer, for time comparisons. It is also relatively easy to extract the components of the date and time, and to calculate their differences. For example, to break-down the date, these formulas, expressed in Pascal, can be used:

year    := 1980 + date_field div 512;
month   := (date_field mod 512) div 32;
day     := date_field mod 32;

STARTING CLUSTER NUMBER: This field is two bytes long, located at offset 26 through 27, in the format of a 16-bit number. This is the entry point to a file's space allocation, and refers to the file's beginning point in the file allocation table (FAT); more is explained in the next section on the FAT. The starting cluster is the first part of the file's data space on the diskette.

FILE SIZE: This field is four bytes long, located at offsets 28 through 31. The file size is given in bytes, in the format of a four-byte unsigned integer, which may be treated as a pair of two-byte numbers.

The file size is not necessarily exact. For all files, the file size should accurately reflect the size of the file, in terms of the number of sectors used. (If it does not, for any reason, the DOS utility CHKDSK will report an error and adjust the size accordingly.) After that, there is some flexibility in the file size value.

For program files in the ".COM" format, and for files built out of fixed length data, the file size in the directory is the only way to determine where the exact end of the file data is. For these files, the file size value is kept accurately.

For some other file formats, this is not the case, and the file size given in the directory entry may be slightly off. The most common instance of this is with ASCII text files, which we will cover in section 5.9. ASCII text files have an end-of-file marker built into them, which is used to mark the precise end of the data. Because of this, some programs which process text files are sloppy about the way in which they cause the file size to be maintained.

For example, if a program writes a text file not byte by byte, but in blocks of 128 bytes, DOS will only be able to keep track of the file size to within 127 bytes of the true size. It can be enormously more efficient for text editing programs to read and write data in large blocks, rather than a byte at a time. This is a common occurrence, and you should not rely on the file size value being exact, at least for ASCII text files. DOS doesn't, and neither should you.

## 5.7 Details of the FAT (file allocation table)

The allocation of diskette space to files is controlled by the file allocation table, or FAT. The use of the FAT, and understanding how to decode it, is somewhat intricate—so we'll lay a little ground work first.

The basic idea of the FAT is that it is simply a table with one entry for every cluster, or chunk of diskette space that can be allocated for files. Entries in the table can indicate that they are in use, or that they are available for allocation. Available, or free, entries are indicated by a zero value in the table.

The space that belongs to a file is connected together by the simple strategy of "chaining." A file's directory entry contains the number of the FAT entry that corresponds to the first part of the file's data. In the FAT table, that entry contains the FAT number of the next part of the file; and that entry points in turn to the next, and the next, until the last part of the file is reached. At the final FAT entry for each file, an end-of-file mark is placed. See figure 5.4 for a diagram of how this works.

This is the simple outline of how the FAT works. But the plot thickens considerably when we get into the details.

First, let's consider the clusters of space that are allocated. For single-sided diskettes, space is allocated one sector at a time. For double-sided diskettes space is allocated two sectors at a time. When there is more than one sector per cluster, consecutive sectors are grouped into one cluster. For double-sided diskettes, a cluster consists of an even and odd sector number, on the same track. So, for double-sided diskettes, each track has four clusters on each side, or eight clusters in all. On each side, the four clusters consist of sectors 1 and 2 for the first cluster, followed by 3 and 4, 5 and 6, and finishing either side of the track, the cluster made of sectors 7 and 8. (Whenever larger-capacity disk devices are added, we can expect to see space allocated in even larger clusters than the two sectors used with double-sided diskettes. In Chapter 4 we mentioned how device handlers can be dynamically added to the BIOS,

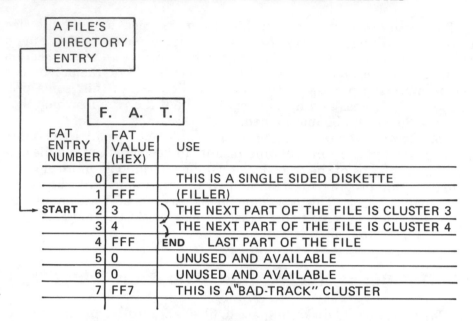

Figure 5.4—A Sample File Allocation Table.

beginning with DOS version 2.00. Part of this scheme allows for disk devices to be added, in a way that is compatible with the existing diskettes. Among the factors which can be set for a new device is the number of sectors in a cluster.)

Allocating diskette space on a double-sided diskette in clusters of two sectors seems like a potential waste of space, since sometimes a file will use only part of the first sector of its last cluster—leaving an entire sector unused. But with double-sided diskettes space is wasted in no greater proportion than it is on a single-sided diskette. The principle reason for allocating space in clusters bigger than one sector, is to avoid an unending growth in the size of the file allocation table, the FAT, as larger and larger diskettes are used.

The data portion of a diskette follows immediately after the diskette's directory, and proceeds, cluster by cluster, from there to the end of the diskette. The first data cluster is number 2 (this seems odd, but we'll see the reason in a moment). Figure 5.5 diagrams the cluster layout for single-and double-sided diskettes.

On both single and double sided-diskettes, two copies of the FAT are stored, on side 0, track 0, sectors 2 and 3. The copies are supposed to be identical. Since the FAT is a critical piece of information, it is stored twice as a precaution. Repairing a damaged directory is simple compared to repairing a damaged FAT. The usefulness of storing two copies of the FAT depends upon many things, such as how extensive or limited any damage to a diskette is, and how intelligent are the programs or people doing any repair work. Prior to release 2.00, DOS did not include much in the way of diskette repair tools.

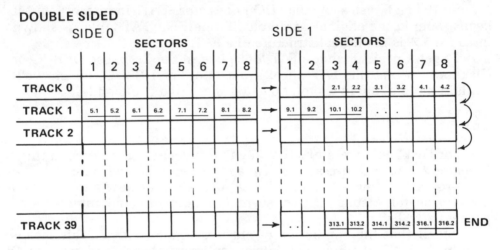

**Figure 5.5—Diskette Diagram: Cluster Numbers.**

I suspect that two sectors are allocated to the FAT not so much to keep two copies, as to allow the size of the FAT to grow in the future. It can't grow indefinitely, but it could double in size and still stay within two sectors.

Next we'll finally see how a FAT is coded in detail. A quick calculation shows that there are more than 300 clusters on a diskette. A FAT entry has to be able to hold the index number of another FAT entry, and the biggest number that you can store in one byte is 255; so each FAT entry has to be bigger than one byte. On the other hand, there isn't room in a 512-byte sector for a FAT with over 300 entries that are each two-bytes big. The solution to this problem is an intricate scheme to use FAT entries that are three hexadecimal digits wide, or one and a half bytes big. Needless to say, this leads to some complications.

The scheme for storing numbers that are one-and-a-half bytes wide looks on paper, to a human, to be very odd. But the method makes simple sense in machine language, and it was designed to be efficiently implemented on the computer, even if it makes us count on our fingers and toes to follow it.

The idea behind how a FAT's information is stored is to scramble the FAT entries in pairs, interweaving two 1 1/2 byte entries, to make a tidy 3 bytes for the pair. To get the value stored in the FAT entry number X, do the following: First, multiply X by 1 1/2 (that really means multiply by 3 and divide by 2). Then, use that number as an offset into the FAT. Load the two-byte number located at that offset into a register. You now have four hexadecimal digits in the register, and you want only three, for a three digit FAT entry. If the FAT entry number was odd, discard the low order digit; for an even entry, discard the high order hex digit. If that is confusing to you, then turn to figure 5.6 to see how to manually scramble or unscramble a FAT entry.

Figure 5.7 shows the relationship between a FAT as stored on a sector and the FAT seen as a table. DOS does store FATs in memory, but it keeps them in the original, scrambled format. The FAT table, as shown in figure 5.7, is the logical structure of a FAT.

To get a peek at what a FAT looks like in the flesh, use DEBUG or DiskLook to read the FAT off of a diskette. For DEBUG, which we'll explain more about in Chapter 6, enter these two commands:

```
L 0 0 1 1
D 0 L 200
```

For DiskLook, press function key f7 to select a sector, type in track 0, sector 2, and then press f6 to display the complete FAT data.

Program listing 5.2 gives a Pascal definition of how a FAT is laid out on a sector. Listing 5.3 gives several programs to read, interpret and process a FAT.

Recall that the numbering of clusters begins with 2. This means that in the FAT, the first two entries (entry number 0, and number 1) aren't used for allocating data. They are reserved for holding one key piece of information—the format of the diskette. For a single-sided diskette the first byte of the FAT has the hex value FE; for a double-sided diskette the byte is FF. Other codes are used for other diskette formats, when they apply. See figure 5.7 again to take a look at these special first two entries in the FAT.

Control programs detect which format a diskette has by inspecting the beginning of the FAT data. In fact the program located on the boot record, which we discussed in the last chapter, has to inspect the FAT to determine where the two system files, IBMBIO.COM and IBMDOS.COM, are located. This is the reason why there was a change in the boot record program between DOS versions 1.00 and 1.10.

A little arithmetic will show that a single-sided diskette has 313 one-sector clusters (numbered 2 through 314) and a double-sided diskette has 315 two-sector clusters (numbered 2 through 316). For single-sided, that's 320 total sectors, minus 1 "boot", 2 FAT, and 4 directory, leaving 313; for double-sided, 640 total sectors, minus 1 "boot", 2 FAT, and 7 directory, leaving 630 sectors, or 315 two-sector clusters. There is

This shows how to scramble and unscramble File Allocation Table entries.  The technique is for use by people, from a visual display; programs do it differently (with the same result).

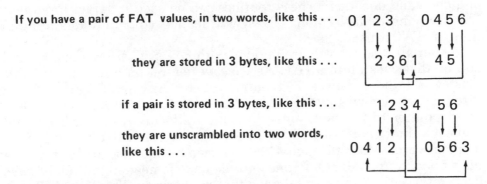

If you have a pair of FAT values, in two words, like this . . .    0 1 2 3    0 4 5 6

they are stored in 3 bytes, like this . . .    2 3 6 1    4 5

if a pair is stored in 3 bytes, like this . . .    1 2 3 4    5 6

they are unscrambled into two words, like this . . .    0 4 1 2    0 5 6 3

Figure 5.6—Scrambling and Unscrambling FAT Entries.

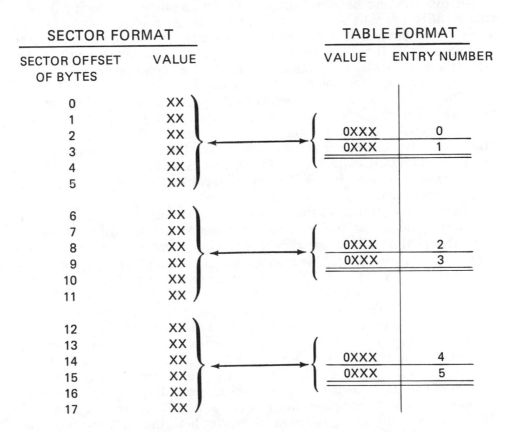

SECTOR FORMAT

| SECTOR OFFSET OF BYTES | VALUE |
|---|---|
| 0 | XX |
| 1 | XX |
| 2 | XX |
| 3 | XX |
| 4 | XX |
| 5 | XX |
| 6 | XX |
| 7 | XX |
| 8 | XX |
| 9 | XX |
| 10 | XX |
| 11 | XX |
| 12 | XX |
| 13 | XX |
| 14 | XX |
| 15 | XX |
| 16 | XX |
| 17 | XX |

TABLE FORMAT

| VALUE | ENTRY NUMBER |
|---|---|
| 0XXX | 0 |
| 0XXX | 1 |
| 0XXX | 2 |
| 0XXX | 3 |
| 0XXX | 4 |
| 0XXX | 5 |

Figure 5.7—File Allocation Table: From Sector to Table. (See figure 5.6 for the scrambling pattern.)

room in a 512-byte sector for 340 FAT entries, so there is some slack space at the end of the sectors which hold the FAT.

Program listing 5.3 contains Pascal routines that map out the FAT, and code and decode it. These routines can be used in larger programs. Just studying them by themselves will deepen your understanding of how the FAT is used.

After all this, we still aren't done with FAT's. There is some special coding that goes on in a FAT. As we saw before, an unused, available cluster is indicated by a FAT entry of zero. Any table value from 2 through 314 (for single-sided diskettes) or 316 (for double-sided), is a valid pointer to the next entry in a file's allocation chain. The eight highest values that can be kept in a FAT entry, hex FF8 through FFF, decimal values 4088 through 4095, are used as signals for the end of a file's allocation chain. Only one end-file code is needed, but eight have been reserved for any special need that might arise. The eight FAT values hex FF0 through FF7, decimal 4080 through 4087, are set aside for any special kinds of reserved clusters, such as bad sectors.

A diskette can have defective areas on its surface, which can't be successfully used to store data. When a diskette is formatted, these areas are detected and removed from potential use. In the original 1.00 version of DOS, these bad sectors were kept out of harm's way by being allocated to a special hidden file which had the file name of "badtrack." Starting with DOS version 1.10, a more elegant method was used.

The FAT value 4087, hex FF7, is used to mark a cluster as unusable, because it could not be formatted successfully. One of the advantages of this method of marking bad clusters, is that it does not occupy a directory entry. DiskLook can be used to see the exact location of any bad sectors on a diskette, something that DOS will not show you.

Any other values in a FAT table entry, anything between 314 (or 316) and 4080 is an improper value.

There are a number of things that can go wrong with a FAT. Two of the most notable are orphan clusters, and cross-linked files. If a FAT entry shows that it is in use (because the entry value is not zero), and yet the entry is not in any file's allocation chain, the FAT entry is a sort of orphan. On the other hand, if two or more different files' allocation chains lead to the same cluster, the files are cross linked. The DOS utility program CHKDSK will report either orphan clusters or cross-linked files, and return orphan clusters to the pool of available clusters.

Orphan clusters are most often created when a program begins to create a file (so that clusters are allocated to it), and then never closes the file, so that the file's directory entry is never completed. The first version of the IBM Pascal compiler does this regularly, when it detects errors in the source program. Regular use of the CHKDSK program will quickly fix any orphaned clusters, no matter how they are created. You should include CHKDSK in a batch execution file with any program that you use that tends to create orphan clusters.

While orphan clusters are not unheard of, cross-linked files are rare. I have only encountered them when I deliberately have created them. If you ever get cross-linked files, each of the files can be copied to another diskette, for later repair, as needed. When this is done, each file will contain a copy of the data from the cross-linked sectors, though the data can only belong to one of them.

You can see a map of the location of any orphan clusters and cross-linked clusters, by using DiskLook's map operation, which is activated by pressing f9.

When DOS is running, it keeps a copy in memory of the FAT for each diskette drive that it is using. Whenever a change is made to the FAT, it is written out to its two sector copies on diskette. Whenever DOS is taking a fresh look at a diskette, it reads the FAT to check the diskette's format.

Now that you have waded through the intricacies of the directory and the file allocation table, we can look at the formats of data files. First we will look at the two most common ways your data will be stored—ASCII text format, and fixed-length record formats. Then we will look at two formats for holding programs, ".COM" files, and ".EXE" files.

## 5.8 File space allocation

Now that we have laid all of the ground work, let's see how data sectors are allocated for files to use. The method is very simple and straightforward.

As file data is stored, clusters of diskette sectors are allocated to it, one by one. As a new cluster is needed, the lowest available cluster is taken. This simple scheme is used when a file is first created, and when an existing file is lengthened (by writing data onto its end).

Unlike some operating systems (like the UCSD p-System), DOS allocates space cluster by cluster, as needed, without regard for keeping the data of a file all located close together, in one contiguous chunk of storage space. All disk space allocation schemes, for all operating systems, face a simple choice—either to allocate space freely, cluster by cluster, and risk scattering a file all over the diskette; or, to allocate space in large contiguous chunks, and complicate the task of space management. DOS was built using the simpler first method.

If a diskette is empty, then all its available space is in one large clean piece. When files are copied to such a diskette, they end up neatly arranged in contiguous chunks of storage. But later, if a file is lengthened, the new addition will be placed in the first available cluster, which could be anywhere on the diskette—even in front of the original piece of the file.

If files are copied to a fresh diskette and left alone, then their space allocation remains tidy. But if data is created and deleted, the space usage on a diskette can become quite tangled.

This happens particularly when a program is creating two files at the same time. As the files grow in parallel, their space allocation becomes thoroughly interwoven. Sometimes a file can end up using every other sector, with its data scattered all over the diskette.

Programs which create temporary files are especially good at scrambling the data space allocation. For example, the IBM Pascal compiler, which creates two temporary files at the same time, and then later creates a third, does this a lot. Programs that read and copy a text file, such as text editors and spelling checkers also can be good at scrambling data space allocation.

It can be very interesting and instructive to see just what is happening with the space allocation on your diskettes. If you have the utility DiskLook, you can inspect the space allocation on your diskettes, see the location of each file, and discover whether or not the data space has become fragmented.

Now DOS's space allocation scheme is quite nice, since it uses all space equally, and requires no attention from us. But it has these advantages at the risk of leaving files scattered all over the diskettes. This can make it take longer to access the files, as diskette drive's reading head must move around looking for the right tracks. Since diskette access is the slowest and most limiting factor in the performance of the IBM/PC, this could become a problem—although usually it isn't.

Because of this, you should be aware of the potential problem of space fragmentation, for diskette files. Most of the time it will not matter to you at all, but sometimes it may be very important. If you feel that space fragmentation is a problem, you can solve it by copying your files to a freshly formatted diskette. If your diskette drives seem to spending a lot of time grinding their way from one track to another and back, then a clean copy may help a lot.

If you do copy your files to a new diskette, then you also have an opportunity to improve their order—either to put the most used files first, or to put them into the order you prefer for the directory listing. Some arrangements of files are particularly useful: a correspondence diskette you might want in chronological order; for a diskette full of many miscellaneous files, you might want to arrange alphabetically, for quick scanning. It can also be very useful to arrange files in order by their filename extension, since that usually indicates their type, or their use. You can do this re-arranging by hand, or you can use utility programs, including some of those in The Norton Utilities, to help you.

## 5.9 Text file format

The most common and important format for a data file on a diskette, is an ASCII text file. ASCII files, or text files, contain ordinary alphabetic information, such as letters and reports.

Text files are the closest thing there is to a universal format among all personal computers. The format is widely supported—nearly every personal computer uses it—and it has many different uses.

Most text editors, including word processors, use the ASCII text format. The editor which comes with the DOS operating system, called EDLIN, creates and uses text files.

The text format is used to hold the source code (or original, untranslated version) of computer programs. Nearly every computer language processor (such as a BASIC interpreter, a Pascal compiler, or an Assembler) expects to read its programs in ASCII text format.

The BASIC interpreter for the IBM/PC works with BASIC program files in three formats, one of which is the standard ASCII text file. To write a BASIC program into the ASCII format, use the "A" option of the SAVE statement, like this:

```
10  SAVE "PROGRAM.BAS",A
```

Batch processing files, which are one of the most powerful and useful features of the DOS operating system, are stored in text format.

ASCII files take their name from the American Standard Code for Information Interchange, or ASCII. This code was developed as a standard form for passing data from one device to another—information interchange.

To understand ASCII files, we have to take the time to understand a bit about ASCII itself. ASCII mostly consists of a coding structure for characters. It assigns certain bit patterns to data; for example, the bit coding for a capital letter "A" expressed in hexadecimal, is 41.

There are 128 different ASCII codes, since ASCII uses only seven bits for its characters. Most computers, including the IBM/PC, use eight-bit characters, and so the 128 ASCII characters occupy half of the 256 different characters that can be represented by eight-bit bytes. For the IBM/PC, and for most computers, the ASCII characters occupy the first 128 codes, from CHR$(0) through CHR$(127).

Loosely speaking there are three different categories of ASCII characters, and two of them concern us. The most obvious ASCII characters are the ones which represent letters of the alphabet, numerals, punctuation and so forth. They are one of the three categories of ASCII characters, and, of course, we make use of them in everything that we do with personal computers.

The next category I'll call formatting characters. These characters have names which indicate their use, such as "backspace," "carriage return," and "line-feed." The formatting characters were developed essentially as commands to a printing device, to tell it things like how to format a string of text into lines and pages. This category is also of use to us, and we'll come back to it shortly.

The third category of ASCII characters I'll call transmission characters. They have names like "start-of-text" and "end-of-transmission," and they are mostly used as control signals when ASCII is used to transmit data across a communications line. These characters allow the two ends of the data conversation to tell each other what is going on. The full explanation of these transmission characters belongs with a full coverage of communications, and we won't go into them any further here. Since these special codes are used for communications, and not for the data or structure of files, they don't concern us here.

Let's summarize this so far: of the three categories of ASCII characters, one is used to code the ASCII data, such as letters, numbers and punctuation. Another is used for formatting, to indicate such things as where one line ends and another begins; these codes are used both to add structure to a file, and to control printing format. Finally, the last category of ASCII characters is used to control communications transmission, and don't have anything to do with ASCII file formats.

The ordinary ASCII text characters are all located in the codes values from CHR$(32), which is a space character, through CHR$(126), which is a tilde character. The ASCII characters in the two special categories—formatting characters and transmission characters—are located in the codes from CHR$(0) through CHR$(31). These codes are all intended to be used for various control purposes, and they normally appear only behind the scenes, away from the data codes that our programs see. Odd things can happen when your programs deliberately use these codes, and appendix 4 covers some of their ramifications.

Here are three simple BASIC programs that show you how to do a little experimenting with the special ASCII values from 0 through 31:

```
10   REM writing to the display screen
20   FOR I = 0 TO 31
30     PRINT CHR$ (I)
40   NEXT I
```

```
10   REM writing to the printer
20   FOR I = 0 TO 31
30     LPRINT CHR$ (I)
40   NEXT I
```

```
10   REM poking to the display screen
20   DEF SEG = &HB800 ' color-graphics
30   DEF SEG = &HB000 ' monochrome
40   FOR I = 0 TO 31
50     POKE I*2,I
60   NEXT I
```

With that out of the way, let's start looking at ASCII text files. An ASCII text file is a file of text, that is ordinary characters, like letters of the alphabet. The characters in a text file are organized into lines, just like writing on a page.

The boundaries between lines are marked with the ASCII formatting characters carriage-return, which is CHR$(13), and line-feed, which is CHR$(10). Any arbitrary end-of-line marker could be used, but these two characters are used together to mark an end-of-line, since they are exactly the two commands that a printer needs to finish printing one line and start the next.

One of the reasons why the new-line function is divided into two parts, carriage-return and line-feed, is to allow overstriking of printed characters. The most common use of this is for underlining. To overstrike a line, a carriage-return is sent to a printer, followed by the overstrike characters. Since no line-feed was done, the new characters will be printed on top of the old. This works for printers, but it doesn't work for display screens.

So the physical commands that a printer needs to end a line, are also the logical markers used to indicate the end of a line in a file. This sensible scheme makes it possible to copy an ASCII text file directly to a printing device, and have the text print out correctly. You can test this yourself, on a PC, by using the COPY command to send a file directly to a printer or the display screen, with these commands:

```
COPY   filename LPT1
COPY   filename CON
```

There is no limit to the length of a line in an ASCII file, since a line continues, character after character, until a carriage-return and line-feed is found. However, most programs which work with ASCII text set a limit of 255 characters to a line; ordinarily this is much longer than we need. (Some text editors and word processing programs limit data lines to what will fit onto one line on the display screen: 80 characters.)

There is more to the formatting of an ASCII file than line marking. One element that is universal to all ASCII files is the end-of-file marker, which is code CHR$(26). This marker is the definitive way of indicating the end of an ASCII file. For DOS diskette files, the location of the CHR$(26) is the true indication of the size of the file, and not the file size given in the files directory entry.

This special character, which has the code value CHR$(26), can be keyed in by pressing the "Z" key, while holding down the "control" shift key; control-Z is a standard way to enter CHR$(26) on a keyboard. If you ever happen across a mention of control-Z in anything written about personal computers, this is the character (CHR$(26)) and the function (end-of-file marker) that is being referred to.

After these three universal codes, carriage-return, line-feed, and end-file, there are other ASCII formatting codes that are used in varying degrees, in different circumstances. The tab character, CHR$(9), is used to replace a series of blank characters. Since there is no universal fixed specification of tab locations, the meaning of the tab character varies, and so it is not used as extensively as it might be.

The form-feed character, CHR$(12), means skip to the top of a new page. Most printers act on this code in the way that you would expect them to, and so some text editing programs use this character as their marker for separating pages. The use of the form-feed character is far from universal, though. You should probably only make use of it as a command to your printer to start a new page.

Text editing programs, especially word processing programs, have a need for more formatting control characters, and they usually define their own codes for their own purposes, such as marking paragraph boundaries, underlining, and so forth. Since there are no universal codes for these purposes, having these codes inside of ASCII text files can cause confusion between one program and another.

Before we finish with ASCII, let's note a few things about the ordinary text characters. Any coding structure defines a collating sequence—the equivalent of the alphabetic order for all the characters. In ASCII, all the customary punctuation characters come before the letters of the alphabet. Upper case letters come before the lower case letters. And, unlike the EBCDIC code used by IBM's main computers, the numerals come before the alphabet.

The upper case letters come 32 places before the lower case letters. You can use this fact to convert text data to all upper or all lower case.

## 5.10 Data record formats

After ASCII text files, fixed-length files are the most common format for data to be kept in. In a fixed length record file, the logical units of information are called records, and their size is uniform throughout the file. This is the sort of file format that is created by BASIC random files, Pascal direct files, and other non-text files. Each read or write command (which in BASIC are known as INPUT# and WRITE#), transfers one record.

While an ASCII text file has markings to show the ends of lines, and the end of the file, a fixed length record file has nothing to separate one record from another in the file. What is stored in the file is pure data, with no punctuation added.

Since the records in this kind of data file are all the same length, pure arithmetic can be used to determine exactly where each record ends and another begins. The DOS services for reading and writing records from files, described in Chapter 4, use this method both for sequential reading and writing of files, and random reading and writing to files. When your programs read or write records to these files, DOS does all the work of finding the records, and your programs do not have to bother with any of the details of locating records.

Let's consider an example. If a file has a record length of 100, and DOS is requested to perform a random read of record number 24, then DOS can calculate that the record begins at a relative byte offset of 24 × 100, or 2,400 bytes into the file. Dividing by the sector size of 512 bytes, gives a dividend of 4, and a remainder of 352. This indicates that the record is located past four sectors, on the fifth sector, at a sector offset of 352 bytes. (This calculation assumes that the records are numbered starting with a record number zero; if the first record was referred to as number one, then the formula would be adjusted accordingly; but the method is the same.)

In a fixed length record file, DOS does not do any padding or adjusting of records—they are stored one right after another. If the record length does not evenly divide into the 512-byte sector size, then some records will span from one sector to another, which will make reading and writing them less efficient.

In our example with 100 byte records, the next record, number 25, is partly contained in the 5th sector of the file, and partly in the 6th. To write this record, two sectors must each be read from the diskette and then written back.

In your own programming, if you can choose a record size that does divide evenly into 512, you will gain some speed in reading and writing the records. However, DOS will handle records of any size easily, and except for the small inefficiency of sector-spanning records, you should not be especially concerned about record size.

As you might imagine, there are many other format besides ASCII text files and fixed length record files that can be used to store program data. What is special about these two formats is that they are widely accepted, and supported in many ways. Other formats for storing data are likely to have structural requirements that complicate the process of reading and writing them—which may involve quite a bit of special programming in order to be able to work with them. The great advantage of these two formats is that they are both very flexible—in different ways—so that they can be adapted to many uses. And since they are supported by so many programs, including the various language processors and operating systems, using them is very convenient. In fact, because the ASCII text format is so easy to manipulate, and is so widely supported by editor programs and various programming languages, it isn't unusual to find that the data format needs of a program will be bent and adjusted to fit into the ASCII text format.

## 5.11 Program file formats

There are two standard file formats for program files. Two filename extensions are reserved for their use: ".COM", and ".EXE". The complete details of programs files belong in a full treatment of DOS, and we won't cover them here, but we will provide the main parts of interest. (BASIC program files, with a filename extension of ".BAS", are not strictly speaking program files—they are data which is read and used by the BASIC interpreter.)

COM program files, with a filename extension of ".COM", are directly loadable programs. They are an exact image of the program as it will appear in memory. They require essentially no processing when they are loaded by DOS, to be run. If you inspect a COM file, for example by using DiskLook, you will see the machine-language instructions and data that make up the program and nothing else. When DOS prepares a COM file program for execution, it constructs the program segment prefix that is required by all programs, loads the program, sets the segment registers to their standard starting values, and passes control to the program.

EXE program files, with a filename extension of ".EXE", are different. Loading them to be run requires some special processing to prepare them for execution. The most notable part of this processing is a service known as relocation.

A program may contain addresses whose values need to be adjusted depending upon where in memory the program is located. If a program does not need this done for it, the program is known as self-relocating. COM programs must be self-relocating, but EXE programs may have relocation done for them by the DOS program loader.

EXE programs begin with a two-byte signature marker, hex 4D5A, which is used as a special check to distinguish them. Following the signature is some control information, including a table indicating what relocation is needed, followed by the program itself.

Besides being relocated, EXE programs may have a stack segment set up for them at load time, and they may request to be loaded into either the low or high ends of the available memory space.

Because the COM format is so simple, it is possible to build relatively short and simple machine-language COM files directly, either with a diskette modification tool like DEBUG or SecMod, or by writing a short BASIC program to write the program bytes right into a COM file. Many interesting and short COM-file programs have been passed around in the form of BASIC programs which use this method to construct their COM files.

The COM format is simpler, more compact, and quicker to load into memory. For programs which do not need the special services available to the EXE format, COM is preferred.

LISTING 5-1   99

```
{  Listing 5.1 -- Diskette directory definitions                    }
{  (C) Copyright 1983, Peter Norton                                  }

{  This listing contains Pascal definitions used to decode the       }
{  diskette directory                                                }

{  See listing 5.3    for programs which operate on the directory    }


{===================================================================}

{ constant values used for directories                              }

const

   directory_sectors_single_sided = 4;
   directory_sectors_double_sided = 7;

   directory_entries_single_sided = 64; { 4 * 16 }
   directory_entries_double_sided = 112; { 7 * 16 }

   hidden_attribute              = wrd (2);
   system_attribute              = wrd (4);

{===================================================================}

{ Following is the definition of the format of a directory entry:   }

type

   directory_entry_type =

     record

         filename                 :  string (8);
         extension                :  string (3);
         attribute                :  byte; { hidden = 2; system = 4 }
         reserved                 :  array [1..10] of byte;
         creation_time            :  word; { hour * 2048 + minute * 32 + secs }
         creation_date            :  word; {(year-1980) * 512 + month * 32 +
                                      day}
         starting_cluster_number  :  word;
         file_size                :  array [1..2] of word;

     end;

{===================================================================}

{ Following is a diskette sector with 16 directory entries  }

   directory_sector_type = array [1..16] of directory_entry_type;

{===================================================================}

{  Following is a complete directory, as it would be stored in a  }
{   program, after being read from diskette.                      }
```

```
complete_directory_type = array [1..112] of directory_entry_type;
    { note -- for single sided diskettes, the first 64 are used.  }
    {  for double-sided diskettes, all 112 would be used.         }

{  end of listing 5.1  directory definitions    }
```

LISTING 5-2    101

```
{  Listing 5.2 -- File Allocation Table definitions                   }
{  (C) Copyright 1983, Peter Norton                                   }

{  This listing contains Pascal definitions used to decode the        }
{  diskette File Allocation Table entries                             }

{  See listing 5.3    for programs which operate on the FAT           }

{=================================================================}

{  The valid FAT values:    }

const

    minimum_cluster                     =      2;
    maximum_cluster_single_sided        =    314;
    maximum_cluster_double_sided        =    316;

    usual_fat_end_of_file               =   4095; { hex FFF }
    minimum_fat_end_of_file             =   4088; { hex FF8 }

    bad_cluster_fat                     =   4087; { hex FF7 }

    single_sided_indicator_byte         =    254; { hex FE  }
    double_sided_indicator_byte         =    255; { hex FF  }

{=================================================================}

{  Here are two ways of looking at a 512-byte sector which holds a FAT }

{  First, a sector viewed as separately addressable bytes, for        }
{    use by the standard FAT algorithm (entry number times 1.5, etc.) }

{  Second, a sector divided up onto its structure of pairs of         }
{    FAT entries, scrambled together.                                 }

type

   fat_sector_type = array [0..511] of byte;

   fat_sector_structured_type  =
     record
       scrambled_fat_pair: array [0..158] {for pairs 0,1 through 316,317 }
of
         record
           scrambled_byte_1 : byte;
           scrambled_byte_2 : byte;
           scrambled_byte_3 : byte;
         end;
       unused_bytes_of_sector : array [1..35] of byte;
     end;

{ Notes: a sector is bigger than a FAT needs, so there are 35 unused bytes}
{  at the end; also, since FAT's are stored in scrambled pairs         }
{  and the valid FAT entries go from 2 through 316 (or 314), the last  }
{  pair contains a dummy 2nd half; finally, FAT entries number 0       }
```

```
{  and 1 are used to hold the indicator for single or double-sided
   diskettes }

{===================================================================}

{ A decoded FAT, as it would be stored inside a program:    }

  fat_table_type  =  array [2..316] of word;


{  end of listing 5.2, FAT definitions    }
```

LISTING 5-3    103

```
{   Listing 5.3 -- Routines for the diskette directory and FAT       }
{  (C) Copyright 1983, Peter Norton                                   }

{ Pascal Routines to Process the Diskette Directory and FAT          }

module Listing_5_3;

{ Here, with two "$include" statements, we will borrow the information  }
{ from the two listings 5.1 and 5.2:                                    }

    {  $include:'5.1'    }
    {  $include:'5.2'    }

{ These type definitions and variables are used in the programs here:     }

type
   diskette_format_type = (format_unknown,   {This defines the possibilities}
                           single_sided,     {for the format of the diskette}
                           double_sided);

  sector_as_bytes_type = array [0..511] of byte;

  lstring12            = lstring (12);


var [external]

   diskette_format        : diskette_format_type;
   work_sector            : sector_as_bytes_type;   { to read sectors into }
   directory_sector       : directory_sector_type;
   diskette_error         : boolean;                {used to signal I/O errors }
   fat_table              : fat_table_type;
   directory              : complete_directory_type;
   hidden_file            : boolean;
   system_file            : boolean;
   end_of_file            : boolean;
   creation_year          : word;
   creation_month         : word;
   creation_day           : word;
   creation_hour          : word;
   creation_minute        : word;
   creation_second        : word;
   side                   : word;
   track                  : word;
   sector                 : word;
   maximum_cluster        : word;
   most_recent_cluster    : word;
   first_sector_of_two    : boolean;

{ Here are definitions of two programs, provided in listing 4.102 on the   }
{ accompanying diskette, which read and write diskette sectors.            }
{   These declarations are given here, so that this program knows about the }
{ two programs, and knows their specifications. This is typical of how a    }
{ Pascal program gets access to routines outside the program at hand.       }
```

```
procedure read_sector (drive    : word;
                       side      : word;    { These are the parameters  }
                       track     : word;    { that the procedure takes  }
                       sector    : word;    { together with their types }
                       data_area : adsmem);

   external; { external means the program exists outside this listing }

procedure write_sector(drive    : word;
                       side      : word;
                       track     : word;
                       sector    : word;
                       data_area : adsmem);
          external;

{==========================================================================}

{ Our first routine finds out the diskette format -- single or double      }

procedure find_diskette_format (drive : word);

  begin

    { read the sector with the formatting code on it }

    read_sector (drive,0,0,2,ads work_sector); { read FAT sector }

    { check for an error, and the defined codes  }

    if diskette_error then
      begin
        maximum_cluster := 0;
        diskette_format := format_unknown
      end
    else if work_sector [0] = 254 then
      begin
        maximum_cluster := 314;
        diskette_format := single_sided
      end
    else if work_sector [0] = 255 then
      begin
        maximum_cluster := 316;
        diskette_format := double_sided
      end
    else
      begin
        maximum_cluster := 0;
        diskette_format := format_unknown
      end

end;

{==========================================================================}

{ The next two routines read, decode, and write the File Allocation Table  }
```

LISTING 5-3    105

```
{===========================================================================}

{ Our next routine will read and decode the File Allocation Table            }

procedure read_and_decode_fat (drive : word);

   var [static]        { variables for local use }
     i     : integer;
     limit : integer;
     offset: integer;
     work  : word;

   begin
     find_diskette_format (drive);   { find out the format -- reads FAT sector}
     if diskette_error then          { if there was a problem, don't procede  }
       return;

     { figure the size of the FAT table }

     if diskette_format = single_sided then
       limit := maximum_cluster_single_sided
     else
       limit := maximum_cluster_double_sided;

     for i := 2 to limit do
       begin

         { find the offset into the sector, for this fat entry     }
         offset := (i * 3) div 2;

         { put together the two bytes that contain the fat value  }
         work := byword (work_sector [offset+1], work_sector [offset]);

         { get rid of the extraneous hex digit, to get a 3-digit value }
         if odd (i) then
           work := work div 16
         else
           work := work mod 4096;

         { save the value found }
         fat_table [i] := work;
       end;
   end;


{===========================================================================}

{ Our next routine will encode and write to diskette the FAT

procedure encode_and_write_fat (drive : word);

   var [static]        { variables for local use }
     i      : integer;
     limit  : integer;
     offset : integer;
     work   : word;
```

```
  begin

    { re-read the old FAT so that we use its slack bytes, etc.              }

    find_diskette_format (drive);   {find out the format -- reads FAT sector }
    if diskette_error then          {if there was a problem, don't procede   }
      return;

    { figure the size of the FAT table }

    if diskette_format = single_sided then
      limit := maximum_cluster_single_sided
    else
      limit := maximum_cluster_double_sided;

    for i := 2 to limit do
      begin

        { find the offset into the sector, for this fat entry     }
        offset := (i * 3) div 2;

        { put together the two bytes that contain the fat value  }
        work := byword (work_sector [offset+1], work_sector [offset]);

        { combine the extraneous hex digit with the new value              }
        if odd (i) then
          work := work mod 16 + fat_table [i] * 16
        else
          work := (work div 4096) * 4096 + fat_table [i];

        { store the two bytes into the sector  }

        work_sector [offset]   := lobyte (work);
        work_sector [offset+1] := hibyte (work);
      end;

    { write the new FAT sector -- to both locations }

    write_sector (drive,0,0,2,ads work_sector); { write 1st copy }
    if diskette_error then
      { you should take some emergency action };
    write_sector (drive,0,0,3,ads work_sector); { write 2nd copy }
    if diskette_error then
      { you should take some emergency action };
  end;

{==========================================================================}

{  The next two routines read, and write the diskette directory        }

{==========================================================================}

{ Our next routine will read and store the complete directory              }
procedure read_and_store_directory (drive : word);
```

LISTING 5-3    107

```
    var [static]        { variables for local use }
       i       : integer;
       j       : integer;
       limit   : integer;
       side    : word;
       sector  : word;

    begin
       find_diskette_format (drive);  {find out the format -- reads FAT sector }
       if diskette_error then         {if there was a problem, don't procede  }
          return;

       { figure the size of the directory }

       if diskette_format = single_sided then
          limit := directory_sectors_single_sided
       else
          limit := directory_sectors_double_sided;

       { loop through the sectors }

       for i := 1 to limit do
          begin
            { figure which sector to read }
            if i < 6 then
               begin
                 side   := 0;
                 sector := wrd (i + 3);   {Note: "wrd" converts integer to word }
               end
            else
               begin
                 side   := 1;
                 sector := wrd (i - 5);
               end;
            read_sector (drive,side,0,sector,ads directory_sector);
            if diskette_error then
               return; {or take some emergency action }

            { now store each of the 16 directory entries on the sector }
            for j := 1 to 16 do
               directory [(i-1)*16 + j] := directory_sector [j];

          end;

    end;

{========================================================================}

{ Our next routine will write a directory to diskette                    }

procedure write_directory (drive : word);

    var [static]        { variables for local use }
       i       : integer;
       j       : integer;
       limit   : integer;
       side    : word;
```

```
    sector : word;

  begin
    find_diskette_format (drive);   {find out the format -- reads FAT sector }
    if diskette_error then          {if there was a problem, don't procede   }
      return;

    { figure the size of the directory }

    if diskette_format = single_sided then
      limit := directory_sectors_single_sided
    else
      limit := directory_sectors_double_sided;

    { loop through the sectors  }

    for i := 1 to limit do
      begin
        { figure which sector to read }
        if i < 6 then
          begin
            side   := 0;
            sector := wrd(i + 3);
          end
        else
          begin
            side   := 1;
            sector := wrd (i - 5);
          end;

        { now store each of the 16 directory entries on the sector }
        for j := 1 to 16 do
          directory_sector [j] := directory [(i-1)*16 + j];

        { write the directory sector;
        write_sector (drive,side,0,sector,ads directory_sector);
        if diskette_error then
          return; {or take some emergency action }
      end;

  end;

{==========================================================================}

{  The next several routines help in processing the directory            }

{==========================================================================}

{ This routine converts the directory filename into a display format     }

function filename_in_display_format (directory_entry : integer) : lstring12:

  var [static]
    work_name : lstring (12);
    i         : integer:
    last      : integer;
```

**LISTING 5-3    109**

```
begin

   work_name := null;  { start with an empty display }

   { scan backwards to find the end of the name }
   for last := 8 downto 1 do
     if directory [directory_entry].filename [last] <> ' ' then
       break; {quit scanning when find last non-blank }

   { move name characters into place }
   for i := 1 to last do
     begin
       work_name.len := wrd (i);
       work_name [i] := directory [directory_entry].filename [i];
     end;

   { check for filename extension }
   if directory [directory_entry].extension <> '   ' then
     begin
       { first add period }
       work_name.len := work_name.len + 1;
       work_name [work_name.len] := '.';

       { find length of extension }
       if directory [directory_entry].extension [3] <> ' ' then
         last := 3
       else if directory [directory_entry].extension [2] <> ' ' then
         last := 2
       else
         last := 1;

       { add extension to the display format }
       for i := 1 to last do
         begin
           work_name.len := work_name.len + 1;
           work_name[work_name.len]:=directory[directory_entry].extension[i];
         end;
     end;

   {return built-up name }
   filename_in_display_format := work_name;

end;

{==========================================================================}

{ This routine checks the directory attribute of hidden or system         }

procedure test_for_hidden_and_system (directory_entry : integer);
  var [static]
    work_byte : byte;

  begin
    work_byte := directory [directory_entry].attribute;

    { test for hidden }
    if (work_byte div 2) mod 2 = 1 then
```

```
        hidden_file := true
      else
        hidden_file := false;

      {test for system }
      if (work_byte div 4) mod 2 = 1 then
        system_file := true
      else
        system_file := false;

    end;

{=========================================================================}

{This routine sets the directory attribute of hidden or system          }

procedure set_hidden_and_system (directory_entry : integer);
  var [static]
    work_byte : byte;

  begin
    {get existing attribute byte, with any stray bits set }
    work_byte := directory [directory_entry].attribute;

    { first reset both bits }
    work_byte := (work_byte div 8) * 8 + work_byte mod 2;

    {add in the hidden and system bits }
    if hidden_file then
      work_byte := work_byte + 2;
    if system_file then
      work_byte := work_byte + 4;

    { put back into directory }
    directory [directory_entry].attribute := work_byte;
  end;

{=========================================================================}

{ This routine decodes the files creation date and time                 }

procedure decode_creation (directory_entry : integer);

  var [static]
    work : word;

  begin
    work             := directory [directory_entry].creation_date;

    creation_day     := work mode 32;
    work             := work div 32;

    creation_month   := work mod 16;
    work             := work div 16;

    creation_year    := work + 1980;
```

LISTING 5-3    111

```
      work                := directory [directory_entry].creation_time;

      creation_second      := work mod 32 * 2;
      work                := work div 32;

      creation_minute      := work mod 64;
      work                := work div 64;

      creation_hour        := work;

    end;
```

{==========================================================================}

{ The next  3   routines are used to trace through the file allocation table }
{ The 2nd    starts tracing a file, and the  3rd    continues from sector to  }
{ sector; each either finds the next sector (and sets the sector specifi-     }
{ cations of side, track and sector number, or sets the end-file signal.      }
{ The 1st is used by the other two, to convert cluster to sector.             }

{==========================================================================}

{ This routine serves the other two, in converting cluster to sector specs}

```
procedure decode_cluster_into_sector;

  var [static]
    work : word;

  begin
    if diskette_format = single_sided then
      begin
        work    := most_recent_cluster + 5;
        side    := 0;
        track   := work div 8;
        sector  := work mod 8 + 1;
      end
    else if diskette_format = double_sided then
      begin
        first_sector_of_two := true;
        work          := most_recent_cluster * 2 + 6;
        track         := work div 16;
        work          := work mod 16;
        side          := work div 8;
        sector        := work mod 8 + 1;
      end;
  end;
```

{==========================================================================}

{ This routine starts the process of tracing a file's sector allocation    }

```
procedure first_sector (directory_entry : integer);

  begin

    { check for end of the space allocation chain or error }
```

```
   if (most_recent_cluster < 2)or(most_recent_cluster > maximum_cluster) then
      begin
        end_of_file := true;
        return;
      end;

    { grab starting cluster number }
    most_recent_cluster:= directory[directory_entry].starting_cluster_number;

    decode_cluster_into_sector;

  end;
```

```
{========================================================================}
```

```
{  This routine finds the next sector for the file being traced          }

procedure next_sector;

  begin

    { for double-sided, check if ready for 2nd sector of a cluster }
    if (diskette_format = double_sided) and first_sector_of_two then
      begin
        first_sector_of_two := false;
        sector := sector + 1;
        return;
      end;

  if (most_recent_cluster < 2)or(most_recent_cluster > maximum_cluster) then
      begin
        end of file := true;
        return;
      end;

    most_recent_cluster := fat_table [ord(most_recent_cluster)];

    decode_cluster_into_sector;

  end;
```

```
{========================================================================}
```

```
end. { of module list_5_3 }
{  end of listing 5.3, Pascal service routines for diskette formats }
```

# 6

# Access to ROM

The programs that reside in the IBM/PC's ROM, or Read-Only-Memory, are the key to making the PC work effectively. In this chapter we'll take an over-all look at the PC's ROM. We'll be seeing what it is used for, how to snoop through it and also how to decode it, and finally, we'll compare the first two versions of the IBM/PC ROM. All this sets the stage for the next five chapters, in which we'll go over the facilities of the IBM/PC in detail.

Our three circles of interest begin to diverge rapidly here. Everything that we have to say here applies completely to the IBM/PC, and, in general, doesn't apply at all to the whole family of MS-DOS computers. For the PC-like computers, nothing can be said for certain about the whole group, for each machine will have its own individual variations. But you can reasonably expect that most or all of the computers that closely imitate the IBM/PC will match it interrupt for interrupt, service call for service call. So while the exact location of ROM service routines is likely to differ among the PC-like computers, you can generally expect that they will correspond to the information given in this chapter and the next five chapters.

## 6.1 ROM and its uses

The ROM programs are extremely important to the IBM/PC because they form the heart of the fundamental control programs that make the PC a usable instrument. And since they are kept in ROM, they are stable and permanent—they cannot be accidentally erased. Also, they are available to any program running on any IBM/PC, regardless of what operating system is being used.

It is possible, however, to over-ride most of the service routines in ROM. In fact, they are carefully written in a way that makes it practical to over-ride them when necessary. The technique for accessing ROM programs is always through interrupts, and the action taken on an interrupt can be redirected at any time by changing the interrupt vector table, as we saw in the discussion of interrupts in Chapter 3.

As we've seen, there are three parts to the ROM storage for the IBM/PC, all placed at the highest address locations of the PC's one million byte address space. At the very top, beginning at segment paragraph FE00, in hex, and extending for 8 K bytes to the end of memory, is the ROM-BIOS, or Basic Input-Output System. The ROM-BIOS is responsible for all the built-in support of the IBM/PC's input-output devices, such as the display screen, and the diskette drives. So ROM-BIOS is at the heart of the operating system programs that make the PC work. The ROM-BIOS is extremely interesting to anyone who wants to master all the special tricks that the IBM/PC can do. And, as we cover the special features of the IBM/PC one by one in the next five chapters, we will explain the ROM-BIOS services that support each feature.

The IBM Technical Reference manual for the PC contains a complete listing of the first version of the ROM-BIOS, and the notes in the listing are quite good in explaining what is being done, how, and, to a lesser degree, why. If you are able to follow an assembly language listing, studying the ROM-BIOS listing will teach you a great deal about how things are done on the PC. The second part of the ROM, beginning at hex paragraph F600 and extending for 32 K bytes, is the ROM-BASIC routines. The ROM-BASIC provides the core of the interpreter BASIC for the IBM/PC. All the cassette BASIC is located in this ROM, and the major portion of disk BASIC, and advanced BASIC ('BASICA'), is actually in this ROM. In fact, all that the two disk versions of BASIC do, is add features to the ROM-BASIC. The ROM-BASIC is, by itself, a complete version of the BASIC language that contains the lion's share of the programs needed by the disk versions.

While a listing of ROM-BIOS appears in the Technical Reference manual, nothing is available to show the contents of the ROM-BASIC program, so we'll use it for our example of how to snoop around in ROM. By itself the contents of ROM-BASIC doesn't seem to be of much interest. Yet buried inside the ROM-BASIC must be a lot of potentially useful subroutines. If BASIC uses them, why not our own programs? Finding and decoding usable fragments of the ROM-BASIC, and then documenting them in a form that would make them accessible to everyone, is a very ambitious project, one that we won't attempt here.

It is possible for a program to directly activate the ROM-BASIC program through an interrupt service. We will show how that is done in Chapter 11.

The third and last part of ROM is the part that isn't there. This is an open possibility for IBM to add new ROM programs, or for users to add built-in programs that customize the IBM/PC. Extra ROM programs can be added nearly anywhere in the one-million byte address space, but the location especially reserved for added ROM is the block that begins at hex paragraph F400, and extends for 8 K bytes, up to the beginning of the ROM-BASIC; if more than eight thousand bytes are needed, a ROM program can begin at an earlier location. It is here that ROM programs can be added to turn an IBM/PC into a specialty computer. Before we start digging deeper into the ROM-BIOS, we'll show you how to snoop around in the ROM, in the next two sections.

## 6.2  Snooping in ROM, part 1: getting to know DEBUG

Here we'll show you how to snoop around inside the programs and data located in ROM. While we'll be specifically covering the ROM routines, the techniques we use can be applied to programs that are stored on a diskette. So everything that we show you here you can also apply to snooping inside the parts of DOS that are on diskette, or inside other programs.

Now you can access any part of the ROM with BASIC, or with Pascal. The addressing techniques that we showed in Chapter 3, let our BASIC and Pascal programs browse around anywhere in memory. As an example, here is a BASIC program which will display chunks of ROM:

```
100   REM display some ROM in hex format
110   PARAGRAPH = &HF600
120   DEF SEG = PARAGRAPH
130   PRINT
140   PRINT "Displaying from paragraph ",HEX$(PARAGRAPH)
150   PRINT
160   PRINT " Decimal       Hexadecimal"
170   PRINT " Offset        Offset              ROM data in hexadecimal";
180   OFFSET% = 0
190   FOR LINES% = 1 TO 16
200       PRINT
210       PRINT OFFSET%,HEX$(OFFSET%),
220       FOR FOUR.BYTES = 1 TO 2
230           PRINT " ";
240           FOR TWO.BYTES = 1 TO 2
250               PRINT " ";
260               FOR ONE.BYTE = 1 TO 2
270                   PRINT " ";
280                   OFFSET% = OFFSET% + 1
290                   IF PEEK (OFFSET%) <16 THEN PRINT "0"; ' pad, for an even
                      display
300                   PRINT HEX$ (PEEK (OFFSET%));
310               NEXT ONE.BYTE
320           NEXT TWO.BYTES
330       NEXT FOUR.BYTES
340   NEXT LINES%
350   PRINT : PRINT
```

But while that sort of program will show us what is in the ROM, it doesn't help us make sense of the data. For that we turn to a very important and interesting tool that comes with DOS, the DEBUG program.

DEBUG provides the three things that we need to snoop in ROM—access to any section of memory, and the ability to list memory in two formats, first in hexadecimal and ASCII, and second in "unassembled" format. DEBUG can also be used to investigate diskette programs. However, there are better tools for that, such as DiskLook, which is included in the diskette package which accompanies this book, and SecMod, one of the Norton Utility programs. Before we go any further, let's explain "unassembly" for you.

Machine-language computer programs are almost completely unintelligible to humans. Even for computers which have relatively simple instruction formats, machine language is difficult to comprehend. And the 8088 micro-processor has a very intricate coding structure for its machine language. Most micro-processors are this way—their designers have sacrificed simplicity for maximum power and compactness of code. As a result, it takes a great deal of labor for someone to look over a listing of machine-language code in hexadecimal, and make sense of it.

The unassembly process—which is a part of DEBUG—takes the brutal labor out of interpreting machine language. Unassembly is simply the process of translating the absolute hexadecimal machine language instructions into corresponding assembly language symbolic notation. For example, in assembly language you might write INC AX (meaning, increment the AX register by adding one to it), and the assembler would translate that into the machine language hex code 40. In reverse, the unassembler would translate hex 40 back into INC AX. Hex code 40 is a relatively easy instruction code to translate by hand, if you have a table of the 8088 instruction codes. Many other codes are much harder, because in many instances various individual bit settings change the meaning of the instruction. All the troublesome task of decoding all the bits, in all their intricate encoding, is taken care of for us by the unassemble command of DEBUG.

While an unassembler can turn machine language into more readable assembler code, it can't reconstruct some of the most useful parts of the original assembly language source code. Obviously it won't create the programmer's helpful comments out of thin air. Also, it won't assign meaningful, and helpful, symbolic names to locations. So where the author's original assembly code might have had something like this:

JMP FINISH    ; Done—go to finish routine

the unassembler can only tell us something like this:

JMP 0E6C

so that we know that it's a jump, but we don't know the significance of it.

Needless to say, unassembly doesn't do all our work for us—in particular, it doesn't make any sense of the program that is unassembled. But at least it tells us what instructions have been found, and gives us clues about whether we are looking at program instructions, or program data.

To show how you can explore ROM programs, let's use the ROM-BASIC routines, and step through the process of using DEBUG to see what's going on. Most of what you need to know for the process will be either explained here, or made clear by example. To fully understand the process of using DEBUG, you should also carefully read the section of the DOS manual which covers DEBUG; it is not the easiest part of the DOS manual to understand, but many of the technical details may eventually become important to you.

If you are a newcomer to using DEBUG, here is some background. DEBUG, like other commands, is invoked by typing its name. While DEBUG is running, it will prompt you for commands with a very terse hyphen; don't expect the more obvious DOS prompt "A".

Most things you do with DEBUG will result in listings appearing on the screen, but you may want copies on your printer for a permanent record, one that you can make notes on. DEBUG isn't set up to send its output to the printer. Remember though, there are two ways that you can get almost anything printed. One is to use PrtSc (print-screen) to make a copy of the current display; the other is to turn on the "printer echo" feature, by pressing Ctrl and PrtSc.

Many users of the IBM/PC don't know about the echo feature. Echo is turned on and off by pressing Ctrl-PrtSc; when echo is in effect, any conventional output to the screen will be copied ('echoed') to the printer. Echo is useful with DEBUG, and other programs, to get a paper copy of work that has appeared on the screen. (Be aware though, that the echo feature only works for printer-type output sent to the screen; most special displays, like those produced by word processors, and by the utility programs DiskLook and SecMod, will not echo. Also, interpreter BASIC programs, which operate under slightly different rules than most DOS programs, do not make use of the echo feature. When you need a copy of the displays produced by programs which will not echo their output, you can usually get them with the print-screen feature.)

We have decided to explore the ROM-BASIC, and happen to know that the ROM-BASIC is located at hex paragraph F600. So we can start DEBUG, and immediately instruct it to start looking there.

But suppose that we didn't know that what we were looking for was at paragraph F600? There are two ways that we might go about searching. One is to successively use the DEBUG command D (meaning "dump" or "display"), until we saw something interesting. The other, and more efficient, way is to have DEBUG search for something that we know—or think—should be present.

As an example, we could search for the BASIC error message, "Illegal function call." Figure 6.1 shows the process of starting DEBUG and telling it to search for this BASIC message. For the example, DEBUG was told to start looking at paragraph F000 (quite a ways before where we know that BASIC begins) and to search for a length ('L') of 65,535 bytes (in hex notation, 'FFFF'). DEBUG reports that it found what we asked it to find. In segmented address notation, DEBUG reports the address as F000:63F4, which means a relative offset of hex 63F4 from paragraph F000. Doing our address arithmetic, we can get the full 20-bit form of the address:

```
A>DEBUG
-S F000:0000 L FFFF "Illegal function call"
F000:63F4
```

**Figure 6.1—Starting DEBUG, and Searching for a Message.**

$$\begin{array}{r} \text{F000} \\ + \ 63\text{F4} \\ \hline \text{F63F4} \end{array}$$

Looking at the address in that form, it's more obvious that the DEBUG found the message not far from the BASIC's beginning at paragraph F600. If we separate the 20-bit address F63F4 into segmented notation, but take paragraph F600 as the base, we get the address as F600:03F4—which means a relative displacement of only hex 3F4, or 1012 bytes, from the beginning of ROM-BASIC.

We can list the surrounding area near where DEBUG found the message we asked it to look for by entering the DEBUG command D F600:03E0 (which means display, beginning at an offset of 3E0—a little before where our message was found—from the base paragraph of F600). Figure 6.2 shows the result of this display command. DEBUG responds by displaying, in both hexadecimal and ASCII, eighty bytes, including our message. What we see is our message, and various other BASIC error messages—just what we might have guessed would be found near our message. If we want to see more, DEBUG will display successive sections in response to just the command "D", without our having to tell it what address to display.

Figure 6.2 illustrates several things worth knowing about the "D" command displays of DEBUG. One is that the displays are formatted with hex on the left and ASCII characters on the right. Another is that byte values which aren't normally printable are converted to periods, in the right-hand ASCII portion. So that the echo feature can be used with DEBUG, DEBUG makes sure that it does not display any unprintable characters which might turn out to be printer control codes. Because of this, be aware that you can't rely on the ASCII portion of a DEBUG display to show everything. Anything that is a standard printable character, or is a printable character with the high-order bit set, will be printed; everything else will be converted to periods. (Note, by the way, that DiskLook, which is part of the diskette package that accompanies this book, will show complete and exact displays of hexadecimal and ASCII, since it sends its display information directly to the screen and bypasses the echo feature.)

```
-D F600:03E0
F600:03E0   74 20 47 4F 53 55 42 00-4F 75 74 20 6F 66 20 44   t GOSUB.Out of D
F600:03F0   41 54 41 00 49 6C 6C 65-67 61 6C 20 66 75 6E 63   ATA.Illegal func
F600:0400   74 69 6F 6E 20 63 61 6C-6C 00 4F 76 65 72 66 6C   tion call.Overfl
F600:0410   6F 77 00 4F 75 74 20 6F-66 20 6D 65 6D 6F 72 79   ow.Out of memory
F600:0420   00 55 6E 64 65 66 69 6E-65 64 20 6C 69 6E 65 20   .Undefined line
F600:0430   6E 75 6D 62 65 72 00 53-75 62 73 63 72 69 70 74   number.Subscript
F600:0440   20 6F 75 74 20 6F 66 20-72 61 6E 67 65 00 44 75   out of range.Du
F600:0450   70 6C 69 63 61 74 65 20-44 65 66 69 6E 69 74 69   plicate Definiti
```

**Figure 6.2—Displaying the Message Found.**

So far we have shown you how to display ROM data with DEBUG, and how to use DEBUG to search for any ROM data that you know of. Next we'll look at the much trickier task of unassembling and interpreting machine language program code.

## 6.3  Snooping in ROM, part 2: making your way through an unassembly

Our next step in learning how to snoop, and how to use DEBUG, is to become familiar with unassembly. The DEBUG command "U"— meaning unassemble— will translate whatever you point it at into a listing of assembly-language like coding. What unassemble will do, is to translate absolute hexadecimal codes into the assembly language mnemonic codes, such as ADD or INC (for increment), complete with register indications (such as registers AX or DS). What unassemble will not do is two-fold.

First, unassemble will not explain what programs mean, or even teach us assembly language. To understand an unassembled listing, you either have to already understand assembly language, or be willing to look up the mnemonic codes in a reference source, to understand what is being done. (To look up the assembly codes, you can use either the IBM Macro Assembler manual, or a reference book on the 8086 instruction set, such as Stephen Morse's "The 8086 Primer", or Rector and Alexy's "The 8086 Book.")

To understand an unassembled program, it isn't enough to be able to comprehend an assembly language listing: you also have to be able to make sense of what the program is doing. Doing that is an interesting intellectual exercise, a variety of puzzle solving. With some experience, it becomes easier than it is at first—partly because you will have to spend less and less time looking up the effect of the instructions, and partly because you will be learning to understand the patterns that assembly language instructions create. We'll have more to say about how to recognize patterns in assembly language as we go further into unassembly.

The second thing the unassemble command will not do for you, is what we might call synchronization. Machine language instructions for the 8088 are variable in length—many are as short as one byte, and some are as long as six bytes. If you point DEBUG's unassembler at some intermediate point in an instruction, or at what is really data and not instructions, DEBUG will dutifully do its best in decoding what it sees into assembly language instructions. And that may turn out to be very garbled indeed.

Now if we know where a stream of instructions begins, there's no problem. But if we don't know, then a little experimentation is in order. The basic approach is to let the unassemble command have a go at what you think is a stream of instructions. Then you must study unassemble's output, to try to make sense of it. If it doesn't make a reasonable pattern (and we'll get into some tricks of recognizing that shortly), then you should try again, having unassemble begin one or two or three bytes further along than it did before. What we are looking for is a synchronization point, from which a sensible series of instructions proceeds. If you don't find the synchronization at first, try again.

Because many instructions are one and two bytes long, synchronization is often easy to find. In fact, more often than you might expect, the unassembly process is self-synchronizing. Even if the unassembler in DEBUG begins at the wrong point, in the middle of some instruction, it often happens that unassemble will stumble onto the proper beginning of a later instruction. Once that happens, the sailing is smooth, at least in the forward direction. (You're on your own going backwards.)

In tracking down an unassembly, you have to be on the look-out for data (as opposed to instructions), which the unassembler will turn into some fanciful assembly listing. The first and fastest check for data is to use the "D" display command, to list the information in hex and ASCII. First you should look for the most obvious—nice fat meaningful ASCII characters, like the 'Illegal function call' message we found above. After that, you should look for other suspicious signs of data.

In ordinary programs—but not in ROM programs—stretches of hex zeros are a common sign of a working data area, one that will be used when the program is running, but that doesn't contain actual data when we are unassembling it. ROM can't be used for working data, since you can't write into read-only memory, so stretches of hex-zero bytes are uncommon in ROM programs.

Other signs of potential data are bytes or two-byte words in which the second, or high-order byte, begins with 0 or F. A large proportion of constants stored in programs are small numbers, either positive (and thus begin with 0) or negative (and begin with F). If you find a series of bytes which show this pattern, then it is very likely that you have found an area used to store data in the form of one or two byte numbers. You would, therefore, not expect that part of the program to be a stream of instructions.

In trying to make sense of an unassembly listing, here are things that you should keep in mind. Ordinary link-edited programs will normally have all their instruction parts together in one place, and their data parts in another. This is a natural by-product of good programming practices, and of the way that the DOS linker works. This characteristic is more true of EXE type programs than it is of COM type programs, but it still is generally true. On the other hand, ROM programs, like those we are exploring, often do not follow such conventions of tidy programming. Their data may well be scattered, interwoven with the program instructions.

If you think that you may have found a stream of program instructions that are followed by some data, there is one sure fire way to tell the difference between finding the true end of a series of program instructions followed by data, and looking at a false unassembly listing.

In a true stream of instructions, the last instruction has to be one form or other of jump or branch instruction, and an unconditional branch at that. Branch instructions include all the Jump instructions, but none of the jump-if-this-or-that instructions qualify as unconditional jumps. The RETurn instruction (return from a subroutine that was called), is a commonly encountered last instruction. The CALL and INTerrupt instructions qualify, although it is rare to use them as the last of a series of instructions.

There are several things that you can look for, when you are trying to decide if an unassembly listing is really a stream of instructions or a false trail. First, consider the registers used. If there are operations done on the registers usually used for arithmetic (AX, AL or AH; BX, BL or BH; CX, CL or CH; DX, DL or DH), but then nothing is done with the results, that is suspicious. Beware, though. One result of doing arithmetic is setting flags—so expect conditional jumps on the flags, like JNC (which is the instruction to jump if no carry flag was set).

Another thing to look for in registers is unlikely usage. Programs don't dance through the registers—they use them in a coherent pattern. And it is relatively uncommon to be setting, or directly referring to, the segment registers—especially the code segment register, CS, and the stack segment register, SS. Setting the data segment, DS, is more likely, but it is still uncommon. On the other hand, the extra segment register, ES, is almost exclusively manipulated by programs, so finding ES being set is nothing unusual. If you do find either the CS or SS registers being set, it should be in a section of program code that is setting up the framework for a program to operate; and there it is most likely that several of the segment registers will be set all together, particularly the CS, SS, and DS registers.

Trying to make sense out of an unassembly listing, and even just making sure that you have a proper unassembly of a true stream of instructions, is a challenging intellectual puzzle. It doesn't, however, require any special skill. In fact, common sense is what you need most to do it successfully. With the helpful clues you have now, and a little practice, you should be able to do it whenever you need to. In the next section we'll decode the start of ROM-BASIC, both to give you an example of how it is done, and to demonstrate that it isn't too difficult.

## 6.4 Snooping in ROM, part 3: decoding BASIC

As an exercise, let's try unassembling some of ROM-BASIC. We'll start at the beginning—paragraph hex F600. Figure 6.3 shows an unassembly of the first 32 bytes. All the zeros at the end (translated into ADD instructions) are obviously data, a nice contradiction to my statement that this is rare in ROM programs. The DB (define-byte) that precedes the zeros is the unassembler's response to any code value that doesn't translate into some instruction (since there are so many instruction codes, this is not too common). Now, is all this data preceded by an

```
-U F600:0000
F600:0000 E98F7E          JMP       7E92
F600:0003 E8A76B          CALL      6BAD
F600:0006 CB              RET       L
F600:0007 E80265          CALL      650C
F600:000A CB              RET       L
F600:000B C1              DB        C1
F600:000C 0000            ADD       [BX+SI],AL
F600:000E 0000            ADD       [BX+SI],AL
F600:0010 0000            ADD       [BX+SI],AL
F600:0012 0000            ADD       [BX+SI],AL
F600:0014 0000            ADD       [BX+SI],AL
F600:0016 0000            ADD       [BX+SI],AL
F600:0018 0000            ADD       [BX+SI],AL
F600:001A 0000            ADD       [BX+SI],AL
F600:001C 0000            ADD       [BX+SI],AL
F600:001E 0000            ADD       [BX+SI],AL
```

**Figure 6.3—Unassembling the Beginning of BASIC.**

unconditional branch instruction of some kind? You bet—a return instruction (RET), used to end a subroutine's execution. So far, so good.

Now, do the first five unassembled instructions make sense? They do look a little odd, since they begin with a jump (JMP). That seems a little peculiar, but most programs begin with some kind of initialization, often calls or jumps to later subroutines. So the beginning jump, while curious, isn't out of the question. And the following four instructions—two pairs of subroutine calls followed by subroutine returns don't make any particular sense, but they at least form a coherent pattern of instructions, and that is one of the indications used to recognize a stream of program instructions. So we might be onto a real instruction stream.

So far it's been pointless—even if what we see in figure 6.3 is an instruction stream, it's only five instructions long, and more or less does nothing. But what it does show us is interesting. If this a valid instruction stream, it has given us the addresses of three places where we might find something more interesting—the locations of the first jump and the two following calls. Shall we follow the jump? The unassembler gives us its address (relative to our starting point of F600) as hex 7E92, so let's try unassembling some of that, which you'll see in figure 6.4.

We seem to have struck pay-dirt. First, we have coherent instructions, no DB's, not one ADD after another. Second, they are just the kind of thing that might reasonably be going on in an initialization routine. The very first thing is a CLI instruction, which we saw in Chapter 3 is used to suspend interrupts—leaving whatever instructions that follow undisturbed by interrupts. This is just the thing that critical start-up code usually begins with, since it usually sets the segment register values necessary when interrupts are handled.

```
-U F600:7E92
F600:7E92 FA              CLI
F600:7E93 BA6000          MOV      DX,0060
F600:7E96 8EDA            MOV      DS,DX
F600:7E98 8EC2            MOV      ES,DX
F600:7E9A 8ED2            MOV      SS,DX
F600:7E9C 32C0            XOR      AL,AL
F600:7E9E A26404          MOV      [0464],AL
F600:7EA1 B591            MOV      CH,91
F600:7EA3 BB0000          MOV      BX,0000
F600:7EA6 BA9A06          MOV      DX,069A
F600:7EA9 8BF2            MOV      SI,DX
F600:7EAB 2E              SEG      CS
F600:7EAC AC              LODSB
F600:7EAD 8807            MOV      [BX],AL
F600:7EAF 43              INC      BX
F600:7EB0 42              INC      DX
F600:7EB1 FECD            DEC      CH
```

**Figure 6.4—Unassembling More BASIC.**

Following that is the very thing that we were talking about: segment register loading. The next four instructions are MOV, or move-data, commands, and they result in loading three of the four segment registers, DS, ES, and SS. While setting these registers is rare, it's expected at the beginning of a program, if anywhere, and setting three of them at once makes perfect sense. (The program relies on the code segment register, CS, to be already set—otherwise, back at the very first instruction, at F600:0000 in figure 6.3, we wouldn't have been able to jump to this part of the program.) So far, so good.

Following the four MOV instructions, that load segment registers, are two instructions that make sense as a pair. First an exclusive-or, XOR, instruction that sets the AL register to zero (since the logical operation exclusive-or, done on the same data always results in zeros), and then that zero value is moved to a particular memory location. There is no indication of why this is done, but at least it is a coherent pattern of instructions — they clearly do something.

If we knew more about how BASIC works, we might know that the zero value that was moved into memory in the last two instructions sets a switch which safeguards protected programs. We might know that when a protected BASIC program is loaded, this switch will be reset to prevent listing the protected program. But at this point, that is beyond what we can learn by studying this listing.

So what we have seen in looking at the first seven instructions look like very sensible instructions. They do coherent, reasonable things, and they fit together into small patterns: the 2nd through 5th do one thing together, the 6th and 7th to another thing. In short, we have found all the critical signs of a proper instruction stream.

Thus we've accomplished our limited objective—of searching for some code, finding it, and even making some sense out of it—which is more than I had hoped for. We would have to do quite a bit more work to decode all the ROM-BASIC, or even to decode a meaningful chunk of it. But we've seen how it is done—and seen that it isn't necessarily a fearsome task.

## 6.5  Two versions of our BIOS

It isn't very widely known, but there are at least two different versions of the ROM-BIOS used in the IBM/PC. In this section we'll take a look at the differences between them, and what significance they might have for you.

Included as part of the diskette package that accompanies this book are two programs which will copy and analyze the BIOS programs. It was an experiment with these programs that first revealed the existence of changed versions of the ROM, something that IBM was not generally admitting to the world. If you have these two programs, you will be able to use them to check your PC system, and to compare your version of ROM with others.

Of all the programs that are used on your IBM/PC the one which must be letter perfect, with no errors or bugs in it, has to be the routines stored in ROM. After all, if you have a bad version of DOS or VisiCalc, it can be replaced at the change of a diskette. Not so with programs stored in ROM. They can only be changed by replacing the memory chips on the IBM/PC's main circuit board—which is not a job for the casual user of the computer. Naturally it would be a major problem for IBM if there were any major bugs in the ROM routines, and they were checked out and debugged with unusual care.

If you think that there is anything that can be done without making any mistakes, you probably also believe in the tooth fairy—and the ROM programs for the PC were no exception. After the PC was first released, IBM found several things worth changing in the ROM programs—but no major errors—and so there are two versions of ROM available. You might be interested in knowing which version you have, and what the differences are between them.

At the very end of the ROM-BIOS program, IBM has placed a date stamp, called a release marker, which identifies the date that the particular ROM routine was officially finished. You can use the DEBUG program to find and display your date marker. After starting DEBUG, enter the command: D F000:FFF5 L 8

DEBUG will then display the release marker for your computer. The original release marker will be "04/24/81". The release marker for the second version will be "10/19/81". If you find a different release marker than either of those two, then you have another and later version of the ROM-BIOS.

Listing 6.1 shows how a program can dynamically inspect the ROM-BIOS release marker, and then take any appropriate action. To do the same thing in BASIC, you can do something like this:

```
10   REM display access and display the ROM release marker
20   REM the program displays the marker, but it could also inspect it
30   REM and act on which ROM version is installed
40   PRINT
50   DEF SEG = &HFFFF
60   PRINT "The ROM release marker is ";
70   FOR OFFSET = 5 TO 12
80      PRINT CHR$(PEEK(OFFSET));
90   NEXT OFFSET
```

If you have an IBM/PC that was bought after October of 1981, you shouldn't assume that you have the newest version of the ROM-BIOS. A check of computer stores a full year after the release of the second version of the BIOS showed that new, freshly shipped PC's had the old, original version of ROM-BIOS installed.

You will recall that the ROM for the IBM/PC holds two things— ROM-BASIC and the ROM-BIOS. The first thing my BIOS checking programs reveal is that there are no changes to the ROM-BASIC program, between the first and second versions of the ROM.

Although some errors have been found in the BASIC, they have all been changed by making changes to the disk versions of BASIC. It was important that the ROM-BASIC not be changed, since that would cause changes in the performance of BASIC programs that we would have no control over. Some BASIC programs might work one way on one IBM/ PC, and another way on another machine, just because of a difference in the ROM.

By making all changes and corrections to BASIC, in the diskette BASIC programs, IBM insured that we would have control over any changes to the language. If any of your programs happen to require the original BASIC, then you could run them with the original diskette version of BASIC. And for the new versions of BASIC, the diskette program can, in effect, update the read-only-memory temporarily, through the technique explained in Chapter 3's discussion of interrupts.

All the changes that did appear in the ROM were in the BIOS, and we'll outline them here, to help you decide if the changes matter to you. If you have the first edition of the IBM/PC Technical Reference manual, you will see that the ROM-BIOS listing in appendix A is for the first version of the ROM, and a look on the last page will show the release marker for 04/24/81. After the end of the ROM-BIOS listing are some slightly confusing notes about the BIOS listing. The 1st, 3rd, and 5th of these notes are about some of the errors that were found in the BIOS and corrected in the second BIOS version.

The first three changes to the ROM-BIOS concern the self-test programs that are automatically executed when the IBM/PC is powered-on. These routines perform fourteen different tests to check for errors in the equipment, before you get a chance to create havoc by running programs on a faulty computer. Of these routines, test number 3 tests that the timer function in the computer's memory controller works correctly. Two of the three changes to the test programs were made to this routine. (Here is a good place to explain that programs, like a BIOS, which work very intimately with computer hardware, are not like ordinary programs. Whether or not hardware test routines, and BIOS routines, work correctly often depends on very subtle characteristics of the equipment they control. Details of timing and the interaction of control signals can be critical to the success of programs like these. At times the only way to debug such programs is through experimentation—logical analysis isn't always enough. That is why, in inspecting the changes made to the test routines mentioned above, I wasn't able to say anything definitive about the changes.)

The other change to the test routines comes in phase three of the tests. This change makes sure that the timer operation is updated, before allowing the video screen controlling interrupts to be moved into place. The original version did not.

Don't feel lost if you don't understand the significance of those changes— they have little practical importance to a system that is operating correctly. The rest of the changes which we'll describe are of more practical importance to us.

The next change is of interest to anyone using the asynchronous communications adapter. The ROM support programs for the communications adapter have the job, among other things, of reporting when there is no response on the communications line. If there is no response after a reasonable amount of time, the ROM communications programs report a 'time-out' condition. Unfortunately, due to a typographic error, the ROM routine does not report a time-out. The actual error was one of those unavoidable problems that come from working with both hexadecimal and decimal numbers; a number was supposed to have been written as "80H", meaning hex 80, but the "H" was left off, and the number was interpreted as 80 decimal, which is hex 50. In this case, the number was being used to set particular bits, and instead of setting the single bit that indicates a time-out condition, two other bits were set— one indicating data is ready (the opposite of a time-out, if you think about it), and the other indicating a parity error, so that the data is probably wrong.

The significance of this mistake is that a communications program may report errors incorrectly. Unless it has been programmed to take the ROM-BIOS error into account, your communications programs are likely to report an un-responsive telephone line as a parity error (and mislead you into thinking that the problem is different, or more severe, than it is).

The next error that was fixed in the second version of the ROM-BIOS is in the printer control programs. Again, the problem is in time-out checking. Your printer can be busy doing work, which the computer should wait for; but it is also possible that the printer is not responding. The control program in ROM-BIOS tests for this by allowing a certain amount of time for printer response. Unfortunately, it did not allow enough time for the longest thing that a printer might have to do—skipping to the top of new page from near the top of the old page. The original time-out test value was not great enough to allow for these long page ejects, and so the new version of ROM-BIOS doubles the time allowed before a time-out is signaled.

After the printer, the next change appears in the cassette support programs. In this case, the order of a few instructions was re-arranged, which made a slight change in the exact timing of how data is collected from the cassette. Since very few IBM/PC's make use of the cassette (and the error is very minor), this change to the ROM is rather insignificant.

The last change is an interesting one, which affects those IBM/PC's which use the color-graphics adapter. Not everyone knows it, but when the color-graphics adapter is used in its graphics mode (rather than its text mode), characters are displayed on the screen by drawing them, like anything else might be drawn. (This is explained in more detail in Chapter 9, which covers video graphics.) There is a table in ROM storage which contains the pictures that correspond to the ASCII characters that might be displayed, such as the letters of the alphabet. When the color-graphics monitor is working in text mode, characters for the display are generated by the color-graphics adapter circuitry. But when the adapter is working in graphics mode, the control programs in ROM display characters by using drawings contained in ROM—and one of these drawings is wrong in the original version of ROM. The CHR$(4) character, which represents the diamonds in a deck of cards, has an extra dot appearing below it in the original version of ROM. The second version of ROM has this drawing corrected.

None of these changes to the ROM-BIOS programs is earth-shaking. The most important one of the lot is probably the incorrect reporting of time-outs on the asynchronous communications line, and that is only an incorrect description of an error, rather than any incorrect operating performance. In fact, very few users of the IBM/PC are likely to be able to notice the difference between them, even if they know what to look for.

But these changes are worth knowing, and it is a little unsettling that changes which will affect the performance of PC programs, even in minor ways, were not publicly announced and documented. It is the sort of thing that makes you worry that more important changes might be made without our knowledge.

## 6.6 Access conventions

In this section we'll summarize the common access conventions used to activate the ROM-BIOS service routines. All the services are invoked using interrupts, for the reasons that we explained in Chapter 3—interrupts allow routines to be invoked without knowing where they are, and interrupts allow the service routines to be over-ridden, when necessary.

To start with, here is a summary table of the interrupts used to activate the ROM-BIOS programs, and closely related routines:

| Number | Hex code | Purpose |
| --- | --- | --- |
| 5 | 5 | print-screen operation |
| 16 | 10 | Video I/O; that is, display screen operations |
| 17 | 11 | Equipment check; used to determine the attached equipment |
| 18 | 12 | Memory check; determines the memory size |
| 19 | 13 | Diskette I/O; numerous diskette operations |
| 20 | 14 | RS-232 I/O; operations for the asynchronous comm adapter |
| 21 | 15 | cassette I/O |
| 22 | 16 | keyboard I/O |
| 23 | 17 | printer I/O |
| 24 | 18 | (not a service routine—invokes the cassette BASIC) |
| 25 | 19 | (not a service routine—causes a system re-boot) |
| 26 | 1A | time and date functions |

There are many more service routines than this list of interrupts. If it was desired, each separate service could have been given its own interrupt number, or they all could have been combined into one interrupt—a sort of master service interrupt.

But instead, quite reasonably, one interrupt was dedicated to each major service area of the computer, so that they are grouped in a logical way. This lead to a manageable number of separate interrupts, with reasonable separations of services.

Although the needs of each service vary, there are some common conventions in how data is passed back and forth, from the caller to the service and back to the caller. If you make use of the interface routines provided in the diskette package which accompanies this book, you will not have to deal with the details of how each service is invoked. It is useful, though, to know how they work.

Except for a few cases, each interrupt has several services under it. The AH register is used to pass a number indicating which sub-service is desired. All parameters are passed back and forth through the registers, and the registers used are kept to a minimum. The service routines take care to preserve any registers that aren't used for passing parameters, so that the calling program doesn't need to safeguard any values that have been left in various registers. When a data area is needed in memory, for example as a buffer for transferring data to and from diskette or cassette, the ES and BX registers are used to specify the segmented address. When a return code or results signal is needed by the service routines, registers AH or AX are used. In a few instances the carry flag, CF, is set to indicate an error, but usually the flags are left undisturbed. For the most part, the general purpose registers, AX through DX, are used in alphabetical priority, as needed, to minimize the usage of and disturbance to registers. In the next five chapters we will go over each of these interrupts and their service routines in detail.

## 6.7 Three odd interrupts

We have mentioned in Chapter 3 that three entries in the interrupt vector table are used to hold the addresses of key system data tables, rather than the addresses of interrupt service programs—the normal purpose of the vector table. Here we'll explain what these tables are for, since they are related to the ROM storage.

The first of these tables, corresponding to phantom interrupt 29, gives the address of the video initialization table, used to control the start-up control codes for the display screens. The table is located in ROM at the segmented address, in hex, F000:F0A4. There are three sub-tables within the video parameters, and each sub-table has four entries, for four video modes—one for the monochrome, two for the two color-graphics text modes, 40-column and 80-column, and finally a single entry for the two graphics modes. One of the sub-tables specifies the length in bytes of the video display buffer corresponding to the current mode being used (which we'll cover in Chapters 8 and 9). Another specifies the column widths, used when performing automatic wrap-around of output from one line to another. There is little or nothing useful that can be accomplished by modifying this table, so we won't cover it in any further detail.

The second table address, corresponding to interrupt 30, points to the diskette parameter table. This table controls such things as the time allowed for various diskette functions. The built-in version of this table is in ROM at the segmented address, in hex, F000:EFC7. When the IBM/PC was first released, it was quickly discovered that some of the timing values in this table were much too conservative, and they caused the diskette drives to work too slowly. One of the many changes made to DOS in release 1.10 was an over-ride of this table to speed up diskette access speed. The classic method was used—when DOS starts up, it builds a new version of the table in regular memory, and resets the address vector for interrupt 30 to point to this table. Since all diskette operations dynamically refer to this table, as soon as the vector address is changed, the new table is in effect. In Chapter 7, where we cover the diskette drives, we will go over the details of this table and the changes that were made to it.

The third table address, corresponding to the unusable interrupt 31, points to the graphics generator table, which is used to create the display screen shapes for the characters CHR$(128) through CHR$(255), when the color-graphics display is used in either of the two graphics modes. There is no default version of this table. While the other two tables we've been discussing do appear in the ROM, ROM doesn't contain a table for this purpose. Since there is no default table, the interrupt vector is set to zero—which is used to indicate that there is no table—and stays that way until a program builds a table, and sets the interrupt vector to point to it. There are many interesting uses for this character generation table, and we'll discuss them in Chapter 9, when we cover graphics.

With these background notes on the ROM out of the way, we've now set the stage for a parade of the rich details of each of the IBM/PC individual features. This will be the subject of the next five chapters. And we will begin with the diskette drives until a program builds a table, and sets the interrupt vector to point to it.

LISTING 6-1    131

```
{  Listing 6.1 -- A Pascal module to check the BIOS date        }
{  (C) Copyright 1983, Peter Norton                             }

{  This simple module shows how a program can dynamically check }
{  the date-stamp on the ROM-BIOS                               }

{$debug-,$line-,$ocode-}

module Listing_6_1;

{ First, we define the data types that we need:                 }

type

   string8       = string (8);
   bios_ptr_type = ads of string8;

{ Next a segmented address variable, which will pointer to the date }

var

bios_date      : bios_ptr_type;

{ Finally, a procedure which will check the date                }

procedure check_rom_bios_date;

   begin

      bios_date.s := #F000;  { Set the segment paragraph }
      bios_date.r := #FFF5;  {Set the relative offset    }

      if bios_date ^ = '04/24/81' then { test the date }
        begin
          { at this point we have the original ROM-BIOS version }
        end
      else
        begin
          { at this point we have another version of the ROM-BIOS }
        end;

   end;

end.

{  End of listing 6.1  }
```

# 7

# Access to Diskette

With this chapter we'll begin the detailed, feature-by-feature, discussion of the facilities of the IBM/PC—starting with the diskette drives. The discussion in this chapter, and the next four, will be organized to follow the ROM-BIOS service routines. However, we'll be covering much more than just what the ROM gives us. For each feature we'll cover all the technical information that is interesting or useful to anyone who wants to understand how these features work and how they can be used.

For our three circles of interest, all the information presented here applies in detail to the IBM/PC. For PC-like computers, we can expect that most of this information will apply, in a degree that varies depending upon how closely each computer mimics the IBM/PC; for any computer which claims to be BIOS compatible, everything here should apply. For the MS-DOS family of computers, the information here is likely to be typical of what is provided on each computer, but you can't count on any of the details being the same.

## 7.1 What's available—three levels of diskette access

There are three ways that we can get access to diskette data—through a programming language (such as Pascal and BASIC), through DOS service calls, and through ROM-BIOS service calls. This amounts to a three-tiered hierarchy of services—with BIOS services being the lowest and most "atomic," or primitive. DOS level services are built atop the BIOS services. Language-level services, the highest level of the three, are built out of DOS services and BIOS services.

There is another, higher, level of services that can be provided by a data-base system, of one kind or another.

Language-level diskette I/O operations normally satisfy all our needs for diskette data manipulation. And, when they don't, it's usually not because of any lack of low-level, or atomic, services, but because of a need for the kind of higher-level services that are usually provided by a data base system. However, sometimes we need lower-level access to the diskette, such as direct reading and writing of diskette sectors. For these services, we turn to the other two levels of diskette I/O, DOS-level and BIOS-level.

In Chapter 4 we covered access to all the DOS services, including the diskette I/O services. One of the greatest virtues of DOS-level I/O services, which you probably noticed in Chapter 4, is the breadth of their range. DOS-level I/O provides functions from relatively high-level (such as searching the directory for files with generic names), through middle level (reading and writing logical records), and low level (absolute reading and writing of sectors).

The range of DOS-level services make them especially attractive to use. The programming languages, such as Pascal, generally provide all their diskette I/O completely through using the building blocks of DOS services. I recommend the use of DOS-level services, if you need to break out of the constraints of the I/O provided by your programming language.

If your primary need for special diskette I/O is simply to read and write complete diskette sectors, then using DOS services, rather than BIOS services, will be better for you. This is simply because the extra layer of service that DOS places on top of BIOS insulates your programs from having to worry about such things as retrying after errors, and allowing sufficient time for the diskette motor to come up to speed. There is much to be gained by letting DOS do as much work for you as possible. Nevertheless, you may want to get direct access to BIOS level diskette I/O, either because you want to circumvent DOS's error checking, or because you want to do things that DOS doesn't permit you to do. So here we'll lay out for you the ROM-BIOS diskette services.

## 7.2 ROM-BIOS diskette services

There are six separate services provided by ROM-BIOS for the diskette drives. They are all performed through interrupt 19, hex 13. In this section we'll take a look at each of them, and see some of the things that they can be used for. Programs 7.101 and 7.102, in the separate diskette package which accompanies this book, provide the assembly language routines needed to use these ROM-BIOS diskette services, and the Pascal definitions and support routines needed to make the assembly language routines easy to use.

The first service, with service code 0, resets the diskette system. This can be used to recover from various diskette problems, or simply to clear the decks. It is analogous to the DOS disk-reset (function call number 13), but takes place on a more primitive BIOS-level. The disk-reset operation sends a command to the diskette controller chip telling it to come to order. Note that this won't do such things as resetting the DOS default diskette drive to drive A; for that the DOS-level reset should be used.

The most obvious use for the diskette reset service is in an error recovery routine. Often the best way for a program to deal with a diskette error is to shut down its operations as gracefully as practical, and leave figuring out and fixing the error to the human user of the computer. After all, most diskette errors come from problems that a program cannot fix—such as damage to a diskette, or a mechanical error in the diskette drive. But it is important for your programs to make every attempt to recover from a diskette error, and this reset service can be an important part of a recovery routine.

The second service, code 1, provides the diskette system status code. The status is set by every diskette operation, so this service reports on the last diskette function performed. You can use this operation to snoop into diskette I/O operations that are out of your direct control. For example, if you are doing conventional language-level I/O, and get an error indication, calling this service may give you deeper indications of what went wrong, so that your program can take appropriate action. These are the individual status codes that may be encountered, in some combination:

| Code | Hex | Meaning |
|---|---|---|
| 1 | 01 | A bad command was issued |
| 2 | 02 | The address mark (used to locate sectors) was not found |
| 3 | 03 | A write was requested for a write-protected diskette |
| 4 | 04 | The requested sector was not found |
| 8 | 08 | DMA (direct memory access) overrun |
| 9 | 09 | DMA data transfer crossed a 64 K boundary |
| 16 | 10 | Read data error, detected by cyclical redundancy check (CRC) |
| 32 | 20 | Diskette controller chip failed |
| 64 | 40 | Seek to the desired track failed |
| 128 | 80 | Time-out: no diskette response within the allowed time |

The third and fourth services, codes 2 and 3, read and write one or more sectors, in a combined block, from a single track. I would recommend using the equivalent DOS services, to get error checking and retrying automatically included in the service. Note that for these two services, and also for the DOS sector read/write services, several sectors can be read or written at one time. If you need to do ultra-fast diskette I/O of bulk data, this can speed up your operations, since you can get up to a track-full of data in the time that it takes the diskette to make one rotation. Reading and writing several sectors one by one takes a full diskette rotation for each sector.

There are disadvantages in multiple sector I/O, though. One is that you must provide a data transfer buffer as large as the number of sectors that you will be reading or writing—which could be up to 4 K bytes, for a full track of data. If you can read or write sector data into the same memory locations where you will be using it, then this is no concern;

but if you have to provide a separate diskette buffer area, to read into or write from, then multiple sector reading and writing will increase your memory requirements. There are other disadvantages to multi-sector I/O. If, during the operation, there are any errors, the error checking and recovery that you may need to do can be more elaborate, since it is less clear which sector caused the problem. This difficulty is reduced, when the BIOS services are used, by a count that is given of how many sectors were transferred; the DOS services do not provide this partial-success count. When you are reading data in multiple sectors, an error part-way through is not much of a problem. But writing data, under critical conditions, can leave you with a very messy error recovery problem, if your programs do not know exactly how many sectors have been written.

The fifth service, code 4, is used to verify data after a read or write operation. It re-reads diskette sectors, using the Cyclical Redundancy Check to detect any errors. This is the service that is used by the "/V", or verify, option of the DOS COPY command. Verifying is not done very much, and for good reason. First, diskette operations are generally quite reliable. Second, nearly any error in data transfer will be reported; it is rare for a diskette read or write to appear to be successful, and the data to be garbled in some way. But when it really matters that no error has been made, the verify service can be used to confirm a diskette data transfer. While using this service will greatly increase the diskette access time of your programs, it is relatively effortless to use—there are no specifications to be set up. To verify a sector read or write operation, this service is requested immediately after the transfer operation is completed.

The sixth and last operation, code 5, is especially interesting. This service formats a diskette track, writing address marks for the sectors, and storing in the data portion of the sector a standard value, hex F6 or CHR$$(246). Separate specifications must be given for each sector, indicating the track, side and sector numbers, and the sector length code. These are more or less the address marks stored on the diskette. Since each sector can have its own size separately specified, a track can be formatted with one or more non-standard size sectors—a common technique for copy protection. Ordinary DOS operations will not read sectors which are not the standard 512-byte length, and this forms the basis for many copy protection schemes. We will see more about this in the next section, which covers the parameters that control the diskette operations.

Formatting must be done a full track at a time—you can't format just part of a track, since the spacing and address marking of the sectors is interdependent. However, if it is necessary to get the effect of reformatting a single sector, there is a way to do that. For example, if you wish to change the formatting of the last sector of a track, and still maintain the existing data in the first seven sectors, do this: Create a program to first read the data from the track's sectors, then reformat the whole track, and re-write the data. This can be done to patch copy protection onto existing data, while seemingly leaving the data undisturbed.

For each sector to be formatted on the track, these items must be specified, each in a one-byte number:

1—track number (0 through 39)

2—side (0 or 1; single-sided diskettes always use 0)

3—sector number (starting with 1; sector 0 is control information)

4—length code (0 = 128 bytes, 1 = 256 bytes, 2 = 512 bytes [standard], 3 = 1024)

Since each sector has its own length code, it is no trick to insert a single non-standard size sector into a track (or to create a full track of sectors that aren't the DOS-standard 512 bytes).

If you use this BIOS-level service call to format a track, be sure that you specify the sector formatting parameters correctly, or you can create quite a mess. If you have any doubts, experimentation is in order; but the process is quite straight-forward, and shouldn't cause you any problems.

## 7.3  Diskette parameters and how to do copy protection

The operation of the diskette drives is controlled partly by a table known as the disk base, or the diskette parameter table (IBM's terminology for this table varies).

The disk base is an eleven byte table containing some key parameters necessary for the operation of the diskette drives, including some key format information for the diskette. Listing 7.1 includes an outline of this disk base table, with notes describing the function of each byte in the table.

As you will recall from Chapter 6, one interrupt vector—number 29, stored at the low memory location 120—is used to indicate the location of this table. The original version of the table, used for DOS release 1.00, was located in the ROM-BIOS, and thanks to this we can see it listed in the Technical Reference manual.

Starting with DOS release 1.10, the ROM table was replaced with one located in ordinary read-write memory. This change, by the way, is an advantage for us. It enables us to monkey with the values in the table, without having to go to the work of setting up a replacement for the ROM table. Any program could set up its own disk-base table, but creating one which will continue in effect after our program ends is more complicated. Accomplishing that involves reserving a small section of storage, and making sure that DOS leaves it alone. But since DOS now has placed the disk-base table in read-write storage, we don't have to go to that trouble to make changes to the disk base.

IBM made only two changes in the disk base table from DOS release 1.00 to 1.10, but they resulted in much faster use of the diskettes. First, they made a 25% decrease in the time allowed for the diskette drive to move from track to track, known as the Step Rate Time, or SRT. In the ROM version of the table, used by DOS version 1.00, the SRT was 8 milliseconds; the new time, starting with DOS version 1.10, is 6 milliseconds.

If you want to look up this item in the disk-base table, it is the first half-byte—or nybble, as half-bytes are sometimes called—in the table. The original value was 12, hex C, and the new value is 13, hex D. I originally misinterpreted this as an increase in the step rate time, but Robert Batten, of Burlington, Vermont, informs me that this controlling parameter is used inversely, so that a larger number sets a shorter, faster, SRT. The SRT is controlled in increments of 2 milliseconds, so that a change from 12 to 13 in the table changes the SRT from 8 to 6 milliseconds.

The second change dramatically increased the speed of diskette access. The "head settle time," a pause for the diskette read/write heads to stabilize, was reduced from 25 milliseconds to zero. Originally IBM had been overly conservative about the performance of the diskette drives, and by eliminating the settle time, diskette access speed became much faster. While most of this table is out of bounds for fiddling with, some parts of it are interesting for the adventurous. The 9th byte contains the byte value that the format operation uses to initialize diskette sectors. The standard value is hex F6, but it could be replaced by you to cause a different initialization value. Some programs check for the hex F6 value to test for sectors which have been used, so it is probably not wise to change this value, unless you have a good reason to do so. If you are doing special formatting for copy protection, then anything goes.

Another very interesting byte is the sector size byte. This controls the size of the sectors to be read or written, and it allows us to work with sectors other than the standard DOS size of 512 bytes. It is by changing this value that other operating systems use other sector sizes. Altering this value is the simplest way of producing a copy protected diskette. To create a sector with a size other than 512 bytes, you will need to use the format service described in the last section. In formatting, the sector size is specified sector by sector. But to later read or write a non-512 sized sector, your programs will need to change with the size indicator in the disk-base table, which is what we are discussing here.

The values used for this parameter are these:

| Value | Sector size in bytes |
|-------|----------------------|
| 0 | 128 |
| 1 | 256 |
| 2 | 512 (the DOS standard) |
| 3 | 1024 |

Program listing 7.1 illustrates, in Pascal, how to gain access to the disk base table and change its values. The same sort of thing can be done in BASIC, although its a touchier business, involving picking up address values byte by byte and putting them back together—tricky, yet interesting. Here is a BASIC program which will work its way through the addressing, and then print out the disk base table:

```
100   REM A basic program to find and print the disk base
110   REM
120   REM First, set up a pointer to the interrupt vector
130   REM
140   DEF SEG = 0 ' beginning of memory
150   OFFSET1 = 30 * 4 ' offset to interrupt vector
160   REM
170   REM Next get the offset part of the vector
180   REM
190   OFFSET2 = PEEK (OFFSET1) + 256 * PEEK (OFFSET1 + 1)
200   REM
210   REM Next get the segment part of the vector
220   REM
230   DEF SEG = PEEK (OFFSET1 + 2) + 256 * PEEK (OFFSET1 + 3)
240   REM
250   REM Now we're ready look at the disk base table itself
260   REM
270   PRINT "Here is the disk-base data, in hexadecimal"
280   FOR I = 0 TO 10
290      PRINT " ";
300      IF PEEK (OFFSET2 + I) = 16 THEN PRINT "0"; = leading zero for evenness
310      PRINT HEX$ (PEEK (OFFSET2 + I));
320   NEXT I
330   PRINT : PRINT
```

If you are interested in copy protection, we provide you with the means, in two forms, to do so.

Programs 7.103 and 7.104, on the diskette which accompanies this book, provide the assembly language and Pascal routines necessary to copy protect a diskette, in a form that you can tailor to your own security scheme. The methods used aren't state-of-the-art by any means, and you can expect that any decent copy-busting program will break through our technique with ease— but using them should give you some amount of copy resistance. In addition, the diskette package contains a complete, ready-to-use, copy protection scheme, if you want to copy-protect diskettes, without having to go to the trouble of working out a customized scheme. This ready-made method can be used from either BASIC or Pascal.

```
{ Listing 7.1 -- Pascal routines to access the "disk base" parameters }
{ (C) Copyright 1983, Peter Norton                                    }


{ This program fragment shows how to gain access to the "Disk Base", or }
{ diskette control table.  This listing is intended to be suggestive, and}
{ would need to be tailored to your needs, before you use it.            }

module Listing_7_1;

type

disk_base_type = array [1..11] of byte;

   { Here is a quick summary of the eleven bytes of the disk base : }

   {  1 : "specify" byte #1  step rate time; head unload time     }
   {  2 : "specify" byte #2  head load time; DMA mode             }
   {  3 : wait time until turning the motor off                   }
   {  4 : bytes-per-sector 0=128, 1=256, 2=512, 3=1024            }
   {  5 : end-of-track (last sector number)                       }
   {  6 : gap length, between sectors                             }
   {  7 : data length (when sector length not specified)          }
   {  8 : gap length, for formatting                              }
   {  9 : format fill byte (stored as data in new sectors)        }
   { 10 : head settle time                                        {
   { 11 : motor start time (how long to allow for start-up)       }

var

   disk_base         : disk_base_type;
   disk_base_pointer : ads of disk_base_type;  { segmented address }
   vector_pointer    : ads of adsmem;          { segmented address }

procedure disk_base_access;
  begin

    { first we set a pointer to the interrupt vector for the disk base }

    vector_pointer.s :=   0;   { segment paragraph 0: start of memory   }
    vector_pointer.r := 30 * 4; { displacement for interrupt number 30   }

    { next we grab the vector to see where the table is located          }

    disk_base_pointer := vector_pointer ^;
    { "disk_base_pointer" now contains the segmented-address that was    }
    { pointed to by the segmented-address "vector_pointer" --            }
    { which means that "disk_base_pointer" now points to the actual      }
    { table that is in effect.                                           }

    { Next we test that the disk base is in read/write memory.           }
    { We could do this by trying to change the table, and then check     }
    { if the value was changed.  Instead, we will just test to see how   }
    { high its address is.                                               }
```

LISTING 7-1   141

```
        if disk_base_pointer.s >= #F000 then
          begin
            { too high-- must be in ROM; you won't be able to change it        }
          end
        else
          begin
            { OK -- it's apparently in read/write memory                       }
          end;

        { Next we make a copy of the table in our own storage                  }

        disk_base := disk_base_pointer ^ ;
        { "disk_base" now contains a copy of the table data that was           }
        { pointed to by the segmented-address in "disk_base_pointer"           }

        { Next, we change the size to 1024 bytes and format byte to AA         }
        { This is done in our copy, which is then moved onto the real          }
        { table; the change could be made directly.                           }

        disk_base [4] := 3;   { change to 1024 sector size                     }
        disk_base [9] := #AA; { hex AA, decimal 170, an arbitrary value        }

        disk_base_pointer ^ := disk_base;  { move our table into place         }

    end;

end. { of module listing_7_1                                                   }

{  end of listing 7.1, access to the disk base table                          }
```

# 8

# Video Access, Part 1— Characters

Practically every program that runs on the IBM Personal Computer will generate output for the video display screens. There are two very different kinds of video display output for the IBM/PC: text (that is, letters of the alphabet and other characters) and graphics. In this and the next chapter, we will go over all the interesting details of how to gain access to the display screens, starting with character text displays.

Unlike most of the information in this book, practically nothing in this chapter or the next applies to the whole of the MS-DOS family of computers. On the other hand, this is one area where we can expect that PC-like machines will match the IBM/PC completely, since many of the most successful programs for the IBM/PC depend upon the exact nature of video output.

## 8.1 Several kinds of video display screens

There are many kinds of video display screens that can be connected to the IBM/PC, and it is easy to be confused about what the characteristics of each are, and what programming considerations apply to them. To reduce the confusion, we'll outline the most important varieties that are used on the PC, and how each of them will relate to the information presented in this chapter and the next.

First, there are two display adapters that can be plugged into the PC as expansion boards. One is the monochrome adapter. The other is the color-graphics adapter.

The monochrome adapter is intended to be used only with the IBM monochrome display screen. The monochrome display cannot produce color, and it cannot generate graphics information. It is only intended to show text character data, and to do the simple kind of drawing that can be accomplished with characters.

The color-graphics adapter may be used with many different display screens. This adapter has output plugs for two different kinds of connections, and different kinds of display terminals may be connected to them.

One output plug produces a single composite color signal. The other produces separate signals for the three primary colors, red, green and blue; this is known as an RGB signal, for the initials of the three colors.

Special display screens, known as RGB monitors, are connected to the RGB output. Composite color display screens can be connected to the composite output. Color TV's can also be connected to the composite output, with a radio-frequency converter. Any of these three types of display screens show color.

It is also possible to connect a black-and-white computer display screen to the composite output. When this is done, the black-and-white display is connected to a color signal, but it cannot make use of the complete color information. Using this kind of display screen sacrifices both color capability, and the high quality and clarity of IBM monochrome display. However, it can be the most economical way to get a display screen.

Different parts of the discussion in this chapter and the next apply to the various kinds of display screens. To avoid confusion, let's summarize what applies to what.

Any information specific to the monochrome adapter applies only to it, and not to any of the color options, including the use of a black-and-white monitor on the color-graphics adapter. A black-and-white monitor may be monochrome, but it isn't used with the monochrome adapter. In IBM/PC terminology, the term monochrome applies only to the IBM monochrome display screen.

Anything specific to the color-graphics adapter, does not apply to the monochrome display, but does apply to all the color displays. Most of the information about the color-graphics adapter applies to black-and-white monitors, except for the color information itself.

Most black-and-white monitors do not handle color signals well. It would be nice if black-and-white monitors produced a reasonably readable screen when they are sent color signals, but often they do not. So any program which may be used with black-and-white monitors should avoid color, or at least be able to convert its various colors to either white or black.

Color TVs generally have a low display resolution, compared to the color monitors normally used with computers. Because of this, color TVs can only be used with the IBM/PC's lowest resolution formats, such as the 40-column mode. For the most part, a color TV will not be able to take advantage of many of the IBM/PC's capabilities, and most important programs for the PC cannot be used with this kind of display screen. Using a color TV with the IBM/PC belongs in the toy category, along with the cassette interface.

## 8.2 Video philosophy

Before we get into the specifics of character displays, we should take a look at some of the fundamentals of video screen displays, to better understand what is happening. There are two common ways that a personal computer can send information to its video display screen. One is for the computer to treat the display screen as it treats any other input-output device. In this approach, the computer sends various commands to the display controller, including commands to display text information. To make this clearer, here is a simplified example of what such commands might be like:

CLEAR-THE-SCREEN
DISPLAY AT LINE 10 AND COLUMN 15 THIS TEXT: "When ready, press enter..."
MOVE-THE-CURSOR TO LINE 10 AND COLUMN 43

The most important thing about this kind of communication between computer and display screen, is that the display is treated like any other peripheral device. There are, naturally, special operations that apply to a screen that don't apply to a printer, for example—you can't CLEAR-THE-PAGE on a printer—but the basic relationship is the same.

There is an advantage in this command approach, for with it display screens are treated like any other computer output device. This makes the software support for display screens potentially simpler, and makes it possible to use any of the literally hundreds of standard computer terminal screens available. The disadvantage in this approach is that the computer can't have an intimate and special relationship with its display screen, and so can't perform magic tricks on the screen. IBM preferred magic, and so they chose the other approach to connecting the IBM/PC to its display screens.

"Memory-mapping" is the term used for the second main way of communicating with a computer display screen. With a memory-mapped display, the computer and the display screen share some addressable memory. The screen continually reads the memory, and shows whatever is in it. The computer's programs can "write" information on the screen by simply changing what is stored in the memory. Among the benefits of the memory-mapped approach, is that a program can seemingly read information off of the display screen by simply inspecting what is stored in the shared memory. The screen and its supporting memory are unified; to read or write in the memory is to read or write on the screen.

The IBM Personal computer actually uses a combination of the command and memory-mapped approaches. For displaying data on the screen, memory-mapping is used. But to control certain aspects of the display, commands are used. In a strictly memory-mapped display, even the cursor is controlled by what appears in the shared memory. But for the IBM/PC, the cursor is positioned by commands sent to the display screen's controller circuits. Commands are used for other things, such as: setting the size of the blinking cursor, clearing and resetting the display, and changing modes (between text and graphics, or between 40 and 80 column displays).

There are two potential disadvantages in using memory-mapping, but IBM found ways to overcome each of them. The first is that memory-mapping uses up memory space—and on the old generation 8-bit personal computers, with their small memory limitations, that was a severe problem. The IBM/PC circumvents that problem in two ways. First, by having an enormous one million byte address space. Second, by giving the display screens their own built-in memory, so that they don't use up any of the ordinary memory that was intended to be used for holding programs and data.

There is an even more important reason why the display adapters are given their own memory, and that is to avoid a problem with conflicting memory access. A memory-mapped display screen must continually read the display memory, and, ordinarily, that would interfere with the micro-processor's ability to use the memory. The two of them would be crowding through the same doorway, fighting to use the memory access circuitry. IBM solved that problem, at the same time that it gave the display screens their own dedicated memory, by providing dual-port access to the display memory. This gives two doorways into the memory, so that both the computer and the display can access the special display memory rapidly.

With dual-port circuitry, there is almost no interference between the display screen and programs which generate display information. If you watch your IBM/PC closely, you can occasionally detect a small amount of interference. When you are using a program which rapidly fills the screen with information, such as a good word processor, occasionally something subtle will happen. If you pay close attention to what the screen looks like when the display is being generated, you may see that usually the display is completely clear, and on a few occasions some temporary "noise" appears on the screen— perhaps the cursor will seem to skip quickly over the screen. This can be the result of the screen's controller circuitry and the computer's program reading and writing the display memory at the same time. There is absolutely no harm in this, but it is interesting to see it happening.

With memory-mapped displays, dedicated display memory, and dual-ported memory access, IBM provided nearly the best possible display format for the IBM/PC. The only real improvement that could be made is to provide a very high resolution character and icon-graphics display, of the sort that was pioneered in the Xerox Star workstation, and used in the Apple Lisa system. In the basic memory allocation for the IBM/PC, 128 K bytes were reserved for display memory. It is a reasonable speculation that IBM set this much memory aside with just this kind of display in mind.

For the moment, that is all the background information that you need. In the next chapter we'll enrich what we've covered above with some more video philosophy concerning graphics. The next section of this chapter will explain the details of the memory-mapping; then we'll go on to discuss display pages and the screen "attributes." And then, for the rest of this chapter, we'll show you how to use and control the display screens for character displays.

## 8.3 A compass for the memory map

Since I've told you that the IBM/PC's displays are memory-mapped, I'd better explain the map to you. It's an interesting layout, with one annoying flaw.

The memory-map that we'll describe here applies to the monochrome adapter, and to the color-graphics adapter, when it is working in a text mode. The graphics modes will be covered in the next chapter, along with the memory-mapping used for graphics. (For a summary of the different modes that the color-graphics adapter can operate in, and a discussion of some of their interesting features, see section 8.11.)

Since the display adapters use a special dual-ported memory, you shouldn't be surprised that the memory is specially located. Physically, the display memory is placed on the display adapter expansion card, a circuit card which also contains the display controller chip and all the supporting electronic circuitry. This card, like other cards for the IBM/PC, is plugged into one of the expansion slots designed to accept optional equipment.

While the display memory is physically located on a display controller card, logically it is like any other memory—and it can be read or written to by programs simply by accessing the memory addresses. The two different kinds of display have their memory placed at different address locations, as we saw in the discussion of the PC's memory usage in Chapter 3, so that both can be installed and used on a single IBM/PC. For the monochrome display, the display storage begins at hex paragraph B000. For the color graphics display, the storage begins at hex paragraph B800.

For BASIC oriented readers, recall that you can access this storage with PEEK and POKE, after you've set the right segment pointer, as with

```
10   DEF SEG = &HB000 ' for the monochrome display memory
20   DEF SEG = &HB800 ' for the color-graphics display memory
```

As we explain the parts of how the memory-mapped display works, you can follow along in the diagram shown in figure 8.1.

The display memory-map begins with the individual character positions on the screen. For each screen position, there are two bytes in memory. Together, these two bytes specify what is to be displayed, and how it is to be shown.

The first of the two bytes, at an even address location, specifies what is to be shown: it contains the ASCII code for the character which is to be displayed on the screen. The second of the two bytes, at an odd location, specifies how it is to be shown. This how-to-show-it byte is

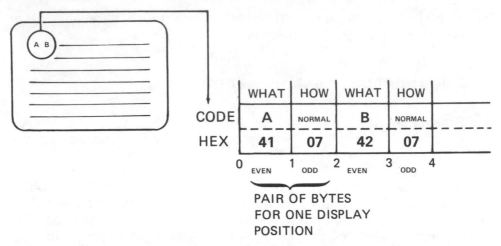

| | WHAT | HOW | WHAT | HOW | |
|---|---|---|---|---|---|
| CODE | A | NORMAL | B | NORMAL | |
| HEX | 41 | 07 | 42 | 07 | |

0    EVEN    1    ODD    2    EVEN    3    ODD    4

PAIR OF BYTES
FOR ONE DISPLAY
POSITION

Figure 8.1a—Display Memory Map, Character Mode.

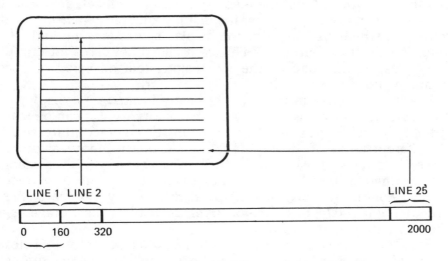

LINE 1  LINE 2                                                    LINE 25

0    160    320                                                   2000

Figure 8.1b—Display Memory Map, Display Lines to Memory Locations.

called the attribute byte. For the color-graphics adapter, the attribute byte controls the color. For the monochrome adapter, the attribute byte controls brightness and underlining—the monochrome equivalent of color. For both adapters, the attribute byte also controls blinking. The full details and capabilities of the attribute byte are covered in sections 8.5 and 8.6.

The first position on the screen, at the top left corner, uses the first two bytes in the display memory. So the offset to this location is zero. The next position, one column to the right, uses the next two memory locations, beginning at offset 2. This continues to the end of the first row of the display screen. For the monochrome display, and for the color-graphics display set to 80-column mode, the last column of the display will use the pair of bytes that are located at offset 158, which is 79 times 2. In 40-column mode, the last position on the first line would use the pair of bytes at offset 78, or 39 times 2.

At the end of each row, the memory-map immediately wraps around, so that the first column of the next line is mapped to the pair of bytes following the last column of the preceding line. There is no gap in the use of memory, and no boundary between where one line ends, and the next begins. No boundary, that is, except for the logical one which can be calculated to determine where the separation lies.

In 40 column mode, the end of each short line is immediately followed by the beginning of the next. So in switching between 80 and 40 column modes, the map of rows and columns is re-drawn.

For the monochrome display, and the color-graphics in 80-column mode, the memory-map takes up 4000 bytes: two bytes for each position, times eighty columns, times twenty-five rows. For 40-column mode, which applies only to the color-graphics adapter, the map is half as big, using only 2000 bytes.

One of the results of this memory-mapping scheme is that the characters displayed are located in every other memory location. This makes it slightly inconvenient to move messages into the display memory. Messages, or other strings of display data, can't be moved into place in one step, unless they are stored in your programs in a form that has the attribute bytes interleaved—so that the message is stored as alternating data and attribute bytes. Since most data displayed on the screen is in the form of strings of bytes which need to be shown with the same attribute, display routines are needed to move the data into place, interleaving it with copies of the desired attribute. Listing 8.2 shows some Pascal service routines which can be used to do this task, and section 8.7 discusses more about the subject.

Because the memory-map has no gap or boundary between one line and the next, messages that are too long to fit in one line can be automatically wrapped around onto the next line, by the successive use of memory locations. This can be a handy way of dealing with the wrap-around of messages, with a minimum of fuss. However, if it matters to you when messages reach the end of a line, then your display routines must include tests for the end of lines.

For the monochrome adapter, 4000 bytes of memory are needed for the display. That is just the amount that is provided, rounded up to an even 4 K, or 4096 bytes. The extra 96 bytes are not used for the display memory, and are left over.

For the color-graphics adapter, there is quite a bit more memory, 16 K in all, thanks to the greater memory needs of the graphics modes (which we'll cover in the next chapter). The PC makes use of this extra memory, when it is not needed for graphics displays, by providing the text-mode with multiple screen images in memory. These multiple images are called pages. We'll cover how pages work, and what you can do with them, in the next section.

# 8.4 Pages on the color-graphics display

This section directly concerns IBM/PCs with the color-graphics adapter attached. But, as you will see toward the end of the section, the concept can be applied to monochrome adapter system. So, even if your interest is only in the monochrome system (or in what can be done on either system), don't skip over this section.

While the monochrome adapter has just enough memory for a screen-full of display information, the color-graphics adapter has quite a bit more than is needed for a text character display—thanks to the greater memory needs of the graphics mode. Rather than let this memory go to waste, IBM put it to work through the concept of display pages.

A display page is a memory-image of what could be shown on the display screen. In 80-column text mode, the color-graphics adapter has four times as much memory as is needed for the display information, and in 40-column text mode, there is eight times as much memory as is needed. So there are either four or eight display pages in the two text modes of the color-graphics adapter.

Each display page is a complete model of the display screen information, complete with data bytes, attribute bytes, and logical division into rows of display characters. In 80-column mode, the color-graphics adapter has four exact replicas of the monochrome adapter's single display image. And in 40-column mode, there are eight replicas, each half-size.

At any one time, the information stored in one of the four or eight pages appears on the display screen. Meanwhile the other pages sit like actors off-stage, waiting for the cue for them to appear. When the command is given, the display adapter switches from one page to another, and the display screen changes immediately.

A program can send display data to any of the display pages by simply writing to the appropriate memory locations, or by using the BIOS services to build output in the desired page. When it is ready, a display image that has been built can instantly appear on the display screen by switching the adapter's active page from one to another. This allows programs to appear snappier in operation than their actual performance, since the user doesn't see the display screen information being laboriously built by a program—the user just sees the quick appearance of the results.

The programming possibilities for using pages are quite interesting. If a program uses several standard formats for the information that it displays, it could do the work of constructing the format outline only once, and leave it in the display page memory. When a change from one format to another is needed, the program can leave the current page showing, write specific information into the outline format in another page, and when it is ready, switch the display adapter to the new page. This kind of technique produces the impression of faster program performance—when information appears, it appears instantaneously. Also, it is kinder to the user of the program because it makes the screen display more stable. Since detailed changes don't take place on the screen, the user can trust the program more—there is no need to look around the screen to see if everything is in place yet, or if things are still changing.

Another potential use for the display pages is to produce smoother animation effects. If the screen display is being directly changed by a program, different parts of the screen will change at different times. But by making all changes "off stage," and moving complete displays into place by changing the active page, there will be no unevenness in the animation effect.

The display pages are numbered 0 through 3, or 0 through 7 for the smaller 40-column pages. As you might expect, page zero is located at the beginning of the display memory, followed by the other pages. The beginning of each page is located at a round number in binary notation. For example, in 80-column mode, each page needs 4000 bytes, for its 25 rows of 80 columns of two bytes of display information. The first page, page 0, begins at relative location 0 in the color-graphics adapters memory—which, again is located at hex paragraph B800. The second page, page 1, doesn't begin immediately following the first page, at relative location 4000; instead it begins at the next kilo-byte boundary, at a displacement of 4 K, or 4096. For 80-column mode, the pages are located at 4 K intervals, and in 40-column mode, they are at 2 K intervals. Figure 8.2 diagrams how the pages are laid out in the display memory.

Control over the display pages is provided in BASIC. It is not directly available to the Pascal user, except through assembly language interface with the ROM-BIOS. In section 8.11 we explain how it is done, and a ready-to-use interface routine is part of the diskette package which accompanies this book.

The monochrome display does not have this display page capability, but the idea can be borrowed and simulated in ordinary memory. Conventional read-write storage can be used by your programs to hold complete screen images, the equivalent of display pages. These off-camera images can be moved into the display memory using the string move capability of the 8088 micro-processor. For Pascal users, the built-in procedure MOVESL will do the trick. I have used MOVESL in some of my programs, and I can testify that it loads the screen so fast that the eye can't see it happening—the display change appears instantaneous, and so has just the same effect as a page change in the color-graphics adapter. This is a very effective technique, and I would recommend it highly in any program which can afford the extra memory required.

There is one simple reason why few programs make use of the paging capability of the color-graphics adapter—most programs for the IBM/PC need to operate equally well on both monochrome and color-graphics systems. Effective use of the paging feature can only be made when a program is specifically writen for graphics system, or when a program is so important that it expects the computer equipment to be

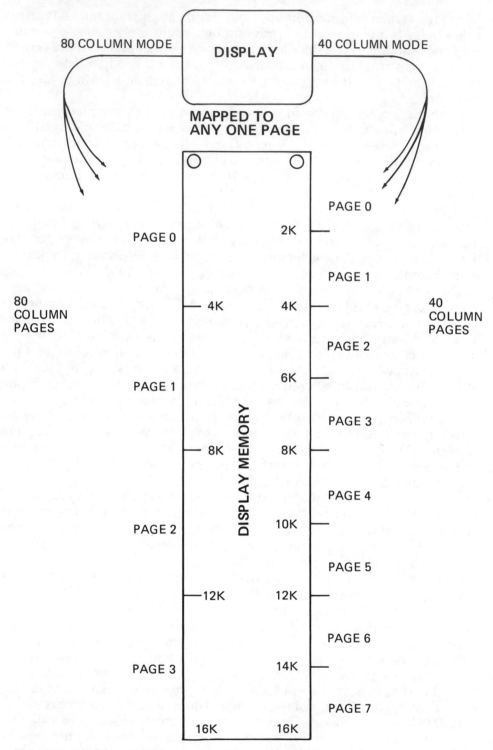

**Figure 8.2—Display Memory Map, Graphics Text-Mode Pages.**

tailored to the program's needs. One prominent example of the latter is the Context MBA program. Nevertheless, the simulation of display paging, described above, can be done on any IBM/PC, provided enough memory is available.

## 8.5 Display attributes

Right after each character byte in the display memory, occupying an odd memory address, is an attribute byte, which specifies how the character next to it is to be displayed. In this section we'll cover the details of how these attributes work.

The BASIC program given in listing 8.1 will demonstrate all possible combinations of the attribute byte, for both the monochrome and color-graphics displays. Running this program will give you a quick insight into how the attributes work, and what their possibilities are.

The attribute byte controls such things as whether or not a character is blinking, and its color (or the monochrome equivalent of color). The attribute byte has eight bits, which are individually assigned different roles in the display process. Figure 8.3 diagrams how the bits work. There are many inconsistent ways of referring to the different bits in a byte. For this discussion, we'll number them from left to right, as shown figure 8.3.

The eight bits are organized into four parts, even though each bit operates separately. What is shown on the screen, in each display position, has two parts—the character itself, and the space around it; these are known as the foreground (the character) and the background (the surrounding space). Since a color display has three color components (red, green and blue), the foreground and background each have three bits in the attribute, dedicated to determining their colors (or the monochrome equivalent of color). So the 6th through 8th bits of the attribute byte control the color of the foreground, and the 2nd through 4th bits control the color of the background. This takes care of two of the four parts of the attribute byte.

The other two parts are intensity and blinking, each controlled by one bit. The first bit of the attribute byte controls whether or not the foreground part of the display position will be blinking; if the bit is set (value 1), then the character blinks. Blinking affects the foreground only, and has no effect on the background.

The final part of the attribute byte is the 5th bit, which controls the foreground intensity. If the 5th bit is set, then the character will be bright on the monochrome display, or a lighter and brighter color on a color display. Some color monitors do not make use of the intensity feature controlled by this bit; on these display screens bright foreground colors are the same as ordinary colors.

To get various colors, the color component bits are set on or off. For example, to get a red foreground color, the red bit, the 6th bit, is set on, and the other two bits off. Combining two of the three display primary

| BIT ORDER | VALUE* | FUNCTION |
|---|---|---|
| 1st | 128 | BLINKING |
| 2nd | 64 | RED COLOR COMPONENT ⎤ |
| 3rd | 32 | GREEN COLOR COMPONENT ⎬— BACKGROUND COLORS |
| 4th | 16 | BLUE COLOR COMPONENT ⎦ |
| 5th | 8 | INTENSITY (PART OF THE FOREGROUND COLOR) |
| 6th | 4 | RED ⎤ |
| 7th | 2 | GREEN ⎬—FOREGROUND COLORS |
| 8th | 1 | BLUE ⎦ |

*The numeric value of the bit's position. This is used when specifying the attributes as a numeric value.
Example: Blinking (128) green (2) on a red (64) background is 128+2+64=194

**Figure 8.3—Attributes for Display Control.**

colors gives more possibilities—for example, green and blue together make a blue-green color known as cyan. With all three color bits off, the color is black, as you might expect. With all three colors on, white is displayed. By looking closely at white characters on a color screen you can usually see the three separate primary colors at the edges of the white.

We'll leave a full list of all the color combinations, and discussion of them, to the next section. We still have a lot to consider, as we go over more aspects of the display attribute, and how it works for both the color-graphics adapter and the monochrome adapter.

Even with a color display screen, the DOS operating system normally works with white characters on a black background. Most of the programs that operate under DOS also format their information in white-on-black. But it is possible to make a temporary change to the normal screen colors, if you have a program to control the screen attributes (such as the Norton Utility programs Reverse and Screen-Attribute). When I am working on a color system, I find that bright yellow characters on a blue background are much easier on the eyes, and so I set my system to have the attributes 00011110 (in hex 1E). If you run the BASIC program shown in listing 8.1, you will have a chance to compare all the possibilities of foreground and background colors, and make your own choice as to which colors you would prefer to work with.

IBM took an interesting approach to the problem of making the monochrome and color displays compatible. First, IBM defined what was needed for the color display (which was three color components for foreground and background, plus blinking and high-intensity); then IBM set up the monochrome display to interpret the color components in as reasonable a way as possible. The resulting attributes for the monochrome display work fairly well, but they are not as consistent and compatible as they could have been. Let's look at the simplest part first, and then go into the complications.

The blinking bit, bit 1, and the bright, or high-intensity bit, bit 5, both work the same for the monochrome display as for the color-graphics display. If blinking is set, the character shown blinks, and if bright is set, the character is displayed in high-intensity.

The rest of the attribute byte specifies the colors for the foreground and background, and for a monochrome display, color is an unknown quantity. If you consider it literally, the monochrome display really has only two colors — phosphor-green and black; that is, showing light (lit) or not. To deal with all the possible color combinations on the monochrome display, IBM simplified things by making all foreground and background color combinations, except for three special cases, show as ordinary green characters on a black background.

The normal color attribute setting for the monochrome display is the same as that for the color-graphics: white characters (color bit settings 111), on a black background (color bit settings 000). While this is the normal attribute color code, any color code (except for the three cases that I will explain), will show in the normal format of phosphor-green characters on a black background.

Of the three special display cases, two you might anticipate. If the color bits are set to black-on-black, that is, all the color bits off, then whatever character might be shown is invisible. If the color bits are set for black-on-white, that is, foreground color bits set to 000 and background color bits set to 111, then the monochrome display shows what is called reverse video, or black characters on a phosphor-green background. Both of these combinations work the same as the color displays, where black-on-black is invisible, and black-on-white is a reverse video effect. Naturally you might expect that a fourth combination of white-on-white would work to produce invisible characters, on a solid phosphor-green background; but IBM didn't do things that way. For the monochrome display, a white-on-white color setting produces the normal format of green characters on a black background, just like all the other miscellaneous color settings.

The one final special display format for the monochrome display is underlined. IBM provided the monochrome display screen with the ability to underline characters. The color setting used to produce this is a blue foreground (color bits 001) and a black background (color bits 000). There is no underlining feature available on the color-graphics adapter, but the same attribute setting, of blue-on-black, does give an equivalent feeling of emphasis.

Since the monochrome display will work in reverse-video, and will produce underlining, you might expect that the two could be used together, but they can't. The color settings that might be used for this, blue-on-white or black-on-blue, both are shown as normal phosphor-green settings, like all the other odd color combinations.

# 8.6 Color details

Here we'll go over the details of color, as they appear on a color screen attached to the color-graphics adapter. Bear in mind that these colors will not show on a black-and-white monitor connected to the color-graphics adapter. Also, many of the popular black-and-white monitors do not treat color signals well, and any screen information sent to a black-and-white monitor using any colors other than white and black may be invisible or difficult to read.

In theory there are sixteen colors that can be used on a color display on the IBM/PC. First, there are eight possible settings of the three color bits that correspond to the primary colors of red, green, and blue. Then, for foreground use only, there are two variations on each of those colors, with or without the bright, or high-intensity, bit set. So potentially there are sixteen colors in all. All sixteen can be used in the foreground, and eight can be used in the background. (In graphics mode, which we'll cover in the next chapter, the same sixteen colors are available, but how they can be used in foreground and background is quite different.)

In practice there are fewer than sixteen colors. One of the eight main colors is black, and it is unclear what a high-intensity black color is; IBM describes it as dark grey, and in principle a color display screen could show such a color—but few do so. That reduces the colors to fifteen possibilities. Also, not all color monitors make use of the bright bit setting, and for those that don't, the color possibilities are reduced to the main eight. For some purposes black is a usable color, but for others it is not, so you may find that there are only seven colors that you can actually use for your displays.

Here is a table of all the sixteen combinations of the four color bits, including the bright or high-intensity bit, with the colors they produce.

| Bright | Red | Green | Blue | Number | Color | Notes |
|---|---|---|---|---|---|---|
| 0 | 0 | 0 | 0 | 0 | Black | no display |
| 0 | 0 | 0 | 1 | 1 | Blue | |
| 0 | 0 | 1 | 0 | 2 | Green | |
| 0 | 0 | 1 | 1 | 3 | Cyan | blue-green to ordinary folks |
| 0 | 1 | 0 | 0 | 4 | Red | |
| 0 | 1 | 0 | 1 | 5 | Magenta | a light purple made of red and blue |
| 0 | 1 | 1 | 0 | 6 | "Brown" | dark yellow; yellow on many displays |
| 0 | 1 | 1 | 1 | 7 | "Light gray" | normal white |
| 1 | 0 | 0 | 0 | 8 | "Dark gray" | bright black (?!) |
| 1 | 0 | 0 | 1 | 9 | Light blue | |
| 1 | 0 | 1 | 0 | 10 | Light green | |
| 1 | 0 | 1 | 1 | 11 | Light cyan | light blue-green |

| 1 | 1 | 0 | 0 | 12 | Light red | |
|---|---|---|---|---|---|---|
| 1 | 1 | 0 | 1 | 13 | Light magenta | |
| 1 | 1 | 1 | 0 | 14 | Yellow | light yellow |
| 1 | 1 | 1 | 1 | 15 | White | bright white |

The column labeled "number" refers to the color number used by BASIC. BASIC's color numbers from 16 through 31 are the same as these colors 0 through 15, with 16 added to the number to turn on the blinking attribute bit.

To help you get the best possible use of colors in your programs, here are some notes on the colors and their uses. There are a few things you should understand about the "high intensity", or bright, colors. First, for color monitors which have only eight colors, and which ignore the bright-bit, the colors that appear usually match the descriptions of the high-intensity colors; for example, color numbers 6 (brown) or 14 (yellow) will show as yellow. For 16-color monitors, what normally happens isn't that the "bright" colors are brighter, but just the opposite—the "normal" colors are displayed with a dim half intensity.

Also, you should understand that the term "high intensity" is used in the narrow sense of more light. To the eye, "low intensity" dark red will be a more visually intense color than "high intensity" light red.

Since display screens generate their colors with active light, the three primary colors of red, green and blue will naturally be dimmer, and more visually intense, than the combination colors. Cyan and magenta may sound visually intense, but since they are twice as bright as the primaries, red, green and blue, they tend to look relatively washed out. Remember that here, brightness is the amount of light produced. More light doesn't always mean stronger colors—often it means washed out colors. On the other hand, since the brighter a yellow color is, the more intense the color appears, yellow is as dramatic a color as red, green, and blue.

The usefulness of the colors will vary depending upon the quality of the display screen, and on the judgment of your eye. I think that most users will find blue, red, yellow, and possibly black, the most distinct colors, and the most useful. Next on the list come green and magenta. Least useful, in my opinion, are cyan and white.

Anyone who intends to make serious use of color on the IBM/PC should consider the color choice very carefully and, if at all possible, test it on several different types of color screen. The wrong choices can lead to information displays that are difficult to read.

## 8.7 Cheating the easy way

There are two basic ways to put display information on the IBM/PC's screen. One, which I'm calling cheating, is to use the memory-mapping feature, and store information directly into display's memory locations. IBM somewhat frowns on this. An early version of their program submission guidelines referred to it as a poor programming practice—for the simple reason that it makes programs that do it dependent upon specific characteristics of the IBM/PC. If another display type is added (which seems like a realistic possibility, as we mentioned in section 8.2 above), or there are other such changes, then your programs may have to be modified to accommodate them.

There is a real advantage in doing all your screen displays via BIOS service calls, for any changes to the computer (or later versions of the IBM/PC) can be expected to incorporate BIOS changes which will automatically upgrade your programs. But frankly, the ROM-BIOS services provided for screen display are not very adequate; in fact, I think they are lousy. And I suspect that they are so inadequate because any reasonable program will circumvent them and go directly to the memory-mapped display storage. Despite IBM's admonition about poor programming practices, I think that it was really intended that programs use the memory-mapped feature whenever they need to do quick or fancy screen displays.

There is a tremendous advantage to generating memory-mapped displays. It is quick, absolute, and very powerful. It is also very easy to do. The program given in listing 8.1 shows how to do it in BASIC, and program listing 8.2 provides a number of service routines for doing direct memory-mapped output in Pascal. The service routines shown in 8.2 can be used to form the core of any display programs which you write in Pascal, or most other languages.

The techniques are quite simple. First, your program must find out if the display type is monochrome or color-graphics. There are two basic ways to do that—one is to find out from the user (for example, by the program first asking, which doesn't produce a very slick impression), and the other is to find out from the operating system. One of the ROM-BIOS service calls, explained in section 8.11, indicates what kind of display is used, and this is the best way to find out.

After finding out what kind of display is used, a pointer is set to the appropriate display memory—hex paragraph B000 for the monochrome adapter, and B800 for the color graphics. In BASIC, this is done with the DEF SEG statement, while in Pascal this is done with segmented address types. Either way is easy to do.

Once you have address access to the display memory, you can display whatever you want, or read what is already displayed. The only tricks concern relative addressing. You must remember to allow for the attribute bytes (in all the odd numbered locations), and if you wish to pay attention to line boundaries on the display, then your programs must make appropriate calculations. If you are using the multiple display page feature of the color-graphics display, then you must also pay attention to the location of the page boundaries, which are at 2 K and 4 K intervals.

Everything that you are likely to need for Pascal is given in listing 8.2. If you need any special features, they should be easy to add using listing 8.2 as a model.

# 8.8  The cursor—faking it, and controlling it

The cursor is a key element in video displays. It is usually used as an indicator of where typed keyboard input belongs, but it is also used as a simple pointer on the screen. Here you'll see how to control the cursor. First, to be fair, I ought to tell you that the blinking cursor that is built into the IBM/PC's displays may not be what you want to use as a cursor. Consider some alternatives.

There are some visual problems in using a blinking cursor. For the IBM/PC there is a standard form of the cursor that takes effect when the PC is powered-on, which is a small blinking underline, that appears under the cursor location. Some people find that form of cursor hard for the eye to spot quickly—it can get lost in a screen full of information.

The cursor can be expanded in size, to cover part or all the character location. For an example of the cursor covering about half of the display character, start up the BASIC interpreter, and press the Insert key. You can use the BASIC statement LOCATE to set the cursor to any size. But you may discover, as many have, that a large blinking cursor is annoying to look at, especially for a long time.

There are two alternatives to using the blinking cursor. One is to use the reverse-video display attribute (hex code 70) at the screen location where the cursor should be. This produces a large lit block, with the character visible inside it—in effect a solid, full-size cursor that doesn't blink. This kind of simulated cursor can be very easy to spot, without bothering your eyes. When BASIC operates with the color-graphics monitor in graphics mode, you will find that it uses a variation of this trick to produce a cursor. Why? Because in graphics mode there is no hardware-produced blinking cursor; so BASIC has to fake a cursor. But even when a blinking cursor is available, a reverse-video blob makes a rather nice working cursor. (Incidentally, the text editor used to write this book, Vedit, uses this kind of cursor.)

Another form of cursor is particularly good when your programs are displaying lists. The cursor isn't always used to indicate a typing position on the screen; sometimes it is used simply as a pointer in a list of choices. This is often the case in programs which present menus, lists of files, and other sets of choices for the user. For these situations, I would suggest that you consider using the two large arrow characters that the IBM/PC can display; these are character codes CHR$(16) for the right-pointing arrow, and CHR$(17) for the left arrow. (DiskLook, which is part of this book's diskette package, and the other Norton Utility programs use the right arrow when selecting from lists.)

But if you don't want to fake the cursor, then you need to be able to control it. (And even if you are faking a cursor, you'll probably want to control it enough to move it off the screen.) There are two things that you can control about the cursor—its size and its position.

The hardware-produced cursor always appears as a number of blinking lines within the display scan lines that generate the display characters. While you can't control each of the cursor lines independently, you can control the range of lines that blink. For the monochrome display there are 13 scan lines, and for the color-graphics display there are 7. By convention, the lines are numbered from the top, starting at number 0, and going down to number 13 (for the monochrome) or 7 (for the color-graphics). The default cursor (which is in effect when the IBM/PC is started up) is lines 12 and 13 for monochrome, or line 7, by itself, for the color-graphics.

You can set the cursor to appear on any range of these lines by specifying the starting and ending scan line numbers. This can produce a full solid cursor, or a partial cursor at the top, middle, or bottom of the character position.

Also, if you specify a starting position that is numerically higher than the ending position (for example, with the starting position at line 12 and the ending position at line 2), the cursor will appear on the scan lines beginning from the starting position, proceed down to the bottom, and then wrap around and back up to the top scan line, and continue to the ending position. This produces a very striking two-piece cursor, with one part at the bottom and the other at the top. This is a dramatic effect, and you may like the look of it, but I would suggest that you think twice before you inflict it on the users of your programs.

If you want to quickly look at a two-piece cursor, fire-up the BASIC interpreter, and enter the command:

LOCATE ,,,6,2

This will demonstrate a two-piece cursor, and you can then experiment with other possible cursor sizes.

The other thing to be controlled about the cursor, of course, is its position. You can locate the cursor at any line or column on the display screen, or even hide the cursor, by placing it on the non-existent line 26. BASIC gives you control over both aspects of the cursor, with the LOCATE statement. But for other languages, you may need some help. Many users of IBM Pascal consider the lack of cursor control to be the greatest flaw in this version of the language.

To give you access and control over the cursor, in Pascal or any other language, we've provided assembly language control routines on the diskette which accompanies this book. How it is done is explained below in section 8.11 along with the rest of access to the ROM-BIOS for video control.

## 8.9 Working the honest way

Working the honest way refers to generating video displays without modifying directly the display's memory-mapped storage. In section 8.11 we show you how to do this through direct ROM-BIOS services. I can't see, however, why anyone would use them (except in an assembly language program), since the output tools that are built into Pascal and other languages are so superior.

There is one trick about using the output facilities built into Pascal, and other languages, which you should know. Output is always positioned based upon the cursor location. So if you manipulate the cursor, using the ROM-BIOS services described in section 8.11, then any conventional output that your program does will follow.

This makes it possible for you to have a reasonable combination of the best of both worlds—full control over where your display data appears, use of your programming language's convenient output facilities, and no "cheating" through direct use of the memory-mapped displays.

While this approach sacrifices some control over what appears on the screen—particularly control over the display attributes—it will give you a programming convention with the greatest likelihood of portability to other personal computer systems.

## 8.10 Character graphics

Character graphics are an interesting and useful alternative to using the full graphics capabilities of the color-graphics display. And programs which use character graphics have the important advantage of being usable on both monochrome and color-graphics versions of the IBM/PC.

Character graphics are displays that are built up out of the extended ASCII character set that the IBM/PC has. Above the conventional 128 ASCII codes are another 128 codes, which have special display forms. About half of these codes are dedicated to characters that are intended for drawing.

First, there are the lines. There is a full set of line characters which make it possible to draw single and double line boxes, graphs, and charts. Many programs for the IBM/PC, including the BASIC sample programs that come with DOS, use these line characters, so you are undoubtedly familiar with them. If you want to make use of them, you will find them occupying forty character positions from CHR$(179) through CHR$(218).

A little less well known are two small sets of drawing characters. One is made up of codes CHR$(219), and CHR$(176) through CHR$(178). These provide full-sized solid character boxes with various degrees of density—from one-quarter solid, through fully solid. They can be used to produce displays of various density, which is especially good for bar charts, and make a good monochrome alternative to the use of color in charts.

The other set of drawing characters, codes CHR$(219) through CHR$(223), provides a solid box, and four half-boxes (top and bottom halves, left and right halves). Unfortunately this set was not completed with some quarter box characters, but you can't have everything. These characters can be used to produce some surprisingly good drawings. For example, the DOS sample program which plays music, draws its keyboard with these characters. Running that program will give you a good example of just how good such simple drawings can be.

## 8.11 Video ROM control

Here we'll describe the ROM-BIOS services that are available for the video display screens. Some of these services apply to the graphics modes, which won't be explained until the next chapter; but we'll outline them here.

Even if you don't plan to making direct use of these ROM-BIOS services you may want to read this section closely, to learn what facilities are available.

There are sixteen separate services provided by ROM-BIOS for the video display screens. All are invoked with interrupt number 16, hex 10. In this section we'll take a look at each of them, and see some of the things for which they can be used. Programs 8.101 and 8.102, on the diskette which accompanies this book, provide the assembly language routines needed to use ROM-BIOS video services, and Pascal definitions and support routines to make the assembly language routines easier to use.

The first of the video service routines, with service code 0, is used to set the mode of the video display. There are eight different video modes, seven of them variations on the color-graphics, and one for the monochrome display. Here is a list of the modes, which we'll follow with some notes:

| Code | Mode |
| --- | --- |
| 0 | color-graphics, text mode, 40-column, black-and-white (color disabled) |
| 1 | color-graphics, text mode, 40-column, color active |
| 2 | color-graphics, text mode, 80-column, black-and-white (color disabled) |
| 3 | color-graphics, text mode, 80-column, color active |
| 4 | color-graphics, graphics mode, 320 by 200 pixels, color active |
| 5 | color-graphics, graphics mode, 320 by 200 pixels, black-and-white |
| 6 | color-graphics, graphics mode, 640 by 200 pixels, black-and-white |
| 7 | monochrome |

If you have the color-graphics adapter, you can use this service to freely switch the mode. You would think that if you had both adapters installed that this service could be used to switch the active display from one to the other, but sadly that is not the case. There is a special code in the ROM-BIOS which checks if the monochrome adapter is installed; and if it is, the BIOS suppresses any request to switch to any of the color-graphics modes. Only through some special coding tricks, which IBM has published, can a dual-display system switch from one to the other. Incidentally, as far as I know, there is no way to have both displays active at the same time.

The black-and-white text modes, codes 0 and 2, work exactly like the full-color modes, but color is suppressed. For the graphics modes, the meaning of "pixels," and the two different sizes, are explained in the next chapter, on graphics.

The second service, code 1, is used to set the cursor size. As mentioned above, the cursor is controlled by setting the starting and ending scan lines, where the cursor is to appear. The top scan line is numbered zero, and the bottom scan line is number 7 (for color-graphics) or number 13 (for monochrome). If the starting scan line is greater than the ending line, then a two-part wrap-around cursor is produced. If you are interested in cursor control, see the special discussion on the cursor in section 8.8, above.

The third service, code 2, is used to move the cursor. Three things are used to specify the cursor location—row, column, and display page. The row and column are calculated with the first positions (at the top left of the screen) numbered zero. If you would rather refer to the rows as 1 through 25 (rather than 0 through 24), your programs must make appropriate adjustments; the Pascal service routines provided in listing 8.102 do just that. The page number applies to the display pages available when using text mode on the color-graphics display; for either the monochrome display, or the graphics modes, the page should be zero. The cursor can be moved to positions off of the screen, to make it disappear. I would recommend using the first column of the line following the last one (if you are numbering rows and columns from 1, that would be row 26, column 1).

Here is one special note for the multi-page color-graphics text modes. When a cursor movement is requested, the page is specified—so you do not have to be moving the cursor on the currently active display page: you can move a cursor on any page. Each page has its own logical cursor position. Some of the video services below, which can be used on any display page, act relative to the cursor position. A cursor position for each separate page makes this more practical.

The fourth service, code 3, reads the cursor location and size. It is the opposite of the last two services, combined. The display page must be specified, and again, that should be zero for the monochrome display or the graphics modes. The values returned are the cursor row and column and the starting and ending scan lines for the cursor.

The fifth service, code 4, is used to read the light pen position for those systems with the light pen installed. This service returns an indication of whether or not the light pen is triggered and, if it is, where it is located. The location is given in terms of the pixel locations, which are discussed in the next chapter, on graphics.

The light pen isn't one of the more popular options for the IBM/PC. The light pen is in kind of a bind—it can only be used with a display which has a very low persistence, that is, one which doesn't continue glowing for long after the scanning beam has passed on to another part of the screen. But that kind of display screen tends to flicker to the eye. So a good display for the eye can't use a light pen, and a light pen display is harder on the eye. Ugh. The IBM monochrome display uses a high-persistence phosphor, known as P-39, which is part of what makes it easy to look at this display screen. We can expect that the light pen will only see limited specialized use on the PC.

The sixth service, code 5, is used to switch the active display page, for the multi-page feature of color-graphics text mode. A proper page number (0-3 or 0-7) should be given. The display screen is instantly switched to show the selected page from the display memory. See section 8.4, above, for a discussion of the display pages.

The next two services, codes 6 and 7, are used to do video scrolling. Scrolling is one of the more interesting features of the IBM/PC's display capabilities, but few programs take advantage of it. Scrolling allows you to move a portion of the screen up or down as many lines as needed. Display characters disappear from the top (or bottom) of the scrolling window, and blank lines appear at the other end. Most interesting of all, the scrolling window can be set to any rectangular portion of the screen, so that you can work with a rolling message board on one part of the display, while leaving the rest of the display undisturbed. And with separate scroll commands, you can manipulate different windows. The possibilities are fascinating, so it is a shame that more programs don't use this feature.

Code 6 scrolls up, and 7 scrolls down. For both, you must specify two opposite corners of the window, the upper-left and lower-right, in row and column notation. You also specify the number of lines to be scrolled, which may be the entire window. And finally, you also specify the display attribute of the filler line, which makes it possible to work with a window that is colored, or in reverse video. If you are going to make use of a window, it can be very valuable to make the window stand out by giving it a different display attribute than the rest of the screen. These scrolling services, by the way, do not insert message text in the new lines of the window—you must take care of that separately.

The next three services are used for character handling. Their purpose is to provide character input-output services without your programs having to resort to accessing the memory-mapped display storage. While I have encouraged you to make use of direct video output, through the use of the memory-mapped display, using these three services will make your programs less dependent upon the exact specifications of the IBM/PC, and more portable to other versions of the PC or to other computers. Besides all that, there are some interesting sidelights to these services.

The ninth service, with code 8, reads the character and attribute that is displayed at the current cursor location. As with some other services, you must specify which page is to be used, although the page applies only to color-graphics text modes. This service works in graphics mode as well as text mode; to understand better how it works, read about character displays in graphics mode in the next chapter. In graphics mode, there is no display attribute (that applies only to text mode, and to the monochrome display), so no attribute is returned. It isn't too difficult to see how a character can be written in graphics mode, but for the interesting story of how a character is read from a graphics display, see the next chapter.

The tenth service, with code 9, writes a character and its attribute to the screen. The eleventh service, code 10, does the same, but uses whatever attribute is already set at that position. The page is specified, and, for code 9, the attribute, but they do not apply for graphics mode. These two services don't just write one character, but any number of copies of one character. There are some very handy uses for this—one is clearing a field with blank spaces; another is quick drawing of horizontal lines with the line drawing characters mentioned in section 8.10. Whatever use you find for this feature, you can save data storage space, or program complexity, by letting these services do the repeated displaying for you. When output from these two services reaches the end of one display line, it wraps-around to the next line, except when displaying characters in graphics mode.

The next three services are used for graphics support. More explanation appears in the next chapter.

The twelfth service, code 11, sets the color palette used for the color-graphics monitor. This service is mainly for use when in mode 4—color graphics with color active, but it can be used with modes 1 and 3, to set the border color that surrounds the working part of the display screen. There are two variations on this service—variation 0 sets the background color, in graphics mode, or the border color, in text mode (remember that in text mode, each display position's attribute byte sets its own individual background color). Variation 1 is used to choose between the two color palettes, of green-red-brown and cyan-magenta-white.

The next two services, codes 12 and 13, are used in graphics mode, to write or read the color that appears at a particular pixel location on the screen. The "color" is the numeric index used to chose from the current palette of colors—in medium-resolution mode, 0 through 3, and in high-resolution, 0 or 1. The pixel location is specified by row and column, starting with 0,0 at the upper left of the screen. One extra frill is added: in the write-color service, code 12, you may 'OR' a color code into the existing code. To request this, set the high-order bit of the color (in effect, add 128 to the color index number).

The fifteenth service, code 14, returns to text character handling, just to confuse the numeric order of these services. This service provides the most elementary typewriter-like output of a single character. For reasons based on the history of computers, IBM calls this service "write teletype." This service treats the display screen as if it were a printer or typewriter, and DOS commands such as TYPE (or a COPY whose target is the console "CON") use this service when they need the screen to act like a printer. In fact, all conventional printer-type output that goes to the display screen, is sent through this service.

To follow teletype conventions, four special character codes are recognized and acted on: The bell-character, CHR$(7), causes the system's speaker to beep. The characters known as "backspace," CHR$(8), "line-feed," CHR$(10), and "carriage-return," CHR$(13), are all treated appropriately. The output character, if it isn't one of four special characters, is put on the screen at the current cursor position, and the cursor is advanced one space. You can specify the display page, for text mode on the color-graphics display, or foreground color for graphics mode on the color-graphics display, but you cannot specify the display attribute, oddly enough. It seems unfortunate that you can't use this service and also set the display attribute, but I suppose that it is in keeping with the spartan nature of a teletype-like service. Unfortunately, this means that our programs can't use the simplest and easiest of all the display-screen output services, and still use emphasis attributes, like underline, high-intensity, and color.

The sixteenth, and last service, with code 15, reads the current video mode. This is the opposite of service code 0, which sets the mode. This service is very useful, particularly for determining if the mono-chrome adapter or the color-graphics adapter is used. If your programs are going to do direct output to the memory-mapped storage, they should use this service to determine which address location to use. If this service returns mode 7, then the monochrome display is in use (and its memory is located at hex segment paragraph B000). If you find modes 0 through 3, the color-graphics display is in use in text mode (and you can use its memory at hex paragraph B800). If modes 4 through 6 appear, the display is in graphics mode, and ordinary-style output to the display memory will cause bizarre results; the display should be set to a text mode first, using the mode setting service. This service, besides returning the video mode, also returns the active page number, which is useful for text-mode color-graphics displays.

Well, that is the works, for ROM-BIOS video display services. Now we will move on, in the next chapter, to unravel the mysteries of the graphics display modes. They are very interesting.

LISTING 8-1    167

```
1000 REM Listing 8.1 -- A program to display all screen attributes
1010 REM                       (C) Copyright 1983, Peter Norton
1020 REM
1030 GOSUB 2000    '   TITLE
1040 GOSUB 3000    '   GET WHICH DISPLAY TYPE, AND SET ADDRESS
1050 GOSUB 2000    '   SET THE TITLE AGAIN
1060 GOSUB 4000    '   BUILD THE SURROUNDING COMMENTS
1070 GOSUB 5000    '   BUILD THE DISPLAY ARRAY
1080 GOSUB 6000    '   FINISH UP AND RETURN TO DOS


2000 REM Title subroutine
2010 KEY OFF : CLS : WIDTH 80
2020 REM
2030 PRINT "                    Programs for INSIDE THE IBM PERSONAL COMPUTER"
2040 PRINT "                        (C) Copyright 1983 Peter Norton"
2050 PRINT
2060 PRINT "                    Program 8-1: Demonstrate all screen attributes"
2999 RETURN


3000 REM Subroutine to inquire about display type
3010 PRINT
3020 PRINT "Before we go any further, is this a color-graphics display? ";
3030 GOTO 3060
3040 PRINT
3050 PRINT "  (answer Y or N)  ";
3060 ANSWER$ = INKEY$
3070 IF LEN(ANSWER$) < 1 THEN 3060
3080 IF LEN(ANSWER$) > 1 THEN 3040
3090 SEGVAL! = 0
3100 IF MID$(ANSWER$,1,1) = "Y" THEN SEGVAL! = &HB800  ' Color segment
3110 IF MID$(ANSWER$,1,1) = "y" THEN SEGVAL! = &HB800  ' Color segment
3120 IF MID$(ANSWER$,1,1) = "N" THEN SEGVAL! = &HB000  ' Monochrome segment
3130 IF MID$(ANSWER$,1,1) = "n" THEN SEGVAL! = &HB000  ' Monochrome segment
3140 IF SEGVAL! = 0 THEN 3040
3150 DEF SEG = SEGVAL!
3999 RETURN


4000 REM     subroutine to build the surrounding messages
4010 LOCATE 11,1  : PRINT "Normal"
4020 LOCATE 12,1  : PRINT "normal"
4030 LOCATE 19,1  : PRINT "Normal"
4040 LOCATE 20,1  : PRINT "blinking"
4050 LOCATE 11,69 : PRINT "Bright"
4060 LOCATE 12,69 : PRINT "normal"
4070 LOCATE 19,69 : PRINT "Bright"
4080 LOCATE 20,69 : PRINT "blinking"
4090 FOR HEX. DIGIT% = 0 TO 15
4100    LOCATE 6,HEX.DIGIT% * 3 + 17
4110    PRINT HEX$(HEX.DIGIT%)
4120    LOCATE HEX.DIGIT%+8,11
4130    PRINT HEX$(HEX.DIGIT%)
4140 NEXT HEX.DIGIT%
4150 LOCATE ,,0
4999 RETURN


5000 REM    subroutine to set the display array
5010 FOR ROW% = 0 TO 15
```

```
5020    FOR COL% = 0 TO 15
5030       POKE (ROW% + 7) * 160 + COL% * 6 + 31, ROW% * 16 + COL%
5040       POKE (ROW% + 7) * 160 + COL% * 6 + 33, ROW% * 16 + COL%
5050       POKE (ROW% + 7) * 160 + COL% * 6 + 35, ROW% * 16 + COL%
5060       POKE (ROW% + 7) * 160 + COL% * 6 + 32, 65 ' 65 is the character "A"
5070    NEXT COL%
5080 NEXT ROW%
5999 RETURN

6000 LOCATE 25,1,1
6010 PRINT "Press any key to return to DOS... ";
6020 IF LEN(INKEY$) = 0 THEN 6020   '  wait for a keystroke
6030 CLS
6999 SYSTEM

9999 REM  End of program listing 8-1
```

LISTING 8-2    169

```
{  Listing 8.2 -- Pascal routines for direct screen output      }
{  (C) Copyright 1983, Peter Norton                             }

module Listing_8_2;

{  These service routines contain most, or all, of what you will  }
{  need to do direct output to the IBM/PC display screens.        }
{     Two assembly language service routines are used, and they are }
{  available, in both source code and read-to-use object code, on  }
{  the diskette which accompanies this book. But, those two         }
{  routines are not necessary, they simply provide a better result. }
{  We also show how to get along without them, so that you can use  }
{  only this Pascal code to do complete screen displays.            }


{=========================================================================}


{  Let's start by defining the types we need, beginning with the  }
{  screen:                                                        }

type

    screen_position_pair_type = (character_byte, attribute_byte);
    normal_screen_type = array [1..25,1..80,character_byte..attribute_byte]
                    of char;


    { Notes-- our screen is set up to number positions from 1; if you }
    {  prefer counting from zero, then change it accordingly.          }
    {  For the less-common 40 column display, use this:                }

    narrow_screen_type =  array [1..25,1..40,character_byte..attribute_byte]
                    of char;

{=========================================================================}


{  Next, here are the variables that we will be using:             }

var [static]

{  To get access to the screen, we need an address variable:       }
    screen_pointer     : ads of normal_screen_type;

    current_attribute : char;          { used to specify the disply attribute }
    row, column       : integer;       { used to specify display location    }
    output_string     : lstring (255); { used to hold data to be displayed    }

    page              : word;          { used to specify which display page  }
    eighty_col_mode   : boolean;       { used to specify 80 or 40 column mode }

{=========================================================================}
```

```
{  Next, we'll define some of the more common attributes used;     }
{  You should add any that you want to use.                        }
const                              { Monochrome  /  Color-graphics  }
  normal_attrib  = chr  (7);   { normal       /   white on black }
  reverse_video  = chr (112);  { reverse      /   black on white }
  bright         = chr  (15);  { bright       /    bright, maybe }
  blinking       = chr (135);  { blinking     /   blinking w-o-b }
  alert          = chr (140);  { bright-blink /    blinking red  }


{======================================================================}


{ Here are two two assembly language routines used:                }

procedure clear_reset;  { This clears and resets the display, and  }
  external;             { also makes sure that 80-column mode is on }
function video_mode : byte;  { This returns the video mode, 0-7     }
  external;

{Now we are ready for some work-horse routines for you to use.     }


{======================================================================}


{  First things first -- we must set our address pointer to the    }
{  right screen buffer, for monochrome or color-graphics.          }
{  If you don't use the "video_mode" assembly language routine,    }
{  then your program must either assume one or the other, or else  }
{  inquire from the user.                                          }

procedure set_video_address;
  begin
    if video_mode = 7 then { monochrome is mode 7; all others color-graphics }
      begin
        screen_pointer.s := #B000; { segment paragraph for monochrome }
        screen_pointer.r := 0;
      end
    else
      begin
        screen_pointer.s := #B800; { segment paragraph for color-graphics }
        screen_pointer.r := 0;
      end;
  end;


{======================================================================}


{ The next routine clears the screen -- with or without the assembly }
{ language routine.                                                  }

procedure clear_screen;
  begin
    { if you have the assembly language routines, just to this: }
    clear_reset;
    return;
    {otherwise, we'll clear the screen the hard way :          }
    for row := 1 to 25 do
      for column : 1 to 80 do
        begin
```

LISTING 8-2    171

```
            screen_pointer ^ [row,column,character_byte] := ' ';
            screen_pointer ^ [row,column,attribute_byte] := normal_attrib;
        end;

    end;

{========================================================================}

{ The next routine is the work-horse of display - it puts data on   }
{ the screen, as needed. This routine picks up its parameters of    }
{ where to put things on the screen, what to put, and which attri-  }
{ bute to use, from variables; if you wish, you could change that   }
{ to have the information actually passed as parameters, but you    }
{ will probably find the method shown to be better.                 }

procedure display_output_string;
  var [static]
    i : integer;

  begin
    for i := 1 to ord(output_string.len) do
      begin
        screen_pointer ^ [row,column,character_byte] := output_string [i];
        screen_pointer ^ [row,column,attribute_byte] := current_attribute;
      end;
  end;

{========================================================================}

{ If you wish to use the color-graphics multi-page feature, this     }
{ procedure will set the screen_pointer to the appropriate paragraph.}

procedure set_pointer_for_page;
  begin
    if eight_col_mode then
      screen_pointer.s := #B800 + page * 4096
    else
      screen_pointer.s := #B800 + page * 2048
  end;

end.

{  end of listing 8.2, Pascal service routines for character output }
```

# 9

# Video Access 2— Graphics

After discussing video fundamentals and characters in the last chapter, we'll cover graphics here.

You shouldn't be surprised that graphics on the IBM/PC is a complicated subject. Graphics in general are complicated, and on the PC they involve color-palettes, numerous modes, and more intricate memory-mapping. It's necessarily a rather messy subject, full of small tricks. In this chapter we'll go over the details. If you need to use graphics, or simply want to understand them, then it's all here; if not, then pass on.

For our three circles of interest, everything here applies to the IBM/PC, and should also apply to the PC-like computers, since they will need to be able to use IBM/PC graphics programs. But, for the family of MS-DOS using computers, little here will apply.

## 9.1 Graphics philosophy

There are two basic ways to generate graphics information on a video display. A visit to an arcade full of electronic games will show you both of them, and will tell you which one is dominant, and even why. I'll explain it here, but you should also visit an arcade and confirm it all with your own eyes.

The two kinds of graphics are usually known as vector scan graphics and pixel or raster scan graphics, but we'll simply call them vector and pixel. Graphics on the IBM/PC are of the pixel variety, so that's what we'll spend most of our time on. (By the way, we've already used the word vector, in discussing interrupts, to mean the pair of words that specify the memory address of the program that will handle the interrupt; here, vector means a line. Both uses of the word have honest roots in mathematics, which I won't go into here. Just don't confuse graphics vectors with interrupt vectors, or you'll be quite mixed up.)

Vector graphics consist entirely of lines drawn on the display screen. To make vector drawings, a computer program specifies the two ends of the line, and the display screen draws a straight line in between. On an ordinary display screen—whether it's your TV set or the terminal of your computer—the electronic spot that generates pictures travels through a standard pattern of scan lines that fills the entire screen: that's the raster scan that I mentioned above. But on a vector-graphics display, the moving spot moves, on command, to draw specific lines between specific points. With vector scanning, the moving spot doesn't spend its time racing around a long fixed path.

Vector graphics have some major virtues—they are very crisp and precise, and they are relatively fast to draw. This makes them very good for things like engineering drawings, or any exceptionally complex or precise graphic display. But vector graphics displays are only line drawings—they can't fill in solid spaces with color, which makes them quite poor for most graphics uses.

Pixel graphics take another approach. The display screen is divided up into a rectangular grid of many small picture elements, called pixels, for short. Each pixel can be lit or not, so that a pixel graphic display is made up of a series of small dots. The size and spacing of the pixels is carefully adjusted so that there is no gap between them—if a bunch of adjacent pixels are on, lit that is, then they don't appear as separate dots. Instead, they look like a solid, lit area. If the dots were small enough they could rival vectors for crispness and precision, but on most pixel display screens they are somewhere in between coarse and fine—fine enough to make a decent picture, but coarse enough to be a little crude.

In principle either form of graphic display could be colored, but often only pixel graphics have color. Color is a strong reason, but not the only reason why pixel graphics dominate vector graphics for both game and business use. The ability to draw full, solid, and seemingly curved shapes, in color, puts pixel graphics far ahead of vector graphics, except for special uses, such as drafting.

Also, while vector graphics must be drawn with a series of commands (each command drawing one small line), pixel graphics can be set up to use memory-mapping, similar to what we saw in the last chapter for character displays. On the IBM/PC, that is exactly how graphics are done—with pixels, controlled through a memory-mapped display format. All the advantages that we discussed for memory-mapped displays, are applied to the pixel graphics on the IBM/PC—particularly the ability to directly read and write display data, simply by accessing the display memory.

## 9.2 Our pixels

Wherever the display screen's scanning spot goes, pixels can appear, at least in the displayable part of the screen. (The scanning spot also goes beyond the display area, into what is called the over-scan area. There are no pixels there, but the over-scan area can be set to a color. BASIC controls it with the border parameter of the COLOR statement, and one of the ROM-BIOS service calls can be used for our programs to set the over-scan color.)

You'll recall that in character mode, the IBM/PC display screens have 25 horizontal lines of text, and when we discussed the cursor, in the last chapter, we saw that the color-graphics display has eight horizontal scan lines for each character position. So it should be no surprise to you that the vertical dimension of the IBM/PC's pixel grid has eight times twenty-five, or 200, lines.

The horizontal dimension of the pixel grid is set a little more arbitrarily. It was worked out based on the limitations of how much memory would be needed to control the pixels and how small a dot size can be shown by moderately priced graphics monitors.

For our IBM/PC, there are two different horizontal dimensions, for two different sizes of dot. Medium-resolution graphics mode has 320 dot positions on the width of the screen, and high-resolution graphics mode has 640 positions. (There is an additional low-resolution mode that could have been used for the IBM/PC, but wasn't. Low resolution mode has a grid of 160 by 100 pixels. The hardware circuitry on the color-graphics adapter can work in this low-resolution mode, but there isn't support for it in the ROM-BIOS.)

So, in medium-resolution graphics, there are 320 dot positions across and 200 down, while in high-resolution graphics there are 640 across and still 200 down. Thus a high-resolution graphics picture is more detailed only in its horizontal dimension. For most purposes, the quality of drawing would be about the same if high-resolution mode happened to be 320 across and 400 down.

Each pixel in the display grid can be individually set to lit or not and, in medium-resolution, a color can be shown. There are no colors in high-resolution mode, partly because of limitations in what displays can show, and partly because of the extra memory requirement needed to specify color.

Let's look first at the memory needs of high-resolution graphics. If all we need to specify about a pixel dot is whether it is lit or not, (and that's all we can specify about high-resolution pixels) then a single bit, with its 0 or 1 values, is enough to control a single pixel. In high resolution graphics, there are 640 x 200, or 128,000, pixels. To control them all, with one bit for each pixel, we need 128,000 bits. With eight bits to a byte, we would need 16,000 bytes, and that is just the amount of memory in the color-graphics adapter (rounded up to an even binary 16 K).

There are only half as many pixels in medium-resolution mode. Using the same 16 K of memory, we can dedicate two bits to serve each pixel. Two bits, taken together, can specify four different values (0,1,2, and 3), and that is half of the secret of how color is specified in medium-resolution mode.

Before we go on to look at the color part of color graphics, let's pause to notice one difference between the way the display memory is used for graphics and for characters. You'll recall from the last chapter, that there are two character modes—80 column and 40 column. Here, in graphics mode, there are also two modes, medium-resolution and high-resolution. In both cases, one mode has only half as many elements to it as the other, which changes the demands made for memory. But what was done with this situation is quite different between character mode and graphics mode. In character mode, the extra memory was used to double the number of display pages. In graphics mode, the extra memory is used to double memory that serves one pixel.

Because of the way that the IBM/PC controls colors, there is a severe limitation to how many colors can be used at one time. The color-graphics adapter and its display screen is capable of showing any of the sixteen possible colors at each pixel—that is no problem. The problem lies in specifying the colors.

IBM could have built the color graphics adapter with enough memory to give each pixel enough bits to specify the full range of possible colors, but they didn't. As we saw above, in high-resolution mode, there is only one bit for each pixel—so in high-resolution, the pixels can only have two colors, either black or white. In medium-resolution mode, with two bits for each pixel, the bit values can only select among four colors.

The problem of choosing which four colors are used in medium-resolution mode was solved in a way that is both curious and ingenious. Only four colors could be active at any time and IBM decided to let us set one of those four to any color we wished. They specified the other three, in what they called a palette. As a bonus, IBM gave us two different palettes to choose from—one palette with the colors green, red, and "brown" (which appears as yellow on many displays), and the other palette with the colors cyan, magenta, and white.

If you are confused by that, let's go over it another way. When we specify the color of any medium resolution pixel, we specify it with one of four numbers— 0, 1, 2, or 3. What do those numbers represent? Nothing fixed. Their meaning is set when we specify the colors to be used. We get to assign any of the 16 color possibilities to the number 0. For the numbers 1 through 3, IBM specified two possibilities (two palettes), and we get to choose which palette we use, but we don't get to choose how the palettes are made up.

Let's pause for a moment to consider what we didn't get, to better understand what we did get. If there were more memory available, we could have had a full choice of color at each pixel. Instead, we got just enough memory to give us two colors for the high-resolution pixels, and four colors for the medium-resolution pixels. We could have been given a full choice of what those colors would be, but we weren't. For high-resolution, we get no choice of what the two working colors will be—they are always black and white. For medium-resolution, we get a partial choice of colors. Of our four working colors, one we get to choose freely. For the other three, we get to choose either of two pre-selected color palettes.

So, for any color display, in graphics mode, we can use four colors. Three of those four will either be from the palette of green/red/brown, or from the palette of cyan/magenta/white.

When a color display is active, you can change any pixels' colors (from among the four colors you are working with) by changing the two-bit numbers of the pixels. Or, you can change the whole display at once, by changing the color definitions: changing the palette, changing color 0, or both. When you make this kind of change, the graphic picture does not change—but the colors that paint it do. (Low resolution mode has enough bits for each pixel to independently have any of the full 16 colors. Low resolution graphics can be used on the IBM/PC, because all the hardware needed is there. What is missing is the software support—in particular the ROM-BIOS routines. But if you provide the equivalent routines in your own programs, low-resolution graphics can come alive.)

## 9.3 Mapping the pixels

Everything is a little more complicated in graphics, and the memory-mapped display storage is no exception. If you use the ROM-BIOS services for graphics (described in section 8.9, under codes 12 and 13), then decoding the memory-mapping is done for you—and that is a strong reason for using them. But if you want to do it yourself, this section will explain it for you.

Like TV sets, computer video displays generate their display screen picture in two passes. The first time through, the moving electronic scanning beam, which draws the picture, scans the even numbered lines; then it goes back to the beginning, and scans the odd numbered lines.

When we are working in text mode, this is of no concern, because the process of drawing the displayed characters is handled by the video display controller. But in graphics mode, it doesn't work that way.

In graphics mode, the display generation circuitry needs to be fed a stream of bits that control the pixels, and it needs to be fed them in the order that the scanning raster passes over the screen—first the even numbered lines, and then the odd numbered lines. To facilitate that, the memory-mapping for the graphics was laid out in the order that the display needed it, not in the order that would be most logical to us and our programs. Figure 9.1 illustrates how this is done.

To match the graphics display scan, the graphics memory-map is organized into two blocks, located 4 K apart. The first block contains the pixel information for all the even lines. The second block contains information for the odd lines. Let's explain it more closely, using high-resolution graphics as an example.

The graphics memory starts with the bits needed to control the first display line, line number zero. There are 640 pixels in a high-resolution graphics line, and each pixel needs one bit to indicate if it is on or off. So the first 640 bits, or 80 bytes, are used to control this first line. The next 640 bits, or 80 bytes, control the next even numbered line, line 2, and so forth. The very first bit controls line 0 column 0, the next control

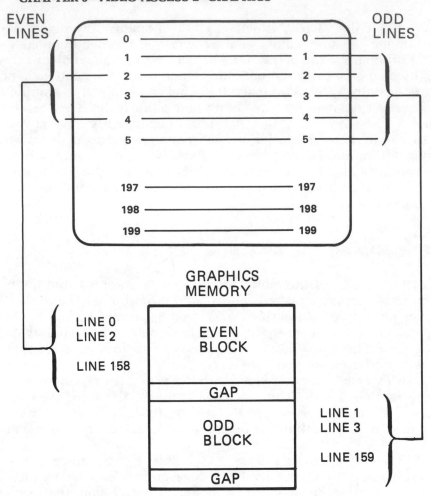

**Figure 9.1—Graphics Mode Memory Map.**

(0,1), then (0,2) and on to the last pixel of the first line (0,639), which is followed by (2,0), and on, and on. Finally the end of the even-line block is reached, and, starting on the next kilo-byte boundary, the odd-line block begins.

For medium-resolution graphics the map is organized the same, but there are only 320 pixels across, and each uses two bits to specify its four color options. It still takes 80 bytes to specify each line, and there are still two memory blocks, one for even and one for odd.

Notice that the ends of the lines are at the same memory locations for both medium and high resolution. One has half the pixels and twice the bits per pixel; the other twice the pixels and half the bits. As a result, in either mode the length of the line in memory is the same—640 bits, or 80 bytes. Program listing 9.1 gives the Pascal routines necessary to get control of all the pixels. It contains the necessary arithmetic to convert pixel locations into the memory-map locations, to save you the tedious labor of calculating bit and byte offsets.

The significance of all this memory-mapping becomes apparent when your programs want to do fast drawing. Any program can laboriously turn pixels on and off to make up any drawing needed—and you can do that either using the ROM-BIOS services described in the last chapter, or the Pascal service routines in listing 9.1. For fast drawing, though, you need to be able to load a part of a picture into the graphics memory all in one piece, not bit by bit. And to do that, your programs will have to break-down their graphics images into their even and odd scan lines, and move the even and odd line data into place separately. This makes the business of fast-loading of graphics drawings complicated, to say the least.

The solution to the problem of fast drawing depends upon your needs, and what compromises you can accept. One trick is to organize your pictures in units that fit into a byte—four pixels at a time for medium-resolution mode, and eight at a time for high-resolution. Provided that you can accept a scheme which always sets pixels four (or eight) at a time across, then you can move drawings into graphics memory in whole bytes. That method eliminates a great deal of processing; otherwise, to set pixel bits, your programs must do plenty of bit manipulation operations, such as shifts, AND's, and XOR's. Working on whole bytes of the picture image roughly triples the speed that you can draw pictures, when you already have the picture image defined.

There is another, cruder, trick to achieve faster picture drawing. It uses character graphics, which we will explain in the next section.

## 9.4 Characters in graphics mode

Even when the IBM/PC is operating its display screen in graphics modes, it can display characters easily. The technique is simple—characters are drawn, in pixels, as if they were any other kind of graphics drawing.

A special scheme is used to describe the drawings of the graphics characters. The space where a character may appear is divided up into a grid of eight positions by eight positions—eight pixels across and eight down. These are coded in the straightforward manner you would expect. Eight bytes are used to describe the drawing of each character. The eight bits of each byte control the eight pixels of one row of the character's drawing. The bits, from first to last, control the pixels of one row from left to right. The bytes, from first to last, control the rows, from top to bottom.

Figure 9.2 diagrams the way a letter's display appears, and how it is controlled by the character drawing table. For a sample, the capital letter A is shown. A quick look at the diagram will show you some things of interest. The bottom row is used for the "descender" part of characters, like the tail in a lower-case Y. The top two rows are used for "ascenders," like the vertical bar of the lower-case letter B, and for the extra height of capital letters. Contrary to what you might expect, let-

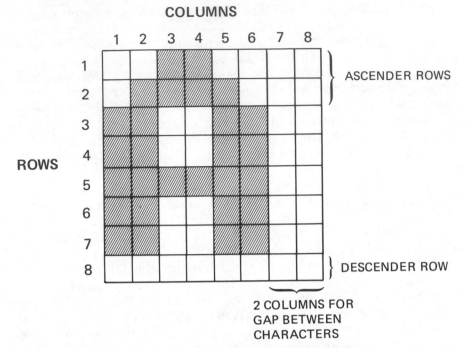

**Figure 9.2—Graphics Characters Drawn with Pixels in an 8 × 8 Grid. (Capital "A" shown)**

ters aren't centered in the eight pixel columns—instead they are left adjusted, and the two right hand columns serve for the normal space between characters.

When a character is written in this mode, the ROM-BIOS looks up the character's drawing in its display table. Then the table's description of the character is translated into pixel setting commands. Finally, the display memory bits are set, with the even and odd lines sent to their own memory banks.

In high-resolution mode, where there are no colors, only black and white, the pixels are turned on or off as the drawing in the character table specifies. In medium-resolution color mode, the current foreground and background colors are used. The background color is whichever color is set as color number 0 — any of the sixteen possible colors. The foreground color is set as color number 3 of the current color palette—white for palette 1, and brown/yellow for palette 0.

The character handling ROM-BIOS routines can read characters off of the screen, as well as write them. Service code 8, described in the last chapter, performs this task. In text mode, there is no problem in reading a character from the screen—after all, the display screen's memory contains just that: the ASCII byte code for the character displayed. But in graphics mode, the display memory doesn't contain an ASCII character; instead, it contains the pixel settings that draw the character. So the ROM-BIOS routine which reads a character does something quite interesting. It reads the pixels, and compares them against the character drawing table—a sort of crude pattern recognition.

The table of character drawings is in two parts, and this is what makes it especially interesting to us. The first part is stored in ROM, and covers the first 128 ASCII codes—that is, all the conventional characters, like the letters of the alphabet. The second half provides the drawings for the highest 128 character codes, codes CHR$(128) through CHR$(255). The first half is located in ROM-BIOS, and the pointers that access it are fixed—so that we can't modify this part of the table, or replace it with our own table. On the other hand, the second half of the table is intended for us to create. In fact, it doesn't exist until we create it.

One of the interrupt vectors, interrupt number 31, hex 1F, located in the vector table at location 124, hex 7C, is used to point to this drawing table. Ordinarily the table doesn't exist, and the vector is set to zero. However if we create a proper table, and place its address location into the interrupt vector, then whatever drawings our table contains will be displayed when the ROM-BIOS is asked to write any of the high characters, CHR$(128) through CHR$(255).

This open, undefined table of 128 character drawings provides the key to some very fast and convenient drawing. If your drawing requirements aren't too demanding, it can be possible to define a repertoire of 128 shapes, each the size of an 8 by 8 pixel character space, and then do all your drawing from those shapes. Obviously the most detailed and sophisticated graphics drawings cannot be produced this way. However, the drawing possibilities of 128 pre-defined modular shapes are enormous, and using them can give your programs a great advantage in speed, simplicity and compactness. In effect, the ROM-BIOS character drawing services (and your table of characters) do the bulk of the work of drawing, and your programs simply write the appropriate characters at the appropriate screen locations.

If you take advantage of this scheme for graphics generation you aren't limited to it, since in graphics mode you can both display characters, and set individual pixels. You can easily use a mixed strategy—using a character table of modular shapes when they will serve your needs, and manipulating pixels when you need to. You can even change the pixels within any characters that you have written to the screen.

The storage requirement for a character display table is 1,024 bytes: 128 characters times the eight bytes needed to draw each character. For medium resolution graphics mode, one single byte code in your program's data can be used to draw a shape of 64 pixels, or eight bytes worth of display information. Under the right circumstances, this technique will compress a large series of complex graphics drawings into one-eighth of its full size.

Before you consider using this technique for drawing, you must consider its limitations—not only in the number of shapes which can be used, but also, for medium-resolution color mode, the restriction to two colors. If you do conventional color graphics, you can make use of a full four-color palette, while character displays use only two colors out of the palette.

Even if you do not make use of a custom character-drawing table for graphics drawings, you can make use of it to produce an enhanced character set, for whatever purposes you wish. This could be a re-creation of the text-mode line drawing characters, or special shapes, or special alphabets. If you have a need to use the IBM/PC for other alphabets—Greek, Cyrillic (Russian) or one of the Japanese kana sets—then this can be a simple and effective way to create them. Arabic and Hebrew can also be written this way, but the right-to-left writing order for these languages adds complications.

LISTING 9-1    183

```
{ Listing 9.1 -- Pascal routines for direct graphics operations }
{ (C) Copyright 1983, Peter Norton                              }

module Listing_9_1;

{ These service routines contain most or all of what you will need   }
{ to understand and do graphics output to the IBM/PC displays,       }
{ using the memory-mapped storage.                                   }

{    Usually any program which generates graphics output has quite   }
{ demanding needs in terms of speed and custom-tailored services;    }
{ so the program code here should be considered to be illustrative   }
{ of what you can do, and how to do it. You will probably want       }
{ and need to develop your own versions, based on what this shows.   }

{    The basic technique here -- that is, using a high-level         }
{ language like Pascal, to produce screen output by manipulating     }
{ the memory-mapped storage -- produces very satisfactory results    }
{ for character output (covered in Listing 8.2), but poor results    }
{ for graphics output, mostly because the kind of "bit fiddling"     }
{ which must be done to manipulate individual pixels is much more     }
{ efficient in machine-language than in Pascal and other high-       }
{ level languages. So for serious graphics programming, you          }
{ should use the ROM interface routines 8.101 in the diskette        }
{ package which accompanies this book.                               }

{=======================================================================}

{ Let's start by defining the types we need, beginning with the      }
{ screen:                                                            }

type

   { Since Pascal doesn't let us work with arrays of bits, we'll use }
   { sets as the most convenient way to get to bits in the map       }

   word_bits_type      = set of 0..15;

high_res_pixel_type    = (off,on);
medium_res_pixel_type  =(color_0,color_1, color_2,color_3;

{ For the display memory map, we must define the even and odd scan lines }

   graphics_screen_type =
     record
       even_pixel : array [0..99,0..39] of word_bits_type; { even lines }
       filler     : array [1..192] of byte;
       odd_pixel  : array [0..99,0..39] of word_bits_type; { odd lines }
     end;

{=======================================================================}

{ Next, here are the variables that we will be using:              }

var [static]

{ To get access to the screen, we need address variables:          }
```

```
    graphics_screen_pointer  :  ads of graphics_screen_type;

    general_screen_pointer   :  adsmem; { to give us ordinary access }

    { For this set of routines, we will number the rows and columns  }
    { from 0, not from 1                                             }

    row, column              : integer;

{ here we will initialize the pointers to the graphics memory:   }

value

    graphics_screen_pointer.s := #B800;
    graphics_screen_pointer.r := 0;

    general_screen_pointer.s  := #B800;
    general_screen_pointer.r  := 0;


{===========================================================================}

{  The first routine will set (or reset) high resolution pixels to  }
{  a "color" value passed as a parameter.                           }

{ The programming here introduces the messy complexity necessary    }
{ to address individual bits in a language such as Pascal.          }

procedure set_high_res_pixel (color : high_res_pixel_type);

    var [static]
      work_byte : word_bits_type;
      work_value: 0..15;

    begin
      { first, get the location of the pixel, and grab its byte }
      if odd (row) then
        work_byte :=
          graphics_screen_pointer ^ .odd_pixel [(row-1) div 2, column div 16]
      else
        work_byte :=
          graphics_screen_pointer ^ .even_pixel [ row   div 2, column div 16]

      { next, get the set-value that corresponds to the pixel bit }
      work_value := column mod 16;

      { set put the color value into the work-byte }
      if color = on then
        work_byte := work_byte + [work_value] { "+" sets bit on }
      else
        work_byte :=work byte - [work_value]; { "-" sets bit off }

      {finally, move put the changed value into the display storage }
      if odd (row) then
        graphics_screen_pointer ^ .odd_pixel [(row-1) div 2, column div 16]
          := work_byte
      else
        graphics_screen_pointer ^ .even_pixel[ row   div 2, column div 16]
```

LISTING 9-1    185

```
                := work_byte;
      end;

{=======================================================================}

{  The second routine does the same pixel setting for medium        }
{  resolution graphics mode, using a color parameter.               }

{  The programming here becomes more complex than what appeared in  }
{  the last routine, since we must set two color bits for the pixel }

procedure set_medium_res_pixel (color : medium_res_pixel_type);

  var [static]
    work_byte : word_bits_type;
    work_set0 : set of 0..15;
    work_set1 : set of 0..15;

  begin
    { first, get the location of the pixel, and grab its byte }
    if odd (row) then
      work_byte :=
        graphics_screen_pointer ^ .odd_pixel [(row-1) div 2, column div 8]
    else
      work_byte :=
        graphics_screen_pointer ^ .even_pixel [ row   div 2, column div 8];

    { next, get the set-values that corresponds to the pixel bits }
    work_set0 := [(column mod 8) * 2];
    work_set1 := [(column mod 8) * 2 + 1];

    { set put the color value into the work-byte }
    if color in [color_2,color_3] then
      work_byte := work_byte + work_set0 { "+" sets bit on }
    else
      work_byte := work_byte - work_set0; { "-" sets bit off}

    if color in [color_1,color_3] then
      work_byte :=work_byte + work_set1 { "+" sets bit on }
    else
      work_byte := work_byte - work_set1; { "-" sets bit off }

    { finally, move put the changed value into the display storage }
    if odd (row) then
      graphics_screen_pointer ^ .odd_pixel [(row-1)   div 2, column div 8]
        := work_byte
      else
        graphics_screen_pointer ^ .even_pixel [ row   div 2, column div 8]
        := work_byte;

  end;

{=======================================================================}

{ The next routine clears the screen-- similar to what is provided }
{ for character-mode screen output.                                }
```

```
procedure clear_screen_graphics;
  var [static]
    i : word;
  begin
    for i := 0 to 16383 do
      general_screen_pointer ^ [i] := 0;
  end;
```

```
{=============================================================================}
```

```
end.
```

```
{ end of listing 9.1, Pascal service routines for graphics control }
```

# 10
# The Keyboard

The keyboard is at the heart of the connection between man and computer. In this chapter we'll cover the details of how the keyboard on the IBM Personal Computer works, and how you can control it. There are some very interesting and unusual features in this keyboard, and you will learn about them here.

## 10.1 Keyboard fundamentals

To me, one of the most impressive things about how IBM designed the IBM/PC is the way that they handled the keyboard. Their approach was simple and elegant, and it provides the two different things that programmers might want to know about keyboard input, in a very tidy way.

On the electronic design level, the keyboard for the IBM/PC is a little computer in its own right. Inside the keyboard unit is a microprocessor, the Intel 8048, which is given the task of watching the keys, and reporting what has happened with them. The 8048 has various jobs to perform, including its own diagnostic error checking (performed when the computer is powered-on), checking for stuck keys, and "debouncing" (keeping one keystroke from being seen as two, due to some bouncing action on the keys).

The 8048 also has the ability to buffer up to 20 key actions in case the PC's system unit can't take the time to accept them. Normally this buffer is completely empty—for it is rare for the system unit in the IBM/PC to not respond to the keyboard computer's request for attention.

It's likely that you have been beeped at, one time or another, when your keystrokes have gotten ahead of a program's ability to accept them. This hasn't been from a full buffer in the keyboard unit itself. The ROM-BIOS routines that support the keyboard maintain their own buffer in the main memory—and when that buffer fills up you get beeped at. While the buffer inside the keyboard unit holds 20 characters, the buffer kept by the ROM-BIOS fills up with only 15. As we progress deeper into understanding the keyboard, you will see how keystrokes progress from the key itself, to the keyboard unit's buffer, to the ROM-BIOS buffer, and then finally to a program.

187

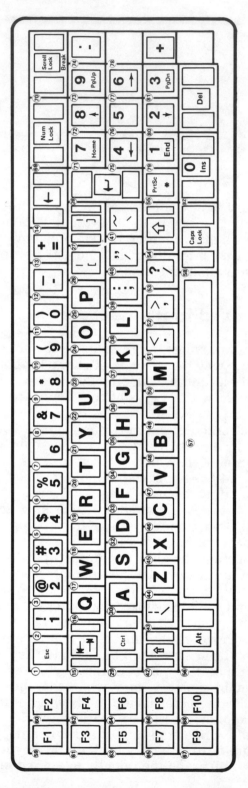

Figure 10.1—The Keyboard and Its Scan Codes.

The keyboard unit considers the keys to have no meaning (i.e., the A key doesn't mean "A"). Instead, the keyboard unit knows each key by its identifying number, called the scan code. The scan codes of the keys are numbered from 1 through 83. See figure 10.1 for the scan codes of the keys. They are numbered in a logical fashion, but not necessarily the way you might have guessed.

When each key is pressed, the keyboard unit reports its ordinary scan code to the system unit. And when the key is released, the keyboard unit reports again, this time with a code for a released key, which is the regular scan code plus 128, or hex 80. This way, there is a separate code for the pressing and releasing of each key.

These keyboard actions are reported using the mechanisms of interrupts and ports. What actually happens, in detail, is this. When a key action (a key pressed or a release) occurs, the keyboard unit sees it, and records the action in its own buffer. Then the keyboard unit generates a keyboard action interrupt, using interrupt number 9. In response to the interrupt, the ROM-BIOS routines read the scan code in from the keyboard port (which is port number 96), and then write back to the keyboard port instructions to clear the key action from the keyboard unit's buffer. If the system unit doesn't respond to keyboard interrupts, then the keyboard unit's buffer will accumulate the scan codes; but this normally doesn't happen. One special scan code, 255 or hex FF, is used for the keyboard unit to report that its buffer is full.

Since keystroke information passes from the keyboard to the system unit through a port, any program which has access to the ports can directly talk to the keyboard. In practice this isn't workable, since the keyboard unit also generates interrupts which are processed by the ROM-BIOS. However, as a curiosity, we can write a little BASIC program to read the keyboard port, and report when it finds something. Below is a sample program to do just that. Since this program is competing with the ROM-BIOS to get to the keyboard first, you'll find its operation spotty. But if you run it, and keep banging on the keyboard, it will occasionally detect a keyboard scan code:

```
100   REM A BASIC routine to try to read the keyboard scan codes
110   X = INP (96) ' read the keyboard port
120   THROW.AWAY$ = INKEY$ ' discard any keystrokes the ROM-BIOS read
130   IF X = 0 THEN GOTO 110 ' if no data, keep looking
140   PRINT
150   PRINT "Keyboard scan code ";X MOD 128; ' report scan code
160   IF X > 128 THEN PRINT " key released"; ' report if key-released code
170   IF X < 129 THEN PRINT " key pressed "; ' report if key-pressed code
180   GOTO 110
```

The keyboard on the IBM/PC has repeat-key action, what IBM calls typematic. The keyboard unit is responsible for keeping track of the time that a key is held down, and generating the repeat-key signals. All keys on the keyboard actually have this repeating action.

The ROM-BIOS routines in the system unit can tell the difference between a regular keystroke and a repeat key, when it needs to, by keeping track of the scan codes for keys being released. If two key-pressed signals are received for the same key without a key-released signal in between, then the key must be held down. This scheme is used by the ROM-BIOS to suppress repeat-action for the keys that shouldn't have it, such as the shift keys.

By now you can see the core of how the IBM/PC handles its keyboard. The keyboard unit is responsible for reporting exactly what has happened on the keys—each press, each release, and in due time, each repeat key action. The ROM-BIOS is responsible for making sense out of the very dumb information that the keyboard sends it. The division of labor is clear and clean. The keyboard unit deals with the mechanics of key action, and the ROM-BIOS programs in the system unit deal with all the logic of interpreting key action.

Most people are unaware that the IBM/PC's keyboard actually signals when keys are released, since this information is usually hidden from the user. But you can see it in action by running the keyboard test in the IBM/PC's diagnostic programs. If you pay close attention, you will see that the screen display changes when you press a key, when you release a key and when you hold a key down long enough for the repeat action to work.

## 10.2 Making sense of the keystrokes

The ROM-BIOS service routine for interrupt 9, the keyboard action interrupt, is responsible for making sense of the key actions. This includes keeping track of the shift states and translating key strokes into their meaning, whether it is a letter of the alphabet, or a function-key signal. Here we'll take a closer look at the subject.

Part of the ROM-BIOS's task, in supervising the keyboard, is to keep track of all the possible shift states. Shift states are a common subject for confusion, especially since the typewriter keyboards that most of us learned to key on have only one kind of shift. Many computer keyboards, including the IBM/PC's, have three different kinds of shift.

First, there is the normal action of the keys without any shifting (for example, to produce lower case letters). Then there is the conventional shift; this is the shift that corresponds to what a typewriter has, and it produces upper case letters, and generally anything that is written on the top half of the key-tops. Then there are two special shift keys, the alternate shift ("Alt") and the control shift ("Ctrl"). These two special shifts work similarly to the regular shift key; but just as lower case "a" is not the same thing as upper case "A", so Ctrl-A and Alt-A also have their own identity. (Some readers may have come to think of the escape key, labeled "Esc", as another kind of shift key. This is because on some old computer terminals, particularly those used like teletypes, the escape key was used in a way that seemed like a shift key. However, when the escape key was used, it wasn't held down like the shift keys—escape was pressed, then some other key was pressed, and the two together were taken as a special key sequence; but they weren't a shift key operation. The escape key isn't normally used this way on the IBM/PC.)

Not all the possible combinations of a shift key and an ordinary key are considered legal. If you enter a combination which is not among the proper combinations, the ROM-BIOS routine will simply ignore it, as if nothing had happened. Later we'll list all the allowable combinations of shifted keys, so that your programs can take advantage of them.

On the IBM/PC keyboard, there are four special "toggle" keys, which act like on-off switches for their particular functions. These four keys are Insert, Caps-Lock, Num-Lock, and the thoroughly neglected Scroll-Lock. Two of these toggle keys, Caps-Lock and Num-Lock, are part of the keyboard shifting mechanism, while the other two, Insert and Scroll-Lock, control their own special information.

Information on the state of these four toggle keys, and on whether the temporary shift keys are held down, is kept by the ROM-BIOS in a location in low memory dedicated to that purpose. Two bytes are used, located at memory addresses 1047 and 1048, or hex 417 and 418. All during the operation of the PC, no matter what programs are run, these two bytes keep track of the shift states, and also the toggle-key states. Naturally when the PC is turned off these bytes are reset to their normal state.

The BASIC program shown in listing 10.1 will display the two keyboard control bytes, and demonstrate the action of the shift and toggle keys on them. The exact bit settings in these bytes are explained below.

For the ordinary shift keys, which must be held down to be active, the ROM-BIOS routine keeps track of whether they are pressed or released, and makes appropriate changes in the interpretation of the ordinary keys. Only for the shift keys does the ROM-BIOS bother to pay any attention to the scan-code sent when a key is released. This makes sense, since only for the shift keys is there any meaning to a key being released.

When the ROM-BIOS receives a scan-code for an ordinary key (other than the shift keys), it checks the state of the various shift possibilities, and then translates the key into its appropriate meaning, which could be an ASCII code, or a special key code.

Although we know that the ROM-BIOS routine will keep track of the shift states, it keeps a record of more than you might expect. If you want to do some clever keyboard programming, you might want to make use of some of these codes. The status of the keyboard is kept in the first thirteen of the sixteen bits in the two keyboard status bytes at location 1047. Here is a table of the control bits for the keyboard, which you can see in action with the program in listing 10.1:

| Byte | Bit | Subject matter | Meaning, when bit is 1 |
|------|-----|----------------|------------------------|
| 1 | 1 | Insert | state active |
| 1 | 2 | Caps-Lock | state active |
| 1 | 3 | Num-Lock | state active |
| 1 | 4 | Scroll-Lock | state active |
| 1 | 5 | Alt shift | key depressed |
| 1 | 6 | Ctrl shift | key depressed |
| 1 | 7 | left-hand shift | key depressed |
| 1 | 8 | right-hand shift | key depressed |
| | | | |
| 2 | 1 | Insert | key depressed |
| 2 | 2 | Caps-Lock | key depressed |
| 2 | 3 | Num-Lock | key depressed |
| 2 | 4 | Scroll-Lock | key depressed |
| 2 | 5 | hold state | state active (from Ctrl-NumLock) |
| 2 | 6 | (not used) | |
| 2 | 7 | (not used) | |
| 2 | 8 | (not used) | |

There are several interesting things about this table. First, for the four toggle keys, note the parallelism in the first four bits of the two bytes; in the first byte, the current state is indicated, while in the second byte these four bits indicate whether the corresponding key is depressed. Second, in the bits indicating the pressing of the four normal shift keys, note that the shift keys on the left and right hand side of the keyboard are treated separately. It may be hard to imagine a sensible use for this distinction, but there it is, if you ever want it.

Also, note that the ROM-BIOS keeps track of the insert status as an on-off toggle function. This is a feature that is generally ignored by programs which make use of the insert key, such as word processing programs. Usually any program which uses the insert key keeps its own record of the insert state, which might easily be the opposite of the insert state that the ROM-BIOS keeps. This has little or no practical significance, but it is interesting and a little ironic.

Finally, notice the hold state bit, which is set when the ROM-BIOS keyboard routine detects a Ctrl-NumLock key. This is used by the ROM-BIOS to control the hold-state, but your programs will have a hard time detecting it since they aren't running in the hold-state. When the hold state is on, the keyboard ROM-BIOS runs in a tight loop, waiting for a key to be pressed to break out of the hold state. During this loop, any interrupts that occur are serviced. And if the interrupt is a keyboard interrupt (for an ordinary key), then the hold state is ended, the keystroke is thrown away, and the ROM-BIOS returns control to whatever program was executing before the hold state was set. If an interrupt occurs for another reason—say for the diskette drive—then that interrupt is serviced, and the hold-state loop continues, waiting for a key to be struck.

The Ctrl-NumLock key combination is one of four keying cases that the ROM-BIOS handles specially. While the keyboard service routine is processing key actions received from the keyboard unit, it is constantly checking for four special cases, which it does not treat as ordinary keyboard input. In effect, the keyboard service routine treats these four cases as commands that the service routine must act on itself. The four are Ctrl-NumLock, PrtSc, Ctrl-Alt-Del, and Ctrl-Break.

As we've already seen, Ctrl-NumLock is used to suspend the operation of the computer. The keyboard routine keeps the computer from proceeding with any program until the suspense is broken with a keystroke.

PrtSc, or print-screen, is a command to write a copy of the screen contents to the printer. Since this operation is done on the most primitive BIOS level, it isn't affected by DOS enhancements, such as redirecting printer output to the communications line. The print-screen service is available to your programs, on an interrupt level, as we will see in Chapter 11.

The Ctrl-Alt-Del key combination is used to request a restart, or reboot, of the computer system. When the keyboard service routine detects this key combination, it passes control to the same program that is used to test the system and start-up the operating system. Supposedly you can do Ctrl-Alt-Del at any time to restart your IBM/PC when it gets into a tizzy. You may have already discovered that this doesn't always work. Sometimes you have to turn the PC off and then on again to get it restarted. Why is this sometimes necessary? Ctrl-Alt-Del will always work, provided that the keyboard interrupt service is working. There are two things that may cripple it. The first, and most common, is the disabling of interrupts. You will recall from Chapter 3, that the CLI (clear interrupts) instruction will suspend interrupts until a STI (start interrupts) instruction re-activates them. Normally a CLI is quickly followed by a STI. But if a program, by accident, leaves interrupts disabled, then our keystrokes, including Ctrl-Alt-Del, will never be seen by the micro-processor. The other thing which can disrupt a Ctrl-Alt-Del reset is a change in the keyboard interrupt vector. If memory locations 36 through 39, where the keyboard interrupt vector resides, have been changed, then nothing on the keyboard will work, including Ctrl-Alt-Del. Naturally the power-on program resets all of the interrupt vectors.

Ctrl-Break is a command that is intended to break out of the current operation. Unlike its three special-status companions, it can be controlled by program software. Interrupt number 27, hex 1B, is reserved for a routine which will be activated when Ctrl-Break is keyed. If a program wants to make use of this capability, then the program inserts the address of its interrupt service routine into the vector location for interrupt 27—at storage location 108, hex 6C. You can experience this facility by using Ctrl-Break with either BASIC, or the Edlin editor that comes with DOS. If a program does not insert the address of an interrupt handler into location 108, then the BIOS and DOS operating system co-operate to break out of the current program or batch processing file.

Since the keyboard unit reports each key action separately, and the ROM-BIOS routines interpret the meaning of the key actions, it is possible for your programs to become aware of the exact action going on at the keyboard. It is rare for a program to want to know more than what the ROM-BIOS service routines normally report about the keyboard, and so no special provision was made for a program to find out about the exact key actions.

If you do want to have more complete knowledge about what is happening on the keyboard, your programs can replace the interrupt vector for the keyboard action interrupt, which is located at memory address 36, hex 24. If you provide your own keyboard interrupt handler, it either could take complete charge of the keyboard, or it could act as a front-end to the regular ROM-BIOS routine. A front-end routine could extract any information that you need and then pass control on to the regular ROM-BIOS routine, to complete the regular keyboard processing.

## 10.3 Key characters

After the ROM-BIOS has processed the keystrokes, they are available in translated form to our programs. There is an interesting range of characters available—in effect two different sets of characters.

The first set is the ordinary extended ASCII character set that we already know about. This consists of all the 256 possible byte codes, except for one (the zero value byte). These extended ASCII characters are the conventional characters described in all the character set diagrams that appear in the various IBM/PC manuals. These codes can be generated on the keyboard either by using the regular keystrokes (A-key for "A", and so forth), or by using the Alt-numeric keys.

To generate ASCII codes by the Alt-numeric method, hold down the "Alt" shift key, and key in the numeric value of the ASCII code; the value must be in decimal (from 1 to 255), and you must use the numeric keys on the right of the keyboard (and not the numbers on the top row of the keyboard). The Alt-numeric method is handled specially by the ROM-BIOS routines, since several keystrokes are interpreted as one keyboard input character. As long as the Alt key is held down, you can key all night on the numeric keys. When you finally release the Alt key, an ASCII character is generated, corresponding to the numeric value you entered. If you have keyed in too large a number, the modulo-256 value is used; for example, if you key in Alt-1000, the character CHR$(232) will be generated. Dividing 1000 by 256 leaves a remainder of 232, so CHR$(232) is the character code that is generated.

The one ASCII value which cannot be entered on the keyboard is the zero, or CHR$(0), value. There are some lame reasons for this (code 0 is defined in ASCII as the null character, which is supposed to be ignored), but the real reason is that zero is used by the ROM-BIOS to indicate the presence of the second set of characters, the special characters. (We'll explain them in a moment.) Although some of the IBM/PC manuals indicate that the zero character can be generated by either using Ctrl-2, or by using the Alt-numeric method, this is incorrect. If you hold the "Ctrl" shift key, and press the numeral "2", one of the special characters will be generated, and that character is supposed to be interpreted as if it were CHR$(0) in the ASCII character set. That isn't really the same thing as generating a true ASCII CHR$(0). And the Alt-numeric method won't work either, whether you key in Alt-0, or even if you try to fool it by keying in a modulo-256 equivalent, such as Alt-256 or Alt-512.

The special characters are used to indicate the special keys such as Home, End, and the ten function keys (there are actually forty function keys, as you will see shortly). The reason for these special character codes is to be able to make use of the special keys, such as the function keys, without using up any of the 256 extended ASCII codes.

The coding mechanism that the ROM-BIOS uses to indicate what character has been keyed (and whether the character is conventional extended ASCII or a special character), is to provide two bytes whenever a keyboard character is requested. If the main byte of the two is not zero, then the input is extended ASCII, and the character is stored in that main byte. However, if the main byte is zero, then the keyboard character is a special character, and the character is stored in an auxiliary byte. Common sense suggests that it would have been better to use one bit of the auxiliary byte to indicate the difference between conventional and special key characters—it would have been simpler, and would have allowed the zero character to be keyed in. But that isn't the way IBM did it.

While there are 256 extended ASCII codes (255 of which can be keyed in), there are only as many special codes as are needed by the intended purposes of the IBM/PC keyboard. For example, there are 40 codes for the function keys (ten regular codes, and another thirty for the three possible shift states—normal shift, alt-shift, and ctrl-shift). Here is a table of the special codes, and which key combinations create then. You will notice that this is a real hodge-podge of codes, without a great deal of consistency to it. Some Alt-key combinations are allowed and others are not; the same is true for the Ctrl-key combinations.

| Special Code Value | Keys needed to generate it |
|---|---|
| 3 | Ctrl-2 (this is supposed to be taken as CHR$(0), the ASCII NULL) |
| 15 | back-tab (shift tab) |
| 16-25 | Alt-Q through Alt-P (top row of letters) |
| 30-38 | Alt-A through Alt-L (middle row of letters) |
| 44-50 | Alt-Z through Alt-M (bottom row of letters) |

| Special Code Value | Keys needed to generate it |
|---|---|
| 59-68 | f1 through f10 (function keys, no shift) |
| 71 | Home key |
| 72 | Cursor up key |
| 73 | PgUp key |
| 75 | Cursor left key |
| 77 | Cursor right key |
| 79 | End key |
| 80 | Cursor down key |
| 81 | PgDn key |
| 82 | Ins key |
| 83 | Del key |
| 84-93 | shift-f1 through shift-f10 (regular shift function keys) |
| 94-103 | Ctrl-f1 through Ctrl-f10 (control shift function keys) |
| 104-113 | Alt-f1 through Alt-f10 (alternate shift function keys) |
| 114 | Ctrl-PrtSc |
| 115 | Ctrl-Cursor-left |
| 116 | Ctrl-Cursor-right |
| 117 | Ctrl-End |
| 118 | Ctrl-PgDn |
| 119 | Ctrl-Home |
| 120-131 | Alt-1 through Alt-= (top row of the keyboard) |
| 132 | Ctrl-PgUp |

As you can see, this table isn't very well organized. Also, you'll see that there are forty variations on the function keys: each of the ten keys, in four shift states (normal, shifted, Ctrl-shifted, and Alt-shifted).

With all these special key codes available, there is no shortage of codes that your programs can use for special purposes. Usually all any program will need is the function keys, and a few special-purpose keys such as Home and the cursor-arrow keys. But if more special key codes are needed, you will find them in this table.

It takes some special methods to get access to these special character codes. In the next two sections, we'll see how it is done.

## 10.4 BIOS services for the keyboard

With that out of the way, lets take a look at the ROM-BIOS service routines that are available for keyboard access and control.

The ROM-BIOS support routines for the keyboard are invoked by using interrupt 22, hex 16. There are only three services, since there aren't very many things that you can ask a keyboard to do.

The first service, with service code 0, returns the next available keyboard character. This service only returns control to the requester when a character is ready, so any program using it doesn't need to check for there being no character ready. Register AL is used to return the conventional character code, and if AL is zero, then register AH contains the special character code; these are the main and auxiliary bytes mentioned in the discussion of the special character codes in the last section. Here is a simple outline of the logic needed to make sense of this way of returning characters:

```
if AL = 0 then
  begin
    special_character := true;
    input_character := AH
  end
else
  begin
    special_character := false;
    input_character := AL
  end;
```

There are a couple of interesting things to note about the values returned by this service. If the input is a normal ASCII character (that is, if AL is not zero), then AH contains the exact keyboard scan code for the key pressed. But if the ASCII character was keyed in by using the Alt-numeric method, then the scan-code given in AH is zero. This can be used by a program to tell how a character was keyed in. Some ASCII characters appear twice on the PC's keyboard—the period, the asterisk, plus, minus/hyphen, and the ten numerals are all duplicated. The scan-code in AH can be used to tell which key used for these characters.

It is worth noting that BASIC gives good, but slightly incomplete, access to the full keystroke information that is passed in registers AL and AH. The INKEY$ function is used to return keyboard information. For special keys, INKEY$ is two characters long—the first CHR$(0), and the second the special key-code. This, of course, is exactly what the ROM-BIOS returns in the AL and AH registers. But if a normal ASCII character is keyed-in, INKEY$ returns only the ASCII character (from AL), and not the scan code (from AH).

The second service, code 1, is used to test if a keyboard character is ready, without waiting for a keystroke. This service returns control to the requesting program immediately, whether a character is ready or not. The 8088 micro-processor's Z flag is used to pass the signal—if the Z flag is 0, a character is ready, and can be read with the first service, described above. One nice addition to this service is that if a character is ready, it is passed to your program in the AL and AH registers, so that you can get immediate access to it. When that happens, the character still has not been officially read, and it remains in the keyboard buffer until service code 0 is used to read it. The primary use of this service, of course, is to allow programs to process keyboard input and still be able to continue operation when no input is available.

Both of these first two services take their input characters from the keyboard buffer that is maintained by the ROM-BIOS. This buffer contains the translated characters that the ROM-BIOS produces from the raw scan-codes provided by the keyboard unit. None of these ROM-BIOS services give your programs access to the raw scan-codes. You can only get them by intercepting the keyboard interrupts, and reading from the keyboard unit's port.

The third and final service, code 2, returns the current shift states, from the first of the two keyboard status bytes defined in the table above. This value is returned in the AL register, and the other keyboard status byte is not presented to your program. Note that you could get to either or both of these bytes by accessing them in memory, but using this service is a safer way to find out about the keyboard shift state. It is safer because this is an official service, which we can expect to be provided by any new versions of the PC; while the memory location where the status bytes are stored could change in revisions to the computer.

Assembly language interface routines, to make these ROM-BIOS services available to Pascal and other languages are provided in listing 10-101, in the diskette package. Supporting Pascal routines are also provided, in listing 10-102.

## 10.5 Language access to the keyboard

Ordinary keyboard input to programs is available in every language used on the IBM/PC, but using that kind of input always involves the program being suspended when keyboard input isn't ready. For many purposes that is adequate, but often your programs need to be able to look at keyboard input without being suspended.

Both BASIC and Pascal have available to them keyboard input services that allow testing for input characters without suspending the execution of the program. BASIC does it through the INKEY$ function, and Pascal does it through accessing the input buffer, via a file pointer (for details of this, see the IBM Pascal manual, particularly page 12-7 in the first edition).

As we mentioned above, BASIC also provides access to the special input codes through the INKEY$ function. When LEN (INKEY$) is two, then a special key was pressed, and INKEY$ has CHR$(0) for its first character, and the special code value for its second character.

However, Pascal does not provide full access to the special key codes. When the special key combinations are pressed, Pascal does recognize the keystroke, but no indication is given if the character is a special code, or an ordinary ASCII character. To make it possible for Pascal programs to properly recognize the special codes, we have provided service routines in programs 10-101 and 10-102, in the diskette package which accompanies this book. These routines will make it possible for Pascal programs to get full use of all the keyboard codes, ordinary and special.

For sophisticated keyboard programming in any language, access to the keyboard shift status bits can be very important. The shift states can be accessed either through the ROM-BIOS service code 2, described in the last section, or by direct memory access, described in section 10.2, and illustrated by the program in listing 10.1.

If you compare the keyboard services that are available in DOS, described in Chapter 4, with the ones that are provided by the ROM-BIOS, you will see that they are considerably enriched from the bare bones BIOS services—providing such operations as clearing the keyboard buffer (a very useful service when handling error conditions). As usual, the ROM-BIOS level services are more primitive and atomic, while the DOS level services are more complete. Both can be very useful to your programs.

```
1000 REM  Listing 10.1 -- A program to display keyboard status bits
1010 REM               (C) Copyright 1983, Peter Norton
1020 REM
1030 GOSUB 2000                    ' TITLE
1040 GOSUB 3000                    ' MISCELLANEOUS INFORMATION
1050 GOSUB 4000                    ' DISPLAY KEYBOARD BITS
1060 GOSUB 5000                    ' CHECK FOR KEYBOARD INPUT TO END
1070 GOTO  1050                    ' CONTINUE DISPLAYING


2000 REM  Title subroutine
2010 KEY OFF : CLS : WIDTH 80 : LOCATE ,,0
2020 REM
2030 LOCATE 5,1
2040 PRINT "            Programs for INSIDE THE IBM PERSONAL COMPUTER"
2050 PRINT "                 (C) Copyright 1983 Peter Norton"
2060 PRINT
2070 PRINT "            Program 10-1: Display the Keyboard Status Bits"
2999 RETURN


3000 REM  Subroutine to display miscellaneous information
3010 LOCATE  11,28
3020 PRINT " Byte 1    Byte 2";
3030 LOCATE  12,28
3040 PRINT "12345678 12345678";
3050 LOCATE 17,10
3060 PRINT "To see the status bits change, press (and hold) any of";
3070 LOCATE 18,15
3080 PRINT "-- left and right shift keys";
3090 LOCATE 19,15
3100 PRINT "-- Ctrl, Alt, Num-Lock, Scroll-Lock, Caps-Lock, Ins";
3110 LOCATE 21,10
3120 PRINT "(beware the effect of the shift and Num-Lock on the Ins key)";
3130 LOCATE 24,10
3140 PRINT "To return to DOS, press any normal input key...";
3999 RETURN


4000 REM     Subroutine to display keyboard control bits
4010 DEF SEG = &H40
4020 CONTROL% = PEEK (&H17)
4030 CHECK% = 128
4040 FOR I% = 1 TO 8
4050    LOCATE 14,27+I%
```

```
4060    IF CONTROL% >= CHECK% THEN COLOR 30,0 ELSE COLOR 7,0
4070    IF CONTROL% >= CHECK% THEN PRINT "1"; ELSE PRINT "0";
4080    IF CONTROL% >= CHECK% THEN CONTROL% = CONTROL% - CHECK%
4090    CHECK% = CHECK% / 2
4100 NEXT I%
4110 CONTROL% = PEEK (&H18)
4120 CHECK% = 128
4130 FOR I% = 1 TO 8
4140    LOCATE 14,36+I%
4150    IF CONTROL% >= CHECK% THEN COLOR 30,0 ELSE COLOR 7,0
4160    IF CONTROL% >= CHECK% THEN PRINT "1"; ELSE PRINT "0";
4170    IF CONTROL% >= CHECK% THEN CONTROL% = CONTROL% - CHECK%
4180    CHECK% = CHECK% / 2
4190 NEXT I%
4999 RETURN

5000 REM    Subroutine to check for ending keystroke
5010 K$ = INKEY$
5020 IF  LEN(K$) = 0 THEN RETURN    ' LOOP UNTIL KEYBOARD INPUT
5030 IF (LEN(K$) = 2) AND (CHR$(82) = MID$(K$,2,1) THEN RETURN ' "Ins" key
5040 CLS : LOCATE ,,1
5999 SYSTEM

9999 REM    End of program listing 10-1
```

# 11

# Miscellaneous Features— Communications, Speaker and More

In this chapter we'll cover a miscellany of features on the IBM/PC, some major, some minor, but none of them complicated enough to need their own chapter. We'll cover the printer, the asynchronous communications adapter, the cassette interface, the speaker, and some odds and ends found in the ROM-BIOS. As you might expect in a mixed bag like this chapter, some very interesting curiosities will turn up.

## 11.1 The asynchronous communications adapter

The asynchronous communications adapter allows the IBM/PC to talk to the world in the standard and widely used communications method that is known as RS-232. For personal computers, RS-232 is normally used for two purposes.

The first use of RS-232 is actual communications, through the telephone network. For this use, the RS-232 adapter is connected to a modem (or modulator-demodulator) which has the job of translating between computer signals and telephone signals. The modem, in turn, is connected to a telephone line. On the other end of the telephone line will be another modem, which is hooked to . . . something. That something on the other end of the line could be anything from a large scale computer (as used by data base services like The Source and CompuServe), through another personal computer, to a simple device such as a printer. This is, shall we say, the normal use of the communications adapter.

The second use of RS-232 is simpler and less far reaching. Some output devices are designed to talk with computers following the RS-232 protocol; this is most common with printers, especially letter-quality printers. So the communications adapter on the IBM/PC is also used simply as another way to talk to its attached equipment, like printers.

Let's pause for a moment to look at the two main ways that personal computers, the IBM/PC included, talk to their environment, particularly to printers. There are two widely used ways, most often called serial and parallel. Serial communications is just another way of saying RS-232 communications. It is called "serial," because the data is communicated over a single channel, and data bits are sent serially, one-by-one. Parallel communications uses another scheme than RS-232—a standard made popular by the Centronics printers, and so it is sometimes called the Centronics parallel interface, or just parallel for short. In the parallel scheme, data is transmitted a byte at a time, and there are enough data channels in the parallel interface for all of the bits of a byte to go out together, in parallel.

The parallel interface is suited for direct connections between computer and output devices, particularly because it can pass data faster—since data goes out a full byte at a time. The Centronics parallel interface is used for the standard printer adapter on the IBM/PC. The serial interface is slower, but has designed into it various features needed for the special requirements of remote communications. These communications features are hardly needed when the serial interface is used locally, to talk to a printer. But it can be a convenient way to make a connection between computer and printer—particularly because the older generation of personal computers which preceded the IBM/PC often didn't have a parallel interface in addition to the serial interface.

Performing remote communications can be very complicated, thanks to all of the things that can go wrong, all the error checking that needs to be done, and all of the many different kinds of equipment that can be talked to on a communications line. But the services that the IBM/PC's ROM-BIOS provides for the RS-232 adapter are quite simple and easy to use.

There are only four communications services, all provided through interrupt 20, hex 14. Register DX is used to indicate which communications adapter is to be used, when there is more than one; zero is used to indicate the first (and usually only) adapter. Program listings 11-101 and 11-102, in the diskette package which accompanies this book, provide the assembly language interface routines and Pascal support programs, needed to make full use of these ROM-BIOS services.

The first service, with code 0, sets the four standard communications parameters: baud rate, parity, stop-bits, and byte-length. These parameters specify the many variations on how communications can be done. The IBM/PC can use any combination of them, and usually what is on the other end of the communications line—whether it's a local printer or a remote data-base service—calls the tune on what parameters must be used. The codes for these variables are taken from register AL, in this manner:

The first three bits specify the baud rate, that is, the transmission rate in bits per second. There are eight possible values, going up to some rather high transmission speeds. For personal computers only two are commonly used—300 bits per second and 1200. Here are the code values:

| Bit code | Baud rate |
|----------|-----------|
| 000 | 110 bits per second |
| 001 | 150 bits per second |
| 010 | 300 bits per second (roughly 30 characters per second) |
| 011 | 600 bits per second |
| 100 | 1200 bits per second (roughly 120 characters per second) |
| 101 | 2400 bits per second |
| 110 | 4800 bits per second |
| 111 | 9600 bits per second |

(Communications overhead—including parity bits and stop bits—increases the number of bits needed to transmit a character. So a baud rate of 300 translates into about 30 characters per second, even though there are only 7 or 8 bits in an ASCII character.)

The next two bits of the parameter byte set the parity used:

| Bit code | Parity |
|----------|--------|
| 00 | no parity |
| 01 | odd parity |
| 10 | no parity |
| 11 | even parity |

The next bit indicates the number of stop bits used, part of the protocol of RS-232 communications:

| Bit code | Stop bits |
|----------|-----------|
| 0 | One bit |
| 1 | Two bits |

The last two parameter bits indicates the size of the byte used:

| Bit code | Byte size |
|----------|-----------|
| 10 | 7-bits (the ASCII standard) |
| 11 | 8-bits (the usual size for computers) |

Normally you will not have a free choice in the setting of these parameters.

Usually it will be determined in advance by the service or equipment with which you are communicating.

The second communications service, code 1, is used to send out a single byte of data. The byte is loaded into register AL, and a completion signal is returned in register AH. If the transmission was not successful, the first bit of AH is set on, and the other seven bits are set as shown for the last service (code 3), below. So, a test for AH less than 128 will indicate success or failure in sending the byte requested. As usual, the interface routines provided in the diskette package for this book will take care of those details for you.

The third communications service, code 2, is used to receive a byte from the communications line. This service waits for completion of the service (which may be a time-out or other error signal).

This service contains one of the most important bugs in the original version of the ROM-BIOS; if the version of the ROM-BIOS is dated 04/24/81, then a time-out error will be incorrectly reported as a parity error, with data ready. You can see which version of BIOS you have by using the DOS tool DEBUG. If you activate DEBUG and enter the command

D   F000:FFF5 L 8

the ROM-BIOS version date will be displayed. For more discussion of the errors in the first version of the ROM-BIOS, see Chapter 6.

If the input service was successful, register AH will be zero, indicating success. Otherwise, register AH will have one or more of the 1st and 4th through 7th bits set, as defined below in the next service.

The last service, code 3, is used to determine the full current status of the communications port (in register AH) and of the modem (register AL). Part of this information is returned for the input and output services, codes 1 and 2. The AH and AL registers are set with these codes:

| Register | Bit | Meaning |
|----------|-----|---------|
| AH | 1st | Time out (except for BIOS version 04/24/81) |
| AH | 2nd | transmission shift register empty |
| AH | 3rd | transmission holding register empty |
| AH | 4th | break detected |
| AH | 5th | framing error |
| AH | 6th | parity error (set when time-out, with BIOS of 04/24/81) |
| AH | 7th | overrun error |
| AH | 8th | data is ready (set when time-out, with BIOS of 04/24/81) |
| AL | 1st | line signal detected |
| AL | 2nd | ring indication |
| AL | 3rd | data set (modem) ready |
| AL | 4th | clear-to-send signal |
| AL | 5th | delta receive line signal detected |
| AL | 6th | trailing edge ring detected |
| AL | 7th | delta data set ready |
| AL | 8th | delta clear-to-send signal |

To make effective use of these services, you need to have a good understanding of the ins and outs of communications, which is subject matter enough for a book by itself. The information here is only enough to satisfy the curious, or to get a communications-wise person started with the IBM/PC.

## 11.2 The printer adapter

The ROM-BIOS provides support services for the parallel printer adapter. (For a discussion of the serial and parallel adapters, see the section above.) Since the printer is even simpler than the communications adapter, the services are simpler—there are only three services, and only six status bits.

Interrupt 23, hex 17, is used to access the three services. Register DX is used to indicate which printer adapter is to be used, when there are more than one; zero is used to indicate the first (and usually only) adapter. Program listings 11-101 and 11-102, in the diskette package which accompanies this book, provide the assembly language interface routines and Pascal support programs, needed to make full use of these ROM-BIOS services.

One of the minor errors in the original version of the ROM-BIOS concerns the printer adapter. When a skip-to-a-new-page signal command is sent to the standard Epson printer, the printer may take longer to do this than the BIOS allows. This will only happen when the page-eject operation is done from near the top of the old page. For versions of the ROM-BIOS later than the original version dated 04/24/81, the time allowed was increased to avoid this problem. The problem doesn't occur often, is very minor, and it only can happen on IBM/PC's with the original ROM-BIOS—so you do not need to consider it very seriously, but you should be aware of it.

The first service, with code 0, is used to send a single byte to the printer. That is so simple and straightforward, that there is nothing much to be said about it.

The second service, with code 1, is used to reset the printer and determine the printer status. This service can be used to get the printer back to normal status, in case any special control codes have been sent to it. The status information is returned in register AH, with these bit signals:

| Bit | Meaning |
|---|---|
| 1st | printer busy |
| 2nd | acknowledge signal |
| 3rd | out-of-paper signal |
| 4th | selected signal |
| 5th | output error signal |
| 6th | (not used) |
| 7th | (not used) |

8th     time out signal (for BIOS version 04/24/81, this may be a false alarm)

The third and last service, with code 2, is used to read the status bits shown above, without the reset operation of service code 1. If you are writing a printer control program, then this service will be particularly useful.

That's it for the printer. It's not a complicated device, and so the ROM-BIOS control services aren't complicated either.

## 11.3 The cassette interface

The next area in the ROM-BIOS, is the cassette interface. Almost no one uses the cassette, and many people, myself included, can see no reason why IBM included it in the PC, except as a marketing ploy. (For more on that, see the hardware discussion in Chapter 2.)

Much of the system software for the IBM/PC was provided for IBM by Microsoft. Bill Gates, the wizard behind Microsoft, has publicly complained about how silly it was to have to support the cassette interface. Nevertheless, the cassette interface is there, and the ROM-BIOS supports it, and so you ought to have access to it.

There are just four simple services provided for the cassette—reading and writing data blocks, and turning the cassette drive motor on and off. There are no commands such as rewinding the cassette: that must be done manually with the controls on the cassette player.

Notice that the commands available are "physical", and that there are no "logical" commands, such as a command to find a file. That sort of command properly belongs at the operating system level, rather than at the BIOS level — after all, BIOS is supposed to provide only the most primitive and atomic services, out of which higher level logical services are built. Unfortunately, there is no support for the cassette in DOS, and so you can only use the cassette within BASIC, or at the primitive BIOS level. This leaves anyone who wants to make serious use of the cassette out in the cold.

Interrupt 21, hex 15, is used to access the four cassette services. Program listings 11-101 and 11-102, in the diskette package which accompanies this book, provide the assembly language interface routines and Pascal support programs needed to make full use of these ROM-BIOS services.

The first service, with code 0, turns on the cassette drive motor. This service returns immediately, without waiting any time for the motor to get up to speed—something that you should allow for.

The second service, with code 1, turns off the cassette drive motor.

The third service, with code 2, is used to read data blocks from the cassette. Data is passed in blocks of 256 bytes, and one or more can be read at a time. If there was an error in passing the data, any of three error signals may be returned in the AH register:

| Error code | Meaning |
|---|---|
| 1 | an error was detected by the cyclical redundancy check (CRC) |
| 2 | some data transitions (used to record the location and information of bits) were lost |
| 4 | no data was found |

The fourth service, with code 3, is used to write data blocks onto the cassette.

With the cassette, we come to the end of the ROM-BIOS support for peripheral equipment attached to the IBM/PC, but we haven't come to the end of either the ROM-BIOS or the IBM/PC's equipment. In the next sections, we'll cover the rest of the goodies. But before we go on to them, there is one more thing to say about the cassette interface.

The IBM/PC's cassette interface was intended as exactly that—a connection to a cassette recorder, which goes unused on almost every PC there is. Some clever people have taken this otherwise wasted connection with the outside world, and have turned it into a data path from the PC to various things. One use that it has been put to is a connection to home-spun modems. Another is an access path to the popular BSR appliance controller. While these uses for the cassette interface are mostly for electronics hobbyists, it is interesting to all of us to know that many unusual and creative uses have been found for this interface.

## 11.4 Miscellaneous ROM-BIOS services

There are a number of interesting and useful services that the ROM-BIOS routines provide besides those we have covered so far. As usual, program listings 11-101 and 11-102, in the diskette package which accompanies this book, provide the assembly language interface routines and Pascal support programs needed to make full use of these ROM-BIOS services.

The first of these services is the print-screen operation. This is normally invoked by the ROM-BIOS keyboard routine, when it sees the "PrtSc" key pressed. The screen-printing is performed by an interrupt handler triggered by interrupt number 5, and this makes it convenient for your programs to do the same operation, by issuing a request for interrupt 5. All that the keyboard service routine does, when it detects the "PrtSc" key, is issue interrupt 5; so if your programs use this interrupt, they will be getting exactly the same service.

Users of BASIC have discovered that the print-screen key doesn't work when BASIC is running. But there is a simple way for BASIC programs to invoke the print screen operation. BASIC changes the keyboard operation, so that pressing the PrtSc key doesn't invoke the print-screen operation. We can't change that, but we can create a simple way for a BASIC program to invoke the operation, by going directly to the interrupt 5 service described above.

BASIC needs a machine-language interface routine to invoke the print-screen operation, and it is a very simple one, consisting of two instructions, occupying three bytes. In assembly language, here is what the interface is:

```
INT   5 ; invoke interrupt number 5 (print screen) (2-byte instruction)
RET     ; return to BASIC (1-byte instruction)
```

Such a small routine can easily be POKEd into memory, and since it's only three bytes, it will even fit inside a single precision number. This short program shows exactly how to do it:

```
100   REM      Here is a simple program which invokes print screen from BASIC
110   REM      We create a 3 byte machine language subroutine inside a variable
120   REM
130   HOLD.THE.CODE = 0 ' this creates a 4 byte single precision variable
140   REM
150   PRINT.SCREEN = VARPTR (HOLD.THE.CODE) ' get a pointer to the memory
160   REM
170   POKE PRINT.SCREEN + 0,205 ' 1st byte of subroutine: interrupt instruction
180   POKE PRINT.SCREEN + 1, 5 ' 2nd byte of subroutine: interrupt number 5
190   POKE PRINT.SCREEN + 2,203 ' 3rd byte of subroutine: return instruction
200   REM
210   REM       Now the machine code subroutine is stored inside "hold.the.code"
220   REM          and pointed to by "print.screen"—so we can call it
230   REM
240   CALL PRINT.SCREEN
```

In this simple routine, lines 120-160 set up the machine language routine, which only needs to be done once. The CALL statement in line 190 can then be done any time your programs want to print the screen. (Interface routines for all of the ROM-BIOS and DOS services are included in the diskette package which accompanies this book, but a simple interface like this one is simple to do directly in BASIC. For more complicated services, you usually will need the complete assembler interface routines, which can be BLOADed by BASIC.)

Next among the miscellaneous services is the equipment list, which is invoked by interrupt number 17, hex 11. When the IBM/PC is first turned on, the power-on routines check what equipment is attached (mostly by the crude but effective method of reading the switch settings on the IBM/PC's system board; these switches are supposed to match the equipment that is attached, but they could be set incorrectly).

Your programs can inquire about the equipment attached by using this interrupt service. When this service is invoked, no new check is made of the equipment, or of the switch settings. All that happens is that two bytes, which contain a summary of the equipment attached, are loaded into the AH and AL registers, where your programs can take a look at them.

Here is a table of the equipment codes:

| Register | Bits | Meaning |
|---|---|---|
| AH | 1st-2nd | number of printer adapters (0 to 3) |
| AH | 3rd | (not used) |
| AH | 4th | game adapter is attached, or not |
| AH | 5th-7th | number of communications adapters (0 to 7) |
| AH | 8th | (not used) |
| | | |
| AL | 1st-2nd | number of diskette drives minus 1, if 8th bit set |
| AL | 3rd-4th | starting video mode (see table below) |
| AL | 5th-6th | amount of memory on the system board (see table below) |
| AL | 7th | (not used) |
| AL | 8th | diskettes are attached, so see 1st and 2nd bits |

Notice that the number of diskette drives, specified by the first two bits of AL, is coded as one less than the actual number, so that a bit setting of 00 means one drive, 01 means two, and so forth. This scheme lets two bits indicate from one to four drives. The eighth bit of AL indicates if there are any drives at all; if so, then the two count bits are used. It would have been simpler just to devote three bytes to an ordinary count of drives, which then could have ranged from zero to seven.

For the starting video mode, this table explains the bit settings:

| Bits | Meaning |
|---|---|
| 00 | (not used) |
| 01 | graphics display, 40 columns, black-and-white mode |
| 10 | graphics display, 80 columns, black-and-white mode |
| 11 | monochrome display |

For the system-board memory, this table explains the bit settings:

| Bits | Meaning |
|---|---|
| 00 | 16K bytes of memory, only |
| 01 | 32 K |
| 10 | 48 K |
| 11 | 64 K |

Your programs can make use of this information to tailor their operation to the system's equipment.

The next service is used to give the size of the memory installed. This is the working memory size, including the memory on the system board (which is indicated by the equipment service above) and memory attachments. Interrupt 18, hex 12, is used to request this service, and the value returned, in the AX register, is the number of blocks of 1 K of memory. This mechanism has the capacity to indicate up to the full one million bytes of memory.

The memory size value is taken from a standard system memory location, and not from direct inspection of the memory or equipment installed. This is to allow the amount of usable memory to be changed by programs.

One of the most useful features that can be installed on an IBM/PC is to get a large amount of memory (such as 512 K), and a system program which will use part of this memory as a very fast simulated diskette drive; various terms are used for this—RAM disk, and electronic disk. This kind of system modification can be extremely useful (and in fact, was used to assist the writing of this book), and is becoming more and more popular. To make it possible for physical memory to be dedicated to some use other than ordinary system memory, the IBM/PC keeps its working record of how much memory may be used stored in a location where it can be changed. And the use of memory, for example in assigning it to programs, is continually checked against this value.

The next of the interesting ROM features is not a part of the ROM-BIOS at all, but is a way of invoking the cassette BASIC that is stored in ROM. If a program invokes interrupt number 24, hex 18, then the cassette BASIC interpreter will take over the operation of the computer. Note, however, that by doing this your program—and the DOS operating system—will lose control of the system, and be gone.

Another service which will wipe your program and DOS off the system, is the boot-strap service, which is invoked by interrupt 25, hex 19. This will reload the operating system from diskette, just like the manual reset operation that is done by pressing the Ctrl, Alt, and Del keys. The only difference is that Ctrl-Alt-Del also performs the same diagnostic routines that are performed when the system is turned on, while interrupt 25 will cause an immediate system load. This is one ruthless way to end your programs, and to guarantee that a fresh copy of the operating system is loaded.

The next of the miscellaneous services is the timer routine. This is used to read or change the internal clock counting routine. Although this routine is referred to as the time-of-day service, it is really only a clock interrupt counter. The count is incremented by one at each tick of the internal clock, which happens about 18.21 times a second. Keeping a record of the actual time of day, and a record of the date, is a DOS operation, based on this raw count.

There are two timer services, each invoked with interrupt 26, hex 1A, one to read the timer, using service code 0, and one to set it, with code 1. The timer count is kept as a pair of two-byte numbers, acting, in effect, as a single four-byte number. This time-keeping service does add one refinement to its simple counting operation—it checks for the count reaching the equivalent of 24 hours. When that point is reached, the count is reset and a note is made. The next time that the read-the-count service is requested, a signal is passed that the timer was reset.

The reason for this scheme is to allow DOS to keep track of the time of day and the date, without having to constantly compute it. When DOS needs to know the time of day, it uses this service to get the raw clock count, and computes the time from it; if it gets a timer-reset signal, then DOS updates the date as well. So DOS only has to do its calculations when the time is needed, without adding any burden to the clock interrupt routine, which must be activated 18 times each second. As long as DOS asks for the time at least once a day, the date will be kept accurately. (You can test this, if you want, by leaving your IBM/PC running for 24 hours, undisturbed; at the end of your test, the time of day will still be correct, but the date will be wrong.)

If you use these ROM-BIOS routines to read or set the timer count, you may interfere with DOS's time-keeping. DOS sets the timer value so that it counts as if it were started at midnight, and DOS relies on the timer-was-reset signal. Any reading or setting that your programs do naturally influence DOS's sense of time. Just reading the count runs the risk of intercepting the timer-reset signal, and disturbing DOS's record of the date.

And that is the end of the services provided in the ROM-BIOS.

You may notice two big gaps in the services. While all of the other standard attachments have supporting services, the game control adapter is completely unsupported. This is not because the game adapter doesn't need ROM-BIOS support—IBM simply didn't provide it. I can only speculate why this is so; one likely reason is that IBM didn't consider the game adapter important enough to give it significant support. Another possibility is that the game adapter was added as an attachment too late in the development of the PC and its ROM-BIOS to include it.

The other missing part of the ROM-BIOS is a set of service routines for the built-in speaker. Why they weren't provided is something of a mystery to me. In the next section we'll cover how the speaker works, and how your programs can make sounds on it.

## 11.5 Making sounds on the speaker

There are, regrettably, no ROM-BIOS general service routines for the speaker that is built into the IBM/PC. Although there are two different subroutines in the ROM-BIOS to sound the speaker, neither one is set up to be used except from within the ROM-BIOS—they are not service routines for our use.

In this section, we will explain how the speaker works, and give you the basics of how to activate it. In the diskette package which accompanies this book, there are assembly language service routines which make the full range of the speakers possibilities accessible to your programs.

Any sound speaker—whether it is part of a hi-fi system, a telephone, or the speaker in the IBM/PC—works by receiving a stream of electrical pulses that drive the speaker's diaphragm in and out, producing the pulses of air movement that make up sound. On an ordinary speaker, the signal pulses going into the speaker vary in strength (volume) and timing (frequency or pitch). For the simple speaker system on the IBM/PC, there is no volume control, and the sound is produced simply by a series of pulses of electricity. The current to the speaker is either on or off, in a strictly binary way. The frequency of these pulses sets the sound frequency of the speaker. For example, if the current is turned on and off 300 times a second, then the speaker produces a 300 cycles-per-second sound.

The circuitry which controls the speaker is very interesting, and is set up to provide two different ways to produce sounds. The pulses that are sent to the speaker are controlled by a combination of a software signal and a programmable timer. The two ways to make sounds depend upon whether or not the timer is used.

First, lets look at how it is done without the timer. To make a sound, an assembly language program must pulse the speaker at the right rate, for the right length of time. Although it's done in assembly language, I'll use an informal kind of Pascal to show you the logic of it. Suppose we want to make a 300-cycles per second tone, and we want it to last for half a second. This is what would be done:

```
repeat 150 times {that's 1/2 second, at 300 cycles per second}
  begin
    pulse the speaker out
    kill time for 1/600th of a second {a half cycle}
    {killing time is done with a do-nothing loop, repeated the right
      number of times}
    pulse the speaker back in
    kill another 1/600th of a second {the other half cycle}
  end;
```

If you study the BEEP/WARBLE assembly language program given in listing 3.2, in Chapter 3, you will see that it works exactly like this Pascal outline.

Now that is a perfectly good way to make a sound, but it doesn't get any work done while the program is generating the sound. In fact, that little program uses the awesome power of the 8088 micro-processor to do nothing but count time, and generate speaker pulses. There is a better way to do that, by using the timer.

One of the hidden features of the IBM/PC is a programmable timer. The timer doesn't really time anything—it counts pulses of the basic system clock. The timer is given a number, called its divisor, and it counts and compares the system clock pulses to the divisor. When the pulse count reaches the divisor, the timer sends out a signal and starts counting again from zero.

The system clock cycle runs at more than one million cycles per second (1.19 MHz). So, if the timer is programmed with a count of 10,000, it will put out a signal about one hundred times a second. Practically any timer output frequency can be generated by loading an appropriate divisor into the timer. When a divisor is loaded into the timer, and the speaker circuitry is activated to be driven by the timer, then the timer's output signal will drive the speaker at whatever frequency the timer is generating, while the computer can go on with its work.

This way of operating the speaker lets programs run while sounds come out of the speaker. That is the secret of the music-in-the-background, or MB, feature in BASIC. You should notice that when sounds are produced by the timer function, they go on forever, and any program which starts a timer-generated sound needs to turn it off after deciding that it has run long enough.

Listing 3.2 can be used as a model of how to generate sounds by the first, non-timer, method. The assembly language program that appears in listing 11.1 shows how to start a speaker tone using the timer.

And that is IBM/PC.

```
;  Listing 11.1 -- "A440" Sound generated with the IBM/PC timer
;  (C) Copyright 1983 Peter Norton

;  This program demonstrates how to generate sounds using the IBM/PC's
;  timer/speaker connection.  It generates a frequency of 440 cycles per
;  second, the musical note A.

;  This program will start a sound which will continue indefinately.

;  As with the BEEP/WARBLE program in listing 3.2, these steps are used
;  to prepare the program for execution.  First enter this program with an
;  editor, into a file named "A440.ASM".  Then complete these steps:

;  1) assemble the program, with      MASM B:A440,B:A440,CON;
;  2) link the program with           LINK B:A440,B:A440,CON;
;  3) convert to "COM" format with    EXE2BIN B:A440.EXE B:A440.COM

a440seg segment 'code'

        assume  cs:a440seg

a440  proc  far

; Step 1 -- prepare the timer to receive its divisor

        mov    al,0b6h ;  timer mode register signal
        out    67,al   ;  output to timer control port

; Step 2 -- send the divisor count to the timer

        mov    ax,2711 ;  divisor for 440 cycles
        out    66,al   ;  output low-order byte of divisor
        mov    al,ah   ;  move high-order byte into output register
        out    66,al   ;  output hight-order byte of divisor

; Step 3 -- turn on the two bits which activate the speaker, and the
;           timer's control of the speaker

        in     al,97   ;  get the current bit settings for port 97
        or     al,03   ;  turn on last two bits
        out    97,al   ;  send back the new value

; Step 4 - return control to DOS

        int    20h     ;  return to system

a440  endp

a440seg ends

        end

;  End of listing 11.1
```

# Appendix 1:
# A Narrative Glossary of Computer Basics

This narrative glossary is intended to provide a very brief run-down of the most common and fundamental terminology used in discussing computers. You can use this narrative glossary in two ways—either by reading it all, or by scanning the word list for the terms you are interested in, and then reading the discussion.

## Numbers and notation

**binary**
**bit**

Computers work only with binary numbers, that is numbers made up of zeros and ones (0's and 1's). Binary digits are called bits, for short. No matter what a computer is doing, it is working with bits. Even if the subject matter is alphabetic characters, or decimal arithmetic, the method is binary numbers.

**hexadecimal**
**hex**
**octal**

Writing many bits, for example 01010100 11101010101, is inconvenient, so several shorthand notations have been developed. The most common is hexadecimal, or base-16, notation. Hexadecimal digits have sixteen possible values, from 0 through 15; they are written as 0 through 9, followed by A (representing the value ten), B (meaning eleven), and C through F (with a value of fifteen). Hexadecimal digits, also called hex, represent four binary digits, or bits, at a time. (Another notation, called octal, uses the digits 0 through 7 and represents 3 bits at a time.)

**byte**
**nibble**
**nybble**
**character**
**alphanumeric**

The bits that a computer uses are grouped into larger units. A group of eight bits is called a byte. Since hex notation represents four bits at a time, it takes two hex digits to represent the value stored in a byte (hex digits are sometimes whimsically called nibbles, or nybbles). A byte can be used to store 2 to the eighth power of values—256 different values. The values can be interpreted as numbers or as characters (such as letters of the alphabet). One byte can hold one character, and therefore the terms bytes and characters are sometimes used interchangeably. The letters of the alphabet and the ten digits, together, are called the alphanumerics, although the term is sometimes used loosely to mean any text data.

**ASCII**
**Extended ASCII**
**EBCDIC**
**ASCII data**
**text data**
**ASCII file**

When bytes are used to hold characters, some code must be used to determine which numeric value will represent which character. The most common code is the American Standard Code for Information Interchange (ASCII). In ASCII, the capital letter "A" has the value 65 (in hex notation, 41), "B" is 66, and so forth. ASCII includes codes for letters, numbers, punctuation and special control codes. ASCII proper has only 128 different codes, and needs only 7 bits to represent it; since ASCII characters are almost always stored inside 8-bit bytes, there is room for the 128 ASCII codes, and another 128 codes. The other codes are sometimes call extended ASCII. ASCII codes are standardized, but extended ASCII will vary from computer to computer. Traditionally IBM computers have not used ASCII coding to represent characters; instead, they used EBCDIC (the Extended Binary Coded Decimal Information Code). ASCII data, or an ASCII file, is data which consists of text—that is, letters of the alphabet, punctuation and so forth—rather than numbers or other data. Sometimes the term ASCII is used loosely to mean text data. Properly speaking, an ASCII file not only contains the ASCII codes for letters, spaces, punctuation and so forth, but also contains the standard ASCII codes for formatting, such as carriage-return and end-of-file.

**unsigned number**
**signed number**

When a byte is used to represent a number, the 256 different byte values can be interpreted as either all positive numbers ranging from 0 through 255, or as positive and negative numbers, ranging from -128 through 127. These are referred to as unsigned (0 to 255) or signed (-128 to 127) numbers.

**word**

To handle larger numbers, several bytes are used together as a unit, often called a word. For different computers different meanings are given to the term "word", but most often it means either two bytes (16-bits) or four bytes (32-bits). For personal computers, like the IBM/PC, a word usually means a two-byte, 16-bit, number.

A two-byte word has two to the 16th power different possible values. These can be used as unsigned numbers, with a range of 0 through 65,535, or signed numbers, with a range of -32,768 through 32,767.

**floating-point**
**single-precision**
**double-precision**
**real numbers**

Integers, or whole numbers, are not satisfactory for some tasks. When fractional numbers are needed, or a very wide range of numbers is needed, a different form of computer arithmetic is used, called floating-point. Floating point numbers involve a fractional portion, and an exponent portion, similar to the "scientific notation" used in engineering. To work with floating-point numbers, computers interpret the bits of a word in a special way. Floating point numbers generally represent approximate, inexact, values. Often more than one format of floating point numbers are available, offering different degrees of accuracy; common terms for this are single-precision and double-precision. Floating-point numbers are also sometimes called real numbers.

**zero-origin**
**base**
**origin**
**offset**

Due to the nature of computer arithmetic and notation, items are often numbered starting from zero for the first element; this is called zero-origin. Counting from zero is especially done when figuring a memory location relative to some starting point. The starting point can be called many things, including base and origin. The relative location is most often called an offset. Starting from any base location in memory, the first byte is at offset zero, and the next byte is at offset one.

## Computer fundamentals

**hardware**
**software**

All of the mechanical and electronic parts of a computer system are called hardware. The programs which a computer uses are called software.

**memory**
**storage**
**location**
**address**

The idea of a computer starts with the concept of memory or storage. A computer's memory consists of many locations, each of which has an address, and can store a value. For most computers, including the IBM/PC, each location is a byte; for others, each location is a word.

The addresses of the locations are numbers. The values stored in each location can be either discovered (read) or changed (written). When reading or writing a value, the address of the location must be given.

**page**
**paragraph**
**segment**
**displacement**
**vector**

Some computers organize their memory storage into large modular units, often called pages. The IBM/PC does not use pages, but for addressing purposes it does divide its memory into units of 16 bytes, called paragraphs (a term that was chosen to suggest a smaller division than a page). The memory addressing mechanism for the IBM/PC uses two parts—a segment value, which points to a paragraph boundary, and a relative value, which points to a byte located at some displacement, or offset, from the segment paragraph. The two values, segment and displacement, are needed to specify any complete address; together, they are sometimes called an address vector, or just vector.

**K**

Amounts of computer memory are frequently referred to in units of 1,024, because 1,024 is a round number in binary notation, and almost a round number in decimal notation. The value 1,024 is known as 'K,' for kilo; 64 K is 64 units of 1,024, or exactly 65,536.

When referring to general capacity, K almost always means 1,024 bytes. However when referring to semiconductor 'chips', K means 1,024 bits. When magazine articles refer to 16 K and 64 K chips, they mean 16 K bits (equivalent to 2 K bytes) or 64 K bits (equivalent to 8 K bytes).

**operations**
**instructions**
**commands**

A computer has the ability to perform operations on the values stored in its memory. Examples of these operations are arithmetic (addition, subtraction) and movement from location to location. A request for the computer to perform an operation is called an instruction, or command.

**program**
**code**

A series of computer instructions which together perform some work, is called a program. Programs are also called code.

**processor**
**micro-processor**

The part of the computer which interprets programs and performs the instructions is called the processor. A very small processor, particularly one which fits onto a single computer "chip," is called a microprocessor. The development of micro-processors made personal computers possible. Properly speaking, a computer is a complete working machine which includes a processor and other parts; but the processor part of a computer is sometimes also called a computer.

The memory of a computer is used to store both programs and data. To the memory there is no difference between programs and data. However to the processor, only those stored values which represent valid instructions can be a program. The processor reads and writes from its memory both to carry out a program, and to access the data that the program uses.

**registers**

To help it carry out its work, a computer may have a small amount of very specialized memory, which does not have addresses. This specialized memory is referred to as registers. Registers are used to make arithmetic more efficient, or to assist in handling addresses.

**stack**
**push**
**pop**
**LIFO**

Many modern computers, including the IBM/PC, use a push-down stack to hold status information. Data is pushed onto and popped off of the top of a stack, on a last-in-first-out (or LIFO) basis.

**bus**

When a computer uses a common data path to pass data from one part to another, this path is called a bus.

**peripherals**
**adapter**
**controller**

The memory and processor are the internal part of a computer. There are many external parts, generally called peripheral equipment, or peripherals. Most peripherals must be connected to a computer through some supporting electronic circuitry, called an adapter. For a complex peripheral, such as a diskette drive, the adapter will include some special logical circuitry called a controller. A controller is often a specialized computer in its own right.

**storage**
**diskettes**
**hard disks**

Peripherals may be of many kinds, but they fall into a few simple categories. Storage peripherals are used to hold programs and data that can be moved into the computer's internal memory. Examples of peripheral storage devices are "floppy" diskettes, cassette tape recorders, and high-capacity "hard" disks.

**terminals**
**CRT**
**display**
**monitor**
**composite**
**RGB**

Other peripheral equipment is used to communicate with people. The equipment used to communicate between people and computers are usually called terminals. A terminal most often consists of a typewriter-style keyboard, and a TV-like display screen, called a CRT (for cathode ray tube). A printer of some kind may be used instead of a CRT. A display screen is called a monitor, or simply a display. A color display may accept its color signal information in a combined form, called composite, or separated into its red, green and blue components, called RGB.

**personal computer**

Large computers may have many terminals, but small personal computers usually work with only one terminal, which may be built right into the computer system. Having only one terminal is a large part of what makes a personal computer personal.

**modem**
**asynchronous**
**communications**
**RS-232**
**baud**
**serial**
**parallel**

Other kinds of peripherals, besides storage and terminals, are printers and telephone connections. Connections between computers and telephones are referred to by the names of some of their parts, such as modems and asynchronous adapters; all of these terms, in general use, refer to the entire computer-telephone connection, which is generally called communications. The most common format for communications connections follows a design standard known as RS-232. The speed, or data rate of a communications line is measured in baud, which is bits-per-second. Three hundred baud is a common speed for personal computer communications; 300 baud is about 35 or 40 characters per second. On personal computers, an RS-232 connection is also called serial, since it transmits data one bit at a time. A parallel connection can transmit more than one bit at a time; the printer adapter on the IBM/PC is a parallel connection.

**dot-matrix**
**letter-quality**
**daisy-wheel**
**thimble**

Computer printers come in many varieties. The standard printer for the IBM/PC is a dot-matrix printer, which creates its printed results by writing a series of dots. Letter quality printers produce results comparable to good typewriters. Most letter quality printers use a print element that is either a flat disk, called a daisy-wheel, or one that is shaped like a large thimble.

**interface**

An interface is a connection between any two elements in a computer system. The term interface is used both for connections between hardware parts, and software parts, as well as the human interface.

**I/O**

Much of the equipment that can be connected to a computer is generally referred to as input/output equipment, or I/O.

**chips**
**board**
**system board**
**mother board**
**slot**

The smallest physical parts that make up a computer may be called "chips." Chips and other parts are wired together electrically, and held mechanically, on boards. If there is one principal board, it is called the system board, or mother board. Openings for the addition of more boards are called expansion slots, into which are placed memory boards, disk boards, asynch comm boards (telephone connections), and other expansion or peripheral boards.

**port**
**interrupt**
**external interrupt**
**internal interrupt**
**software interrupt**

A micro-processor interacts with its world through three means, memory accesses, interrupts and ports. Ports have a port number, or port address, and are used for passing data to or from peripheral devices. Interrupts are used to get the computer's attention. There are three kinds of interrupts (although all three are handled the same). An external interrupt is from the outside world (for example, from a diskette drive). An internal interrupt reports some exceptional logical situation (for example, division by zero). A software interrupt is a request from a program for some service to be performed; a software interrupt is an alternative to using a "call" to activate a subroutine. Memory accesses are used to read or write from the computer's memory.

**RAM**
**ROM**
**memory-mapped**

The computer's memory can be of several types. Ordinary memory, which can be read or written to, is called RAM (random access memory). Memory which contains permanent data is ROM (read only memory). Memory can be dedicated to some use, for example, to hold the data that appears on the computer's display screen. If a display screen uses the computer's memory to hold its information, then it is a memory-mapped display.

## Programs and programming languages

**program**
**subroutine**
**function**
**procedure**
**subprogram**
**routine**

Series of computer instructions are called programs. Parts of programs which are partially self-contained are called subroutines. Subroutines may be procedures if they only do some work, or functions, if they also result in a value ("open the door" is analogous to a procedure; "tell me your name" is analogous to a function). Subroutines are also called subprograms, and routines.

**parameter**
**return code**

Many subroutines use parameters to specify exactly what work is to be done; for example, a subroutine which computes a square root, needs a parameter to specify what number to use. Many subroutines will indicate how successful their operation was, through a return code.

**machine language**
**assembly language**
**macro-assembler**

Computers can only execute programs which appear in the detailed form known as machine language. However, for the convenience of people, programs may be represented in other forms. If the details of a machine language program are replaced with meaningful symbols (such as the terms ADD or MOVE), then the programming language is know as assembly language (also called assembler, symbolic assembler, or macro assembler).

**low-level**
**high-level**
**compiler**
**assembler**

Assembler is called a low-level language, because assembly programs are written in a form close to machine language. Other forms of programming languages are more abstracted, and produce many machine instructions for each command written by the programmer. These are called high-level languages; examples are BASIC, Pascal, Fortran, Cobol, PL/I, C and Forth. Programs which translate high-level language programs into a form usable by the computer, are called compilers; for low-level languages, the translators are called assemblers. There is no real difference between a compiler and an assembler—they both translate from a human programming language to a form of machine language.

**source code**
**object code**
**link editor**
**load module**

When a person writes a computer program, the form it takes is called source code, or source. When the source code is translated (by an assembler or compiler), the result is often called object code. Object code is nearly ready to be used, but it has to undergo a minor transformation, performed by a link editor, or linker, to produce a load module—which is a finished, ready-to-use program.

**bug**
**debug**

An error in a program is called a bug, and the processing of trying to find errors, or trying to fix them, is called debugging.

**algorithm**

There are usually many ways to accomplish an objective with a computer program. The scheme, formula, or method that a program uses, is its algorithm. For many tasks—even as simple a one as sorting data into alphabetic order—there are dramatic differences in the efficiency of different algorithms, and the search continues for better and better methods.

variable
type
string
file

A program works with symbolic entities call variables. In effect a variable is the name of a place that can hold data of some type. Specific data can be moved into and out of a variable, and the purpose of the variable is to provide a mechanism for manipulating data. Variables usually have a fixed type, which indicates what sort of data it can accommodate; for example, integer type, single and double precision floating point, and string (a collection of text characters). In a program, a file is just a special kind of variable, one which can be connected to a diskette file or some device, such as the display screen.

## Human roles

On a personal computer, one person may do everything that is to be done. However, in traditional large computer systems, there is a division of labor, separating human involvement with a computer into various roles. Users of personal computers may wonder about the meaning of various job titles used.

user

The user, or end-user, is the person for whom computer work is done.

analyst

The systems analyst, or analyst, determines the details of the work that the end user needs done, and decides on the general strategy of how a computer will perform the work.

programmer

The programmer converts the analyst's general strategy into the detailed tactics and methods to be used. This usually includes writing (and testing) the actual program. However, actually writing and testing the program is sometimes left to a coder.

coder

The coder turns the programmer's detailed methods into the program instructions.

operator

The operator runs the program on the computer, to produce the results needed by the user.

## Data organization

**file**
**record**
**field**

Data is organized and viewed differently, depending upon who or what is looking at it. To the computer itself, data consists of just bits and bytes. To programmers who manipulate data, there are some traditional logical boundaries for data. A complete collection of related data is a file (as an example, a mailing list file). One complete unit of the information that is in a file, is called a record; in a mailing list file, all of the information connected with one address would be a record. Finally, within a record are fields, the information of one type; for example, the zip-code would be one field, in an address record, in a mailing list file.

**logical record**
**physical record**

The records that a program reads or writes, are logical records. Logical records are placed in the storage medium's physical records—which are the pieces actually read or written to a diskette. A program sees logical records, while the operating system performs any translating necessary between logical and physical records. On a diskette, a physical record is called a sector.

**data base**
**data base manager**

The terms data base and data base manager are used, and abused, so widely, that they have no precise meaning. When data is large, complex, and spread across several files, it might be called a data base. A data base manager is a program—usually large and complex in itself —which can control and organize a data base. Full scale data base management is far beyond the capabilities of a personal computer.

# Diskette vocabulary

**sector**
**track**
**cylinder**
**seeking**

Data on a diskette is stored on sectors, which can be individually read or written; on the IBM/PC, a sector holds 512 bytes. Sectors are the diskette's physical records—the units that are actually read or written. A track is the collection of sectors that will fit into one circle on a diskette; for the IBM/PC, there are eight sectors in a track. If there is more than one surface on a disk or diskette drive, then a cylinder is all of the tracks that are the same distance from the center. Sectors that are in the same cylinder can be read without moving the disk drive's read-write mechanism. Moving the read-write heads from one track/cylinder to another is called seeking, and it is relatively slow. On the IBM/PC, there are forty tracks on each surface of a diskette (so that a double-sided diskette has eighty tracks of eight sectors each).

**directory**
**VTOC**
**FAT**
**file allocation**
**boot record**

A diskette needs a table of contents for its files, called a directory on the IBM/PC. On some other systems, a directory is called a VTOC (Volume Table Of Contents). Some means must be used to keep track of used and unused space on a diskette, and on the IBM/PC it is done with the FAT (File Allocation Table). The first sector of each diskette is dedicated to holding the first part of the operating system's start-up program, called the boot-strap loader, or boot record. So, on each diskette there are four kinds of sectors—boot record, FAT, directory, and data space (where files are stored).

**floppy**
**flippy**
**hard disk**
**Winchester**

A diskette is flexible, thus it is called a floppy. A diskette which can be turned over, to use the other side is a flippy. (Double sided diskettes are not turned over.) A hard disk has a rigid platter in place of the flexible plastic of a floppy; the rigid shape allows more precise data recording, and thus higher density and more capacity. The sort of hard disks installed on personal computers today use a collection of methods called Winchester technology, so they are also called Winchester disks.

## Operating systems

**operating system**

An operating system is a program which supervises and controls the operation of a computer. Operating systems are complex and consist of many parts.

**BIOS**
**driver**
**device handler**

One element of an operating system is its BIOS, or Basic Input-Output System. The BIOS is responsible for handling the details of input-output operations, including the task of relating a program's logical records to a peripheral device's physical records. At the most detailed level, the BIOS contains routines tailored to the specific requirements of each peripheral device; these routines are called drivers, or device handlers.

**logical I/O**
**physical I/O**
**services**

Usually an operating system is organized into a hierarchy of levels of services. At the lowest level, the device handlers insulate the rest of the operating system from the details of each device. At the next level, relating logical data to physical data is performed. At a higher level basic services are provided—such as accepting output data from a program to be placed into a file.

**loader**
**relocation**
**error handler**

Besides device and data handling, an operating system must supervise programs, including loading them, relocating them (adjusting their internal addresses to correspond to their exact location in a memory), and recovering from any program errors, through an error handler.

**command processor**

Another element of an operating system is the command processor, which accepts and acts on commands given by the computer's user. Commands usually amount to a request for the execution of some service program.

Boundaries are usually drawn in operating systems, isolating the parts which are specific to peripheral devices, and the parts which are specific to a particular computer. Depending upon which level of services is used, for example, a program may work on any computer, any computer which uses the MS-DOS operating system, only on the IBM/PC using MS-DOS, or only the IBM/PC with MS-DOS and the monochrome display.

# Appendix 2:
# A brief tutorial on Pascal

If you are completely new to Pascal, here's a brief introduction for you. Don't expect a full tutorial—you'll find that in any of the many beginner's books on Pascal. Here I'll give you enough of a taste so that you can read and understand Pascal programs, and know what Pascal's virtues are, which can help you decide whether you want to make use of Pascal.

There are reasons for using Pascal for programming the IBM/PC beyond any advantages that it may have as a language. Any serious programming effort needs to make use of a modern, structured language. There is no excuse for the personal computer world repeating the mistake of the traditional large computer world, the mistake of using languages like Fortran and Cobol which make it difficult to produce reliable, maintainable programs. By those standards—reliability and maintainability—BASIC is worse than Fortran, and much worse than Cobol. For computers like the IBM/PC, there are only two realistic choices of language—Pascal and C. For the IBM/PC, Pascal is the natural choice, because both IBM and Microsoft support its use as a system development language. Since Microsoft is producing the DOS operating system, we can expect that their Pascal compiler will advance in parallel with advances in DOS and its successors.

So, let's take a look at Pascal. In all the examples we show here, Pascal keywords will be shown in capital letters. This should make it easier for you to recognize what's fundamentally Pascal, and what is just our examples. We'll be talking about the IBM/PC version of Pascal, which has many useful enrichments over ordinary standard Pascal.

Pascal programs start with an outline like this:

```
PROGRAM sample_program;
  BEGIN
  END.
```

Between the BEGIN and the END, we put our program logic. (Many important and interesting things fit between the PROGRAM name and the BEGIN—we'll come to that later.)

Pascal has a full complement of program logic features. First, the usual IF statement, used to execute part of the program, based on a true or false condition:

```
IF some_true_or_false_condition THEN
    execute_some_statement
ELSE
    execute_some_other_statement;
```

Naturally the ELSE is optional; if you don't need it, you don't use it.

Then, there are three different looping statements, used to repeatedly execute part of a program. One is the usual loop-with-a-count (which in BASIC is done with a FOR, in Fortran a DO, and in Cobol a PERFORM VARYING):

```
FOR i := 1 to 25 DO
    some_statement;
```

The other two loops continue until some logical condition is met; the difference between the two is that one tests the condition before looping (and thus may never execute its loop), and the other tests after looping (so it always executes at least once). Here they are:

```
WHILE some_condition_is_true DO          REPEAT
    some_statement;                          any_statements
                                         UNTIL some_ending_condition;
```

Notice the reversal of the condition—in a WHILE, the condition must be TRUE to continue; in a REPEAT-UNTIL, the condition must be FALSE to continue.

There's one more logic statement, called CASE, a generalization of the IF statement. While the IF selects between a TRUE or FALSE value on the condition, the CASE statement can select among many possible values. For our example, we'll assume that we are selecting a letter of the alphabet.

```
CASE letter_variable OF
    'A'           :  statement_for_case_a;
    'B'           :  statement_for_case_b;
    'C'..'G'      :  statement_for_cases_c_through_g;
    OTHERWISE        statement_when_the_variable_is_anything_else;
END;
```

One major virtue of Pascal is the completeness of its control logic statements. This is part of what makes good structured programming practical, and leads towards reliable, maintainable programs.

Often in your programs, you need to group several statements together—for example, under the control of an IF statement. Anywhere one statement can appear, a group of statements can appear, enclosed in a pair of BEGIN-END. Notice that in a series of statements, semicolons separate the statements.

For example—

```
IF some_condition THEN
```

```
BEGIN
    one_statement;
    another_statement;
    the_last_statement
END;
```

Notice one inconsistency in the way Pascal's logic statements are formatted. The IF statement, the FOR, the WHILE, and the various cases of the CASE statement, each need a BEGIN-END to control more than one statement. But the form of the REPEAT-UNTIL statement acts as its own enclosing format, and so can contain any series of statements without using a BEGIN-END pair.

There are two different kinds of subroutines, and Pascal provides them both. PROCEDUREs that simply do something, and FUNCTIONs which return a value (as trigonometric function returns a number value). Subroutine declarations are part of what appears between a PROGRAM name and its BEGIN statement, and they are structured very much like a PROGRAM. Here are some typical subroutines:

```
PROCEDURE some_procedure;
    BEGIN
        some_statements
    END;

FUNCTION some_function : type_of_value_the_function_returns;
    BEGIN
        some_statements;
        { including assigning some value to the function name: }
        some_function := some_value
    END;
```

Notice two things we've snuck in above—comments can appear anywhere, and are enclosed in braces {}. They can also be enclosed like this:

```
(* comment *)
```

Also, the assignment symbol is not the equal sign used by BASIC, Fortran, and PL/I. Instead it is a colon-equal combination ( ":=" ).

To execute a subroutine, you simply use its name—there is no "CALL" keyword needed. So we could execute the two subroutines defined above, like this:

```
IF some_function = some_value THEN
    some_procedure;
```

The working part of a subroutine, the part that appears inside its BEGIN-END, doesn't have to be present in your program—it might be provided elsewhere, in a separate Pascal routine, or in assembly language. When that's the case, the subroutine is still declared, but its body (BEGIN-END) is replaced with the word EXTERNAL:

```
PROCEDURE solve_all_my_problems;
    EXTERNAL;
```

Next, let's cover variables and value types. Unlike BASIC and Fortran, Pascal requires that every variable be declared. This may seem like a nuisance, but actually it is very beneficial to you, because it eliminates a major problem with BASIC—a typographic error becoming a separate orphan variable. Since every variable is declared, if clumsy fingers mis-key a variable name, the Pascal compiler will complain about an undeclared variable—and catch your mistake.

Variables must be of some "type"—a number, a string of characters, or whatever. Types are one of the innovative features of Pascal. Pascal has some very nice types built into it, and you can add your own types endlessly. What is available in Pascal types?

First, there are numeric types, for arithmetic. There is REAL (that is, floating point, corresponding to BASIC's single-precision type). Then there are four types of integers, with different sizes and ranges of values that they can accommodate:

| Type name | Range of values | Number of bytes |
|---|---|---|
| INTEGER | -32768 to +32767 | 2 |
| WORD | 0 to +65535 | 2 |
| SINT | -128 to +127 | 1 |
| BYTE | 0 to +255 | 1 |

(All of these numeric values are taken from the first release of the IBM Pascal compiler. The second release should include major enrichment, including double-precision REAL and four-byte integers).

For logical conditions (as used in the IF statement), there is the BOOLEAN type, consisting of FALSE and TRUE. The BOOLEAN type is the first instance of a remarkable innovation—the enumeration data type. Very often in programs we need to code a series of values; for example, marital status values of single, married, divorce. In traditional programming languages, you would have to assign some arbitrary coded values to the cases (say, single = 1, married = 2, and so forth), and then keep track of the codes. With an enumeration data type, you can define a new type (calling it, for example, "marital_status"), and give meaningful names to its values ("single", "married", and so forth). Then you can use those meaningful names in your program, and not have to keep track of any arbitrary codes.

There is another very interesting data type in Pascal, which can make some of your programming both simpler and clearer: the set data type. A set is a list of values (such as numbers, or letters of the alphabet). As an example of the usefulness of sets, consider this example. Suppose we had a character variable, "c", and we wanted to check if it was a vowel. Without sets, the programming task would be rather laborious:

IF (c = 'a') OR (c = 'e') OR (c = 'i') ... and on and on ...

With sets, we could test quickly and cleanly:

```
IF c IN ['a', 'e', 'i', 'o', 'u'] THEN
```

Here, then, is what some type and variable declarations look like:

```
TYPE
   marital_status_type    =    (single,married,divorced,widowed);
   honorific_type         =    (Miss,Mrs,Ms,Mr,Dr,Prof,Rev);

VAR
   i                 :   INTEGER;
   x                 :   REAL;
   error_found       :   BOOLEAN; {which is (FALSE,TRUE); }
   marital_status    :   marital_status_type;
   honorific         :   honorific_type;
```

There are more pre-defined types that you should know about. For handling ASCII characters, there is the type CHAR, which holds a single character. If you want to convert between numeric types and characters, similar to the BASIC CHR$ operation, you do things like this:

```
i := ORD (c);     { convert character to integer }
c := CHR (i);     { convert integer to character }

IF 'A' = CHR (65) THEN
   { indeed ASCII code 65 is a capital A }
```

There are string types in Pascal, used to hold a series of characters—both fixed length (STRING) and variable length (LSTRING). Here's a quick sample of what you can do with variable length strings, and how to do it:

```
VAR
   xxx : LSTRING (20); { xxx can be up to 20 characters long }

xxx := 'blaise pascal'; { we set it to some length and value }

xxx [1] := 'B'; { We change two of the individual characters }
xxx [8] := 'P'; { in the string. }

IF xxx.LEN < 20 THEN { if the current length of the string is under 20}
   BEGIN
      xxx.LEN := xxx.LEN + 1; { lengthen the string by 1 }
      xxx [xxx.LEN] := '?'; { and set the new end character to "?" }
   END;
```

Pascal naturally has arrays, the same thing that BASIC creates with the DIM statement, which are declared and used like this:

```
VAR
   a :    ARRAY [1..100] OF REAL;
   b :    ARRAY [101..200] OF REAL;

FOR i := 1 to 100 DO
   b [i+100] := a [i] * 3.14159;
```

Unlike BASIC, Pascal lets you set the lower bound of an array, which is very handy at times. For example, if you were keeping track of annual information, you could declare an array like this:

```
VAR
   gross_income : ARRAY [1945..1990] OF REAL;
```

From the common use of brackets [ ], you may have guessed that STRINGs and LSTRINGs are actually ARRAYs of CHAR with some special features thrown in.

Pascal allows you to define a co-ordinated group of data, called a RECORD. RECORDS are the same thing as structures in Cobol and PL/I. For example:

```
TYPE
  complete_name_record_type =
    RECORD
      honorific  : honorific_type;
      first      : LSTRING (20);
      middle     : LSTRING (1);
      last       : LSTRING (20);
      suffix     : LSTRING (4);
    END;

VAR
  name : complete_name_record_type;

name.honorific   := Mr;
name.first       := 'Blaise';
name.middle      := null; { that's nothing—a string of length zero}
name.last        := 'Pascal';
name.suffix      := 'Jr';
```

The main purpose of RECORD types is to allow you to move all of that data around quickly and easily, like this:

```
IF name = name_searching_for THEN
  temp—name := name;
```

One safety virtue of Pascal is strict typing. Just because WORD and INTEGER are both whole numbers, you can't freely mix them together—they are different types, and must be kept separate. If you need to mix types (and sometimes you do), there are explicit ways to do it. The philosophy here is to avoid errors by forbidding mixing types—unless you say, in effect, I know what I'm doing, this isn't a mistake.

Another of the ways that Pascal adds safety to programming, is by introducing sub-ranges. In the array example above, we used "i" as the index to the array "a." The only legal values for "i" should be from 1 through 100. If we declared "i" to be an INTEGER, though, then "i" could be set to any value from -32768 to +32767. Instead, we could declare "i" to be a sub-range, like this:

```
VAR
  i : (1..100);
```

Then, if we have automatic error checking active, assigning any value to "i" outside this range will be caught. This kind of feature may seem insignificant in small simple programs, but it becomes very important when programs become large and complex.

When variables are declared, you can specify an initial value for them. It is done this way:

```
VAR
```

```
  year : INTEGER;
VALUE
  year := 1776;
```

It is a good practice to replace constant values in programs with variable names. This does two nice things—it allows a meaningful name to replace a number and centralizes the appearance of the value to one place (very handy when constants need changing). Unfortunately, variables can be modified by a mistake in the program—making what you intend to be a constant into a true variable. Pascal solves this reliability problem by letting you define "named constants." Named constants work just like variables, except that they can't be changed while the program is running. Constants are declared like this:

```
CONST
  pi = 3.1459;
  norman_invasion = 1066;
  atomic_age = 1945;
```

Putting all these pieces together, we can show you the skeleton of a complete Pascal program. Besides illustrating all the parts of a normal Pascal program, it also shows how clear Pascal programs can be, compared to BASIC.

```
PROGRAM horse_race;
TYPE
  position = (nowhere, show, place, win);

VAR
  finish : position;
  kitty : REAL;
  bet : REAL;
  meet_over : BOOLEAN;

VALUE
  kitty := 100.00;
  bet := 50.00;

CONST
  bus_fare = 0.75;

FUNCTION odds : REAL;
  EXTERNAL;

PROCEDURE place_bet;
  BEGIN
    IF odds > 0.5 THEN
      bet := kitty / 2
    ELSE
      bet := kitty / 10;
    kitty := kitty - bet;
  END;

PROCEDURE run_race;
  EXTERNAL;

PROCEDURE collect_winnings;
  BEGIN
    kitty := kitty + bet / odds;
```

```
    END;
BEGIN
  REPEAT
    place_bet;
    run_race;
    IF finish ' nowhere THEN
      collect_winnings;
  UNTIL meet_over OR (kitty " bus_fare);
END.
```

There is much more to know about Pascal, needless to say. We'll briefly cover one more topic, files, and then call it quits.

Like any other language, Pascal needs to do input and output, and it is done with files. Files are declared like this:

```
VAR
  real_file        : FILE OF REAL;
  people_file      : FILE OF complete_name_record_type;
  character_file   : FILE OF CHAR;
  ascii_file       : TEXT;
```

Generally a FILE OF something reads and writes individual units of the something. If it's a file of a record type (like the people file above), then it reads and writes complete records. The special file declaration TEXT is used to manipulate the common ASCII files found on the IBM/PC. A TEXT file is similar to a FILE OF CHAR, but it recognizes the organization of characters into lines, so that complete lines can be read or written. A Pascal text file is the same thing as an ASCII text file, discussed in chapter 5.

Two TEXT files are automatically available in Pascal; one, named INPUT, is for reading from the keyboard. The other, named OUTPUT, is for writing to the display screen.

Files can be read and written sequentially or by random access, when they are disk files.

As with most programming languages, files can be opened, closed, read, written, and processed sequentially or randomly. File declarations inside a Pascal program can be dynamically redirected to different diskette files, either when the program is invoked, or inside the logic of the program.

This hasn't been an exhaustive treatment of Pascal, but it should be enough to get you started, and to give you the ability to read and understand the programming examples used in this book.

# Appendix 3:
# The Pascal / Assembly
# Language Connection

If you do sophisticated programming on the IBM/PC, using Pascal, it's likely that you will need to make use of some assembly-language support. Here we will show you the fundamentals of how it is done. In the diskette package which accompanies this book you will find many examples of how it is done, and you will also find there ready-to-use assembly object modules. These object modules are there so that it will not be necessary for you to use the assembler yourself to gain access to the full power of the IBM/PC.

It's likely that you will want to customize the assembly routines that I have provided, to tailor them to you particular needs. And you may want to add to them. Or, you may just want to understand the basic ideas of how the connection is made between Pascal (and other high-level languages) and assembler routines. The purpose of this section is to show you how it is done.

To explain all of this fully would nearly take a book in itself, so we'll cover the most straight-forward situations only. What we show here is enough to allow you to accomplish anything that you need to do. When you put any of these methods into practice, you should experiment and explore to make sure that things are happening the way you expect them to be. Some very innocent appearing changes can radically alter the results you get.

Let's start with the Pascal end, and see what goes on there.

## A3.1 The Pascal side of the border

First, to be able to use an assembly language routine, it must be declared in Pascal terms, with the EXTERNAL directive, indicating that the routine's working code lies elsewhere:

```
PROCEDURE assembly_routine;
  EXTERNAL;
```

235

The assembly routine may need parameters, and it may be a function, which returns a value. Any of these characteristics will have to be included in the declaration of the routine.

There is a simple DOS convention for how a value is returned from a function, for values of one or two bytes, and Pascal follows this convention. Single byte values are returned in the AL register, and two-byte values are returned in the full AX register. Pascal automatically picks the values up from these registers, a very efficient operation. (While writing Pascal code, you don't need to know about AL and AX—that's out of your hands. But when it comes to your assembly language code, it's another matter.) So it is reasonable for you to declare your assembly routines as FUNCTIONs, provided that the value being returned is a one or two byte number (in Pascal terms, BYTE, SINT, WORD, or INTEGER).

However, longer or more complex returned values (such as strings and records), are passed back by a much more intricate mechanism. If you need to return anything other than a one or two byte number, I suggest that you pass back the value through the parameter list (explained below), since that method is much simpler.

Passing parameters between a subroutine and its caller is accomplished through the micro-processor's stack. There are several variations on how this is done. It is important that you understand them, for this is the most common area of difficulty in connecting Pascal, or other languages, and assembly language.

From the point of view of the Pascal language, there are two main ways to pass a parameter, with or without the VAR option:

PROCEDURE subroutine (parm1 : WORD; VAR parm2 : WORD);

With VAR, the called subroutine is being given permission to modify the variable that is being passed—so, one way or another, the subroutine must be given the memory address of the variables location. On the other hand, without VAR, the subroutine is forbidden to change the variable, and to protect the variable, the subroutine must only be given access to a copy of the original variable.

All of this has great impact upon what happens in the stack, upon how the assembly language routine must operate, and, incidentally, upon the efficiency of the Pascal code. So it is important that you understand very accurately how this all works.

When the VAR option is used, the subroutine needs the address of the variable—so it is the memory address of the variable that is placed on the stack during the calling sequence. Since there are two kinds of addresses (single-word offset addresses, and double-word segmented addresses), there are two variations on the VAR option. VAR passes a single-word relative address, and VARS passes a double-word segmented address. (The CONST option is simply a variation on VAR, and passes a relative address.)

When VAR is not used, then the subroutine must be given a copy of the value to be passed. When this is done, there are two very different things that can happen which have nothing to do with the Pascal language—they have to do with practical matters in the computer. If the value being passed is sufficiently small and simple, the value itself is pushed onto the stack— which is very efficient for both the caller and the called routine. But if the value is not simple, then a copy of it is made in memory and the address of the copy is pushed onto the stack. A copy needs to be made, for fear that the subroutine might try to change the value—heaven forbid. This is quite inefficient from the points of view of both caller and called. Both of these two ways of protecting a variable from being changed by a subroutine accomplish the same end, but they have very different effects on efficiency, and on how the called assembly language routine must be written to access the values.

Just for the sake of efficiency, it is valuable to always use the VAR option for parameters that aren't short and simple, and generally good not to use VAR for simple parameters. I don't know just what rules the compiler uses to decide whether a parameter is simple enough to push onto the stack. I think that only one and two byte numbers, and one and two word addresses are the only values considered simple enough. If you need to know more exactly, then you can find out by compiling an example, and inspecting the compiler's object code listing (which usually is the best way to find out about the efficiency of your Pascal code).

To recap: to let an assembly language routine get addressing access to your variables (for example, to pass back a long or complex value), use the VAR and VARS options—this is necessary. If the assembly language routine only needs to access parameter values, then VAR can be used, or not. For efficiency, don't use VAR for simple variables, but do use it for complex ones—this is advisable, but not necessary.

Any assembly-language routine must know exactly what its caller places on the stack, and in what order. You can deduce what is placed on the stack from the principles explained above. But the best way to actually find out, and be sure, is to inspect the Pascal compiler's object code listing. It will show exactly what is done with the stack.

The method that I recommend is this: First, declare the subroutine parameters in Pascal the way that you think is best. Then compile a sample program that calls the subroutine, and inspect the object code listing. If the stack manipulation is what you expected (or, anyway, is in a form you can work with) then proceed to tailor your assembly routine to the stack as Pascal sets it up. If the stack manipulation isn't workable for you, then tinker with the declaration of the subroutine in Pascal, until it is workable.

To help you, here is a step by step example of what goes on with the stack during a call from Pascal. We'll take our example right out of the pages of the Pascal manual (first edition, page 10-23, if you care to follow along), since that very example has instructed so many people, and confused so many others.

The subroutine declaration is:

FUNCTION uaddok (a, b : WORD; VAR c : WORD) BOOLEAN;
  EXTERNAL;

When Pascal calls this routine, here is what it does. First the parameters are pushed onto the stack, in the order declared. Variable "a" is not VAR, and it's simple—so its two-byte value is pushed right onto the stack. The same happens with variable "b". Variable "c" is declared VAR, so its offset address is pushed onto the stack. The stack now holds six bytes connected with this call. Then the routine is called, and the calling process pushes the return address onto the stack; since this is an external routine, the call is "far," and the return address is a full double-word segmented address, consisting of the CS segment register value, and the IP instruction pointer (updated to point past the call instruction). So at the point of entry to the subroutine, there are ten bytes loaded on the stack for this call—six bytes for the parameters, and four bytes for the return address. We'll see how these stack contents can be used by an assembly language routine, after we've covered an introduction to assembly language.

## A3.2 The Assembly language side of the border (May I see your passport, please?)

Obviously, you aren't going to be able to do any assembly language coding for the IBM/PC if you can't handle assembly language. However, there seem to be quite a few people who have done assembly language programming on other computers—so that they generally know how to handle assembly language— and get really stuck on some of the peculiarities of 8086 assembly language.

So, to help you get started, here are some very elementary assembler fundamentals, showing you how to wade through some of the peculiarities of the 8086. Don't expect this to be complete—it's just the minimum needed to get started.

Here's the minimum we need for a routine that does nothing but return to its caller:

```
tests   segment   'code'   ; the segment is named "tests"
                           ; "code" is a classification you can ignore

        public    test     ; our subroutine is named "test"- making it
                           ; public gives the world access to it, by name

test    proc      far      ; declaring our routine, a procedure named "test"
                           ; the attribute "far" is very important

; so far everything has been declarative overhead—no executable
; code at all. The next line begins (and ends) our code.

        ret                ; a return instruction. Since the proc was
                           ; declared "far" this is a far return- it pops
                           ; both a CS and an IP off of the stack

; now we complete the overhead, ending everything in sight.
```

```
test    endp            ; end the procedure

tests   ends            ; end the segment

        end             ; end the assembly
```

There is one additional bit of overhead that you will need if you have any labels and branching instructions. The assembler will require an "assume" statement to tell it what is loaded in the code segment register, CS. This is needed, even if all of your addressing is in the short relative form, which pays no attention to the CS register; apparently it's a little too tricky to expect the assembler to tell when it does and doesn't need to know the CS contents. So if you have any labels for jump commands, add something like this to your routine:

```
assume cs:test
```

(If all of your jumps are in the short relative form—which is common for simple routines, including all of the assembler examples in this book and the accompanying diskette package—you can get away with any "assume cs:"; but if the assembler uses your assumption to produce a true relative address, then you had better declare the real value that will be in CS.)

The next thing we need to provide is some programming conventions, which don't have any obvious function. They are needed, in general, to support stack control, through a mechanism known as a frame pointer. For a full explanation of the why and wherefore of this, you should consult a good guide to 8086 assembly language programming. Your assembler routines may be able to get along without them, but it is probably better to include them in all of your assembly language routines. Here they are, three instructions—a PUSH and MOV at the beginning, and a POP at the end:

```
test    proc    far

        push    bp      ; save the old frame pointer on the stack
                        ; this in effect completes the calling sequence

        mov     bp,sp   ; establish a new frame pointer—the stack
                        ; pointer after the call sequence is complete

; at this point the working part of your assembler routine will appear
; the frame pointer can be used to access the parameters on the stack
; regardless of what else is now pushed onto the stack

        pop     bp      ; before returning, pop the old frame pointer

        ret
test    endp
```

There are actually two reasons for doing this. One, as mentioned, is to keep a frame pointer. The other is to be able to address the contents of the stack. While the SP stack-pointer register points to the current location on the stack, you cannot use the SP as an addressing register to access the stack. You must load the SP value into some other register which can be used for addressing. And what better register than the BP base-pointer register?

There are two more essential things that you need to know about setting up assembly language routines, and this is as good a place as any to cover them. The first is the notation for direct and indirect values. When we refer to a register with its simple name, like the instruction above "mov bp,sp", then we mean the direct contents of the register. So, "mov bp, sp" takes the value stored in the SP register, and moves that value into the BP register. But if BP had been in brackets, like this "[bp]", that means use the contents of BP to specify an address in memory. So, "mov [bp],sp" would mean take the value stored in the SP register (no difference so far), and move it, not into BP, but into the memory location that BP points to. You will find the bracket notation [] used in the examples below, and in the example on page 10-23 of the Pascal manual.

The second thing we need to cover is stack control when returning from a subroutine. When a subroutine finishes, and returns to its caller, it is responsible for cleaning up the stack. First, it must undo anything that it has pushed onto the stack itself. That could be accomplished either by popping anything that was pushed, or by a simpler expedient—moving the frame pointer, which ought to be sitting in the BP register, into the stack pointer, SP, thereby automatically popping any garbage off of the stack.

While cleaning your own use of the stack is important, there is another essential part of cleaning up the stack—removing the subroutine calling sequence from the stack. In calling a subroutine, two things are put on the stack—parameters, and the return address. The return instruction, ret, takes care of popping the return address off—but you must also specify how many bytes of parameter were placed on the stack, so that the return instruction can also pop them off. This means that your subroutine must know exactly how many bytes of parameter were placed on the stack. In the example above, the subroutine named "test" does a simple RET instruction—taking no parameters off the stack. But the subroutine uaddok, given on page 10-23 of the Pascal manual, had six bytes of parameter (three two-byte parameters), and so it ends with a "ret 6" instruction. The "6" is necessary to clean those parameters away. So if you are coding any assembly language routines from our skeleton example, be sure to add the length of the parameters on the the final RET of the subroutine.

With that out of the way, how does our assembler routine gain access to the parameters on the stack? Since the BP register, as frame pointer, points to the stack with the parameters, the stack parameters can be accessed using addresses relative to BP. Since the stack runs backwards (from high addresses to low), accessing the parameters that were placed on the stack before the frame pointer, in the BP register, will be done with positive relative displacements. With a "backwards" stack, negative displacements move ahead on the stack, and positive displacements look back.

To diagram this, here is a table of the stack contents, for the example above, of the uaddok function:

| Relative offset from BP pointer | Significance of the contents of the stack |
|---|---|
| 0 - 1 | the old frame pointer, pushed from BP |
| 2 - 3 | return address, segment part (CS register) |
| 4 - 5 | return address, offset part (IP register) |
| 6 - 7 | last parm pushed: address of variable "c" |
| 8 - 9 | previous parm: value of variable "b" |
| 10 -11 | first parm: value of variable "a" |

With these stack contents, a reference to [bp + 10] gets the value of "a", while a reference to [bp + 6] will yield the address of "c". So the value of "a" can be loaded into a working register to do arithmetic on it, as with the instruction:

mov ax,[bp + 10]

We can move the address of "c" into an addressing register, like this:

mov bp,[bp + 6]

That lets us then use that address to change the value of "c" back in the calling program, like this:

mov [bp],ax

There is one additional thing that you need to know about the use of the stack in passing parameters. All push and pop operations onto and off of the stack work two bytes at a time. If a one byte parameter value is pushed onto the stack, then two bytes are placed there—the first byte, located at an even offset from the SP or BP register, will the be actual value, and the second, at an odd offset, will be some filler value. If you are coding an assembly language routine which takes one-byte parameters, you need to take this into account when figuring stack offsets, and so forth.

This should give you all of the basics that you need to get started in assembly language coding on the IBM/PC, and also what you need to know to effectively make the connection between Pascal code, and assembly code.

# Appendix 4:
# Some Odd Characters

There are few areas of more confusion than the meaning and use of the first 32 ASCII characters, CHR$(0) through CHR$(31). These characters have traditionally been used and interpreted in a hodge-podge of ways. In the original ASCII definition of these characters, some are used for printing control, like skipping to a new page, some are used for communications control, and some are intended to be used as needed.

Different printing devices interpret these codes in different ways. There is little consistency in the way that special control signals are defined and used.

On top of all of the existing confusion, IBM added a small measure to the confused use of these codes, by giving them character shapes for use on the IBM/PC's display screen—some of them very useful shapes.

If you have looked up these ASCII codes in various computer manuals, or tried to make use of them in your programs, you may have become quite confused about them. In this appendix, we'll try to clarify things a bit.

This is not a definitive treatment of these ASCII codes—possibly one can never be written. What we will do here is explain some of the most useful things to know about these characters as they apply to the IBM/PC. For each character, we'll give the standard ASCII name for the character—a two or three letter abbreviation—and the customary ASCII meaning or use for the character.

Next we'll describe the shape as it appears on the IBM/PC's display screen. When you can get the character on the screen, this is how it will appear. The BASIC program given in listing 1.1 will demonstrate the actual appearance of all these characters.

When your programs try to write these characters to the display screen, various things can happen besides showing the character shape on the screen. In the table below, we show what happens when you write these 32 characters in either BASIC or Pascal; there are some surprising inconsistencies in what happens. The only way to display all 256 different characters is by direct memory usage, as with the POKE in listing 1.1, or the Pascal methods in listing 8.3.

To complete the listing below, we give the effect of sending these characters to the standard printer for the IBM/PC, the Epson MX-80 matrix printer. This doesn't show all of the control codes used by the MX-80—that is subject enough for a small book by itself—but just the main uses of CHR$(0) through CHR$(31).

Since some of these codes are for printer control, this is a good place to explain one important difference among printers. Some printers, like the MX-80, have a line buffer which accumulates characters to be printed, and then prints an entire line at a time. Other printers, without buffers, must print characters immediately as they are received.

In a buffered printer, like the MX-80, the backspace code automatically rubs-out the previous character, keeping it from printing. With an unbuffered printer, backspace can be used to over print characters, but not to erase them. Subtle differences between printers like this can produce very different results.

Here, then, are the odd character codes:


0—numeric code
    ASCII code name: NUL; null character, which should be ignored; as you'll see below, it is sometimes treated as a space character; also, see the special discussion of this character and the keyboard, in chapter 10.
    Shape shown on screen:    blank, like the space character
    When written by BASIC:    above shape appears (instead of NUL operation)
    When written by Pascal:    above shape appears (instead of NUL operation)
    Use by Epson MX-80:    no special use
  1—numeric code
    ASCII code name: SOH; start of header (used for communications)
    Shape shown on screen:    happy face
    When written by BASIC:    above shape appears
    When written by Pascal:    above shape appears
    Use by Epson MX-80:    no special use
  2—numeric code
    ASCII code name: STX; start of text (used for communications)
    Shape shown on screen:    reverse happy face
    When written by BASIC:    above shape appears
    When written by Pascal:    above shape appears
    Use by Epson MX-80:    no special use
  3—numeric code
    ASCII code name: ETX; end of text (used for communications)
    Shape shown on screen:    hearts card suit
    When written by BASIC:    above shape appears
    When written by Pascal:    above shape appears
    Use by Epson MX-80:    no special use
  4—numeric code
    ASCII code name: EOT; end of transmission (used for communications)
    Shape shown on screen:    diamonds card suit

When written by BASIC:    above shape appears
When written by Pascal:    above shape appears
Use by Epson MX-80:    no special use

5—numeric code
  ASCII code name: ENQ (used for communications)
  Shape shown on screen:    clubs card suit
  When written by BASIC:    above shape appears
  When written by Pascal:    above shape appears
  Use by Epson MX-80:    no special use

6—numeric code
  ASCII code name: ACK; acknowledge transmission (used for communications)
  Shape shown on screen:    spades card suit
  When written by BASIC:    above shape appears
  When written by Pascal:    above shape appears
  Use by Epson MX-80:    no special use

7—numeric code
  ASCII code name: BEL; audible sound, bell or buzzer
  Shape shown on screen:    small solid circle
  When written by BASIC:    buzzer sounds
  When written by Pascal:    buzzer sounds
  Use by Epson MX-80:    buzzer sounds

8—numeric code
  ASCII code name: BS; backspace (see notes above)
  Shape shown on screen:    reverse small solid circle
  When written by BASIC:    above shape appears, rather than backspacing
  When written by Pascal:    back spaces on display, without rubbing out
  Use by Epson MX-80:    no special use

9—numeric code
  ASCII code name: HT; horizontal tab
  Shape shown on screen:    circle
  When written by BASIC:    skips to the next tab position
  When written by Pascal:    skips to the next tab position
  Use by Epson MX-80:    no special use

10—numeric code
  ASCII code name: LF line feed, e.g. move paper up one line
  Shape shown on screen:    reverse circle
  When written by BASIC:    skip to beginning of next line (as if CR + LF)
  When written by Pascal:    true line-feed: cursor stays on the same column
  Use by Epson MX-80:    space up one line

11—numeric code
  ASCII code name: VT vertical tab (when there are any)
  Shape shown on screen:    Mars/male symbol
  When written by BASIC:    home operation; cursor moves to top left

When written by Pascal:      above shape appears
Use by Epson MX-80:          move to next vertical tab setting

12—numeric code
ASCII code name: FF form feed; skip to top of page, or equivalent
Shape shown on screen:       Venus/female symbol
When written by BASIC:       screen clears (a good equivalent of form-feed)
When written by Pascal:      above shape appears
Use by Epson MX-80:          skip to top of next page

13—numeric code
ASCII code name: CR carriage-return (i.e. move to beginning of same line)
Shape shown on screen:       single musical note
When written by BASIC:       moves cursor to the beginning of the line (CR)
When written by Pascal:      moves cursor to the beginning of the line (CR)
Use by Epson MX-80:          print line buffer; line-feed if switch set

14—numeric code
ASCII code name: SO shift out; for some printers this means red-ribbon
Shape shown on screen:       double musical note
When written by BASIC:       above shape appears
When written by Pascal:      above shape appears
Use by Epson MX-80:          set double width mode

15—numeric code
ASCII code name: SI shift; for some printers this means black-ribbon
Shape shown on screen:       sun burst
When written by BASIC:       above shape appears
When written by Pascal:      above shape appears
Use by Epson MX-80:          set compressed mode

16—numeric code
ASCII code name: DLE data link escape (used to begin special codes)
Shape shown on screen:       right-pointing triangle
When written by BASIC:       above shape appears
When written by Pascal:      above shape appears
Use by Epson MX-80:          no special use

17—numeric code
ASCII code name: DC1 device control #1
Shape shown on screen:       left-pointing triangle
When written by BASIC:       above shape appears
When written by Pascal:      above shape appears
Use by Epson MX-80:          activates printer

18—numeric code
ASCII code name: DC2 device control #2
Shape shown on screen:       up-down arrows
When written by BASIC:       above shape appears
When written by Pascal:      above shape appears

Use by Epson MX-80:        turn off compressed mode

19—numeric code

ASCII code name: DC3 device control #3
Shape shown on screen:        double exclamation mark
When written by BASIC:        above shape appears
When written by Pascal:        above shape appears
Use by Epson MX-80:        deactivate printer

20—numeric code

ASCII code name: DC4 device control #4
Shape shown on screen:        paragraph symbol
When written by BASIC:        above shape appears
When written by Pascal:        above shape appears
Use by Epson MX-80:        turn off double width

21—numeric code

ASCII    code    name:    NAK    negative    acknowledge    (used    for
        communications)
Shape shown on screen:        section symbol
When written by BASIC:        above shape appears
When written by Pascal:        above shape appears
Use by Epson MX-80:        no special use

22—numeric code

ASCII code name: SYN synchronization (used for communications)
Shape shown on screen:        thick lower bar
When written by BASIC:        above shape appears
When written by Pascal:        above shape appears
Use by Epson MX-80:        no special use

23—numeric code

ASCII    code    name:    ETB    end    of    transmission    block    (used    for
        communications)
Shape shown on screen:        underlined up-down arrows
When written by BASIC:        above shape appears
When written by Pascal:        above shape appears
Use by Epson MX-80:        no special use

24—numeric code

ASCII code name: CAN cancel
Shape shown on screen:        up arrow
When written by BASIC:        above shape appears
When written by Pascal:        above shape appears
Use by Epson MX-80:        clear print line buffer

25—numeric code

ASCII code name: EM end of medium
Shape shown on screen:        down arrow
When written by BASIC:        above shape appears
When written by Pascal:        above shape appears
Use by Epson MX-80:        no special use

26—numeric code

ASCII code name: SUB substitute
Shape shown on screen:        right arrow

When written by BASIC:    above shape appears
When written by Pascal:    above shape appears
Use by Epson MX-80:    no special use

27—numeric code
   ASCII code name: ESC escape; this is the same as the PC's "Esc" key
   Shape shown on screen:    left arrow
   When written by BASIC:    above shape appears
   When written by Pascal:    above shape appears
   Use by Epson MX-80:    used to begin special codes

28—numeric code
   ASCII code name: FS file separator
   Shape shown on screen:    L-shape
   When written by BASIC:    cursor moves right one space (with
      wrap-around)
   When written by Pascal:    above shape appears
   Use by Epson MX-80:    no special use

29—numeric code
   ASCII code name: GS group separator
   Shape shown on screen:    left-right arrows
   When written by BASIC:    cursor moves left one space (with wrap-
      around)
   When written by Pascal:    above shape appears
   Use by Epson MX-80:    no special use

30—numeric code
   ASCII code name: RS record separator
   Shape shown on screen:    upward pointing triangle
   When written by BASIC:    cursor moves up one line (and stops at
      top)
   When written by Pascal:    above shape appears
   Use by Epson MX-80:    no special use

31—numeric code
   ASCII code name: US unit separator
   Shape shown on screen:    downward pointing triangle
   When written by BASIC:    cursor moves down one line (and stops
      at bottom)
   When written by Pascal:    above shape appears
   Use by Epson MX-80:    no special use
   Use by Epson MX-80:    no special use

# Appendix 5:
# The accompanying
# diskette package

Scattered throughout this book are many references to the accompanying diskette package. If you only have this book, you may be a little uncertain about what all is in the diskette package, and whether or not you might want it.

Here is a guide to the contents of the diskette package. In summary, the diskette package contains the programs necessary to give you full access to all of the special features of the IBM/PC. Although there are many extras in the package, its main content is a series of Assembler and Pascal routines that make it easy for your programs to access and control the IBM/PC's features. Each of these routines comes already assembled or compiled, so that you can make immediate use of them. Each of them also comes in source statement format, fully commented, so that you can study them to learn more about how the PC works, and adapt them to your special needs. I know of no better way to extend your knowledge of the IBM/PC beyond what this book provides, than to study the source code of the access routines in the diskette package.

Here is a detailed list of the contents of the diskette package, by category:

*Power tools:*

1.  The power-tool program DiskLook appears in the package, in the program file DL.EXE. DiskLook provides you with a complete information and exploration source for investigating your diskettes. DiskLook will show you:

● A complete map of the space utilization of each diskette

● The location of any bad sectors, conflicting file allocation or temporarily unusable sectors

● Complete directory information for each file, including information that is not otherwise available

- A map of the location of each file, indicating space fragmentation problems
- The names of all files erased from the diskette, and an indication if each can be recovered
- A complete file directory listing, sorted by name, extension, date and time, or file size
- A display of any data on the diskette, shown in either hexadecimal format or text-file line format

## BASIC demonstration programs:

Four BASIC language programs, which demonstrate and explore parts of the PC, are included. These programs are:

2.  CHARS.BAS, corresponding to listing 1.1, will demonstrate all of the display-screen characters, including those which cannot be displayed by conventional BASIC language methods.

3.  ATTRIB.BAS, corresponding to listing 8.1, will demonstrate all of the possible combinations of screen attributes, including all color combinations.

4.  MEMLIST.BAS, corresponding to listing 3.1, will find and display the location of all the active memory on your PC system.

5.  KEYBITS.BAS, corresponding to listing 10.1, will display the keyboard status bits, and dynamically demonstrate their action.

## Sound demonstration programs:

Four assembly language programs demonstrate three variations on how to produce sounds on the IBM/PC. Each appears as a source listing (with the file name extension of '.ASM', and as an executable program file (with the file name extension of '.COM').

6.  BEEP, in the files BEEP.ASM and BEEP.COM, demonstrates a pure sound, generated by a program. This corresponds to listing 3.2.

7.  WARBLE, in the files WARBLE.ASM and WARBLE.COM, demonstrates a program generated sound, altered by the effect of clock interrupts. This corresponds to listing 3.2.

8.  UPSCALE, in the files UPSCALE.ASM and UPSCALE.COM, demonstrates a changing sound pitch, generated by a program.

9.  A440, in the files A440.ASM and A440.COM, demonstrates a sound generated by the system programmable timer, which continues without program intervention. This corresponds to listing 11.1.

## Port exploration program:

10.  PORTTEST, in the executable program file PORTTEST.EXE and the two program source files PORTEST.PAS and INPORT.ASM,

explores all of the ports in the IBM/PC, reporting which ones appear to possibly be active. This corresponds to listing 3.3 and 3.4.

## ROM exploration programs:

Two programs are provided to read and compare the ROM-BASIC and ROM-BIOS installed in an IBM/PC.

11. ROMSAVE, in the executable program file ROMSAVE.EXE, will report the release marker on a version of ROM, and copy the complete ROM to diskette, for comparison and analysis.

12. ROMCOMP, in the executable program file ROMCOMP.EXE, will read and compare any two copies of the ROM, as produced by ROMSAVE. This program will display both versions of ROM, in hex and ASCII, and search for differences. When differences are found, the program will pause, and highlight the differences.

## Pascal access examples:

Three program listings are provided to illustrate how Pascal is used to access three parts of the system. These programs are illustrative only, and so appear only in source format.

13. BIOSDATE, in the source file BIOSDATE.PAS, illustrates how a program can dynamically test the version of the ROM-BIOS that is being used. This corresponds to listing 6.1.

14. DISKBASE, in the source file DISKBASE.PAS, illustrates how to access, copy, and modify the diskette controlling parameters in the disk base table. This corresponds to listing 7.1.

15. VIDEODEM, in the source file VIDEODEM.PAS, illustrates how to do direct memory-mapped output to the display screens in Pascal. This corresponds to listing 8.2.

16. GRAPHDEM, in the source file GRAPHDEM.PAS, illustrates how to do direct memory-mapped graphics output to the display screens in Pascal. This corresponds to listing 9.1.

## Diskette system processing routines:

Three program listings are provided to give Pascal access to the diskette directory and file allocation table (FAT). These programs provide a thorough set of tools to access the diskette directory, decode the directory and FAT, trace file allocation, and more.

17. DIR/FAT/DIRFAT, in the Pascal source files DIR.INC, FAT.INC, DIRFAT.PAS and DIRFAT.INC, and the linkable object file DIRFAT.OBJ provide the diskette processing tools. This corresponds to listings 5.1, 5.2 and 5.3.

## Copy protection scheme:

This set of Pascal and assembly programs provides a simple but workable means of making diskettes copy protected. The method is not state-of-the-art, and every method that I know of can be relatively easily broken by available programs intended to bust copy protection. These programs, though, will give you an ordinary and usable degree of copy protection for your diskettes.

18.    PROTECTA, in the source file PROTECTA.ASM and the assembled object file PROTECTA.OBJ, provides the assembly language service routines needed to do copy-protected formatting, data storage and data retrieval. This corresponds to listing 7.103.

19.    PROTECTP, in the source file PROTECTP.PAS and the compiled object file PROTECTP.OBJ, provides the Pascal language service routines needed to do copy protection, giving access to the facilities of PROTECTA for your own programs. This corresponds to listing 7.104.

20.    PROTECT, in the source file PROTECT.PAS and the ready-to-use program file PROTECT.EXE, provides a complete copy protection service which can be used to copy-protect batches of diskettes quickly. Naturally, when you copy-protect a diskette, your programs must check the copy-protection when they are run, and the Pascal source file PROTECT.INC provides a routine which your programs can use to do this.

## Complete access routines:

These five sets of Pascal and assembly-language routines provide complete access to all of the features of the ROM-BIOS and DOS. The programs are organized to correspond to the chapters of this book; they may be used in that form, or you may combine separate parts of these programs to get just the sections that you need in a compact form.

Each of the programs listed below contains numerous usable routines within it.

21.    DOSA provides assembler access to the many DOS service routines. The source file DOSA.ASM and the object file DOSA.OBJ give the routines themselves, while the source file DOSA.INC provides the Pascal declarations needed to use these routines. This corresponds to listing 4.101.

22.    DOSP provides Pascal support routines to make the use of the DOSA routines easier and more effective. The source file DOSP.PAS and the object file DOSP.OBJ give the routines themselves, while the source file DOSP.INC provides the Pascal declarations needed to use these routines from your programs. This corresponds to listing 4.102.

23. DISKA provides assembler access to the ROM-BIOS diskette service routines. The source file DISKA.ASM and the object file DISKA.OBJ give the routines themselves, while the source file DISKA.INC provides the Pascal declarations needed to use these routines. This corresponds to listing 7.101.

24. DISKP provides Pascal support routines to make the use of the DISKA routines easier and more effective. The source file DISKP.PAS and the object file DISKP.OBJ give the routines themselves, while the source file DISKP.INC provides the Pascal declarations needed to use these routines from your programs. This corresponds to listing 7.102.

25. VIDEOA provides assembler access to the ROM-BIOS display service routines. The source file VIDEOA.ASM and the object file VIDEOA.OBJ give the routines themselves, while the source file VIDEOA.INC provides the Pascal declarations needed to use these routines. This corresponds to listing 8.101.

26. VIDEOP provides Pascal support routines to make the use of the VIDEOA routines easier and more effective. The source file VIDEOP.PAS and the object file VIDEOP.OBJ give the routines themselves, while the source file VIDEOP.INC provides the Pascal declarations needed to use these routines from your programs. This corresponds to listing 8.102.

27. KEYA provides assembler access to the many ROM-BIOS keyboard service routines. The source file KEYA.ASM and the object file KEYA.OBJ give the routines themselves, while the source file KEYA.INC provides the Pascal declarations needed to use these routines. This corresponds to listing 10.101.

28. KEYP provides Pascal support routines to make the use of the KEYA routines easier and more effective. The source file KEYP.PAS and the object file KEYP.OBJ give the routines themselves, while the source file KEYP.INC provides the Pascal declarations needed to use these routines from your programs. This corresponds to listing 10.102.

29. MISCA provides assembler access to the miscellaneous ROM-BIOS service routines, including those for the cassette, printer, asynchronous communications adapter, print-screen, system-reset, ROM-BASIC, and others. The source file MISCA.ASM and the object file MISCA.OBJ give the routines themselves, while the source file MISCA.INC provides the Pascal declarations needed to use these routines. This corresponds to listing 11.101.

30. MISCP provides Pascal support routines to make the use of the MISCA routines easier and more effective. The source file MISCP.PAS and the object file MISCP.OBJ give the routines themselves, while the source file MISCP.INC provides the Pascal

declarations needed to use these routines from your programs. This corresponds to listing 11.102.

# Appendix 6:
# The XT, IBM Fixed Disk,
# & More on DOS 2.00

On March 8, 1983, after the first edition of this book was prepared, IBM announced several interesting new additions to the Personal Computer. This appendix provides you with supplementary information about these new products from IBM.

## What's New, and What Does It Mean?

Here is a quick summary of what IBM announced in the spring of 1983, and how it relates to previous releases of IBM personal computers.

The best place to begin, in order to make sense of what IBM announced, is with the fixed disk system. It has been easy to see that the greatest flaw in the original IBM/PC was the lack of a high-capacity storage disk system. IBM removed this flaw by adding a winchester-type fixed hard disk to the PC, with ten million bytes of storage space. This ten-megabyte disk has the capacity of over 30 double-sided diskettes, or over 60 single-sided diskettes. With this addition to the PC, IBM has created the "Winchester version" of the PC, which we talked about in Chapter 2.

The next step in understanding IBM's new PC equipment is to look at how the fixed disk system was added to the PC. The fixed winchester disk could not be just plugged into an old PC, for one very simple reason—the power supply in the original PC, with a 63-watt capacity, is too small to handle the needs of a winchester disk. IBM solved the power problem by designing a new 130-watt power supply, and providing two ways to put it and a fixed disk onto a PC.

For a conventional PC system, the new power supply and the fixed disk system are supplied in an "expansion unit." The expansion unit is a case that is identical in size and shape to the PC's system unit. Just like the PC's system unit, the expansion unit contains two spaces for disks in the front, and inside it has room for a number of expansion cards to be plugged in. In effect, the expansion unit is a second PC sys-

255

tem unit, but without the brains (the 8088 micro-processor chip). The expansion unit connects to the PC's system unit with an "umbilical" connector, which passes signals back and forth between the two units. By plugging an expansion unit into a PC, the PC gains the fixed disk system, and some additional space for expansion cards. Incidental from our point of view (but critical from an engineering point of view), the PC also gains a higher-powered power supply, for the use of any parts that plug into the expansion unit.

The main disadvantage of an expansion unit, however, is that it doubles the physical size of the PC's system unit. Except for PC users who need the extra expansion board slots, this is an unnecessary and expensive addition to the equipment of a PC. To solve that problem, IBM developed the XT model of the PC.

In essence, the Personal Computer XT is nothing more than an old PC, with the new larger power supply and the fixed disk system installed. There are actually some differences between the original PC and the new XT model, but the differences are relatively minor. Basically, the XT model is simply an original PC and its expansion unit brought together into one box.

So far, we have the essence of the hardware changes that IBM added in March, 1983. There were important software changes as well, in the release of DOS version 2.00.

From the point of view of hardware support, the key thing about DOS 2.00 is that it provides support for IBM's ten megabyte fixed disk system. However, from a software point of view, DOS 2.00 is a radical departure from what has appeared in previous releases. These changes to DOS are mostly internal and hidden from us, its users—so they have little practical importance to us in the short term. But these changes will have an important long-term effect on the future of our use of personal computers. We'll cover more of this below.

When all of the new hardware and software that IBM announced in March 1983 is carefully analyzed, it reveals a very important message from IBM to the world. It is clear that IBM moved very carefully in the design of its new equipment, to do as little harm as possible to the community of software and hardware suppliers that had sprung up around the PC. Many observers of IBM have noted a historical tendency for IBM to be less than friendly with some of the businesses that make a living on the edges of IBM's own market. If that has been true, it certainly doesn't seem to be true in the PC market place. Many signs indicate that IBM's attitude toward the PC after-market is very benign. A few of IBM's actions may harm some PC-related businesses—for example, companies that sold add-ons or winchester disks for the PC now must compete directly with the IBM fixed disk system. But, on the whole, it is clear that IBM is moving very carefully to do as little damage to the PC market place as possible.

This, clearly, is the most interesting and important significance to what IBM announced in March, 1983. The message is that IBM is making the PC environment as stable as possible, and so they are protecting all of us PC users from having our computers made obsolete. This is a very comforting message to buyers and sellers alike of PC equipment.

There is one other important message IBM has delivered in the form of the XT model—where the future of personal computing is going. We'll hold off discussing that message until the end of this appendix.

## Specifics About the XT

As we mentioned above, the XT model of the Personal Computer is basically an ordinary PC with the new larger power supply and the fixed disk system. But under the skin there are a number of interesting changes in the XT version of the PC.

The XT has a slightly re-worked and re-designed system board from the original PC. All of the basic design, and all of the major circuit chips, which were discussed in Chapter 2, remain the same. The empty co-processor socket remains in place, although IBM still does not officially support the 8087 arithmetic co-processor, which this open socket was designed to accommodate.

The most important change in the XT's system board is that it now contains room for up to 256 K bytes of memory. The original PC's system board had room for only 64 K, and any additional memory had to be accommodated on expansion boards. By re-arranging the system board, and by using higher density memory chips, IBM allowed 256 K to be placed on the system board. Although large amounts of memory can be put to good use, most PC systems have no real need for more than 256 K, and so the majority of XT systems will probably not need any memory on expansion boards.

There were two other changes to the circuitry and physical layout of the XT model. First, the almost completely unused cassette interface was eliminated. This means that those few PC users who found something to do with the cassette interface (such as using it for a modem port), will not be able to do the same things with the XT. The other change is a narrowing of the width of the expansion slots in the XT.

In the XT, and in the expansion units for the PC, the expansion slots have been narrowed in size so that there is now room for eight slots, instead of the five in the original PC. Room was made for three more slots not only by narrowing the space, but also by using some of the space to the right of the original expansion slot space—the space behind the first, or A, diskette drive. Because of this, two of the eight expansion slots are short, and will only take half-size expansion boards; the other six slots are full length.

Some of the expansion boards that have been developed for the PC are rather fat, particularly the ones which contained circuitry piggy-backed onto two physical boards. Some of these fat boards will not fit into the new reduced slot space, and they can be used only by taking up two slot spaces. However, most of the expansion boards developed for the PC will fit very nicely into the new narrower space.

Besides these design differences in the XT, there is an interesting marketing difference, one which has two meanings. The marketing difference in the XT concerns the minimum equipment which is sold with it. Originally, IBM sold rather bare-bones versions of the PC. The original PC was sold with 48 K of memory as a minimum, and it could even be ordered with only 16 K. However, the XT comes with a minimum of 128 K of memory; IBM now considers 128 K as the lowest reasonable amount of memory to have on a PC (I and many others agree).

So the XT version of the PC comes with 128 K of memory, and, naturally, one diskette drive and one 10 megabyte fixed disk drive. But it comes with one other surprising piece of standard equipment—the asynchronous communications adapter. There is nothing special in this communications adapter—it is the standard one that has been used on the original PC; and it is not designed into the XT, it is on an expansion card, just like any other optional equipment for a PC or a XT.

What makes this piece of standard equipment so interesting, is that it is "unnecessary." There is no compelling reason for the communications adapter to be on all XTs, except that IBM wants it to be there. The XT is what I referred to in Chapter 2 as the "winchester machine"—it is the standard serious user's version of the PC. So IBM has equipped all XT's with what it considers to be the minimum gear for a serious personal computer. Now the 10-megabyte disk and the 128 K of memory are naturals for a serious machine. But what is interesting is that IBM is saying, in effect, that any serious personal computer user needs to be equipped for communications. That is a very interesting and important message which IBM has for us, and one we wll come back to later.

## New Diskette Formats

One of the changes that IBM made in the 2.00 release of DOS was to create a new set of diskette formats. Whereas the old single- and double-sided formats placed eight sectors of data on a track, the new formats squeeze nine sectors into the diskettes. Practically everything else remains the same—the 512-byte size of the sectors, and the 40 tracks per diskette.

So, now with DOS 2.00, there are four different diskette formats—all the combinations of single- and double-sided, eight and nine sectors. As it was when DOS added double-sided formats with release 1.10, the new DOS 2.00 will automatically use the larger nine-sector format, unless it is specifically told not to.

This change to nine sectors per track increases the storage capacity of diskettes by about 12%, and also brings about some minor changes to the way that diskette data is controlled.

The "boot record," which is the first sector on each diskette, remains one sector in size, but the program on it has been changed so that it will now deal with four different disk formats. The boot record also has a boot-id marker on its last two bytes—they are set to hexadecimal 55AA. There is one additional change to the boot-record format. With DOS 1.10, the same boot record was used for either single- or double-sided format; but with DOS 2.00, two different formats are used—one for eight sector (single or double) and one for nine sector. The eight-sector boot record does not have the 55AA boot marker, nor the DOS version ("IBM 2.0") that appears on the nine-sector version.

The allocation of diskette space, which is controlled by the file allocation table (FAT), is unchanged for nine-sector format. Space is still allocated the sector at a time for single-sided diskettes, and two at a time for double-sided. Since there is an odd number of sectors per track in nine-sector format, double-sided diskettes have one cluster on each track that wraps from side to side: the cluster's first sector is sector 9 of side 0, and the cluster's second sector is sector 1 of side 1.

The first byte of the FAT still identifies the format of the disk—as before, hex FE identifies a single-sided eight-sector diskette, and FF, double-sided; FC and FD identify nine-sector single- and double-sided. F8 is used for the fixed disk system.

With a 12% increase in diskette space, the size of the FAT has grown accordingly, and it now no longer fits onto one sector. There are still two copies of the FAT stored on the diskette, so that nine-sector format diskettes now have four sectors dedicated to the FAT, which moves the location of the diskette's file directory.

There are no changes to the directory for nine-sector formats. The directory is still four or seven sectors, with room for 64 or 112 directory entries. There are, however, profound changes to the file directory for DOS 2.00, which apply to all disk format.

## The New File Directory

There are many changes to the file directory for DOS 2.00. However, there has been no change to the format of the directory entries, as defined in Chapter 5. The ten reserved and unused bytes in the 32-byte format remain unused.

The change has been made in the filename part of the directory entry. Previously, unused directory entries were marked in the same way as erased directory entries, with a hex E5 in the first character. This meant that a search of the directory required reading every directory sector (and there are 32 of them in the fixed disk system). To shorten this search, when a disk is formatted the entries are now marked as unused, with a hex 00; this allows directory searches to stop at the first unused entry.

There are many other changes to the directories, and all of them involve parts of the attribute type in the directory entry. For simplicity, we'll discuss them in terms of the attribute byte.

The eighth bit of the attribute byte now marks a file as "read-only." If a file is marked as read-only, DOS will not allow the file to be opened for output, which protects a read-only file from being changed using the

normal DOS file services. The read-only bit cannot be set or reset by
any DOS commands, but there is a DOS programming function call
(CHMOD) that can be used to control it, and my Norton Utility programs also provide control over this read-only attribute. On the DOS
diskettes, only the two hidden-system files, IBMBIO.COM and
IBMDOS.COM are marked read-only. All the others may be changed,
including COMMAND.COM.

The hidden and system bits remain the same, and there continues
to be no special treatment of the system bit.

The 5th bit of the attribute is now used to mark a directory entry as
the disk's volume id label. The volume label is used to provide an identifying name for a disk or diskette. The id name occupies the eleven
bytes of the filename and filename extension, but it is considered to be
a unified 11-byte name, without a period for punctuation. There should
be only one volume id label on a disk. DOS does not allow labels to be
placed on eight-sector format diskettes, and labels can only be created
when a disk is formatted; DOS provides no commands for changing,
removing or adding labels (but the Norton Utilities do provide full
label-changing services). DOS 2.00 reports the volume id label whenever the DIR and CHKDSK commands are used on a disk, and with
some other commands as well.

The 4th bit of the attribute is used to identify the name of a directory. DOS 2.00 now supports a tree-structured directory system, which
means that each disk can have subdirectories under its main directory
(and those directories can have other directories under them). Subdirectories add two main things to DOS. First, they make it possible to
break through the limit in the number of files that a fixed directory size
imposed. With subdirectories, there is no arbitrary limit on the number
of files that can be accommodated; this is because subdirectories can
grow to accommodate any number of files. Second, subdirectories
allow the logical organization of files into groups. All the files that
belong together can be placed in the same subdirectory, apart from
other files.

Each subdirectory is itself a file, stored in the ordinary file data
space on the disk. Unlike a disk's root directory, subdirectories can
grow as needed, just like any other file—this allows them to accommodate any number of files. Since subdirectories are, from one point of
view, like other disk files, something is needed to mark their special
status as directories. The 4th bit of the file attribute byte (which is a
part of each file's directory entry) is used to identify those entries that
are subdirectories, and not ordinary files.

There are three kinds of entries that will have this directory bit set.
If the first character of the filename is not a period (.), then the directory
entry defines a subdirectory under the current directory—and the location of the subdirectory is given, as with any other file, by the starting
cluster number field. But if the filename begins with "." or "..", then this
directory entry is used to provide information about the connection
between directories. Each subdirectory has a "." and a ".." entry (but

the disk's root directory does not have either). The ".." entry is used to provide a pointer to the directory that owns this subdirectory; the starting cluster number in this ".." entry points to the beginning of the directory under which this directory is located. If the parent directory is the disk's root directory, then a zero is given in the starting cluster number field, and it's understood to mean that the directory's parent is the disk's root directory. This ".." parent entry allows DOS to easily thread its way backwards from a subdirectory. The "." entry provides a similar pointer, but it points to the first cluster of the subdirectory itself. If I am a subdirectory, "." tells me where I begin, while ".." tells me where my parent directory is. There is no real need for the "." entry, and it seems to have been included just to make life a little easier for DOS.

The next and last of the new attribute bits is the 3rd bit (the first two attribute bits remain unused). This bit is called the archive bit, and it is used to help control the backup and restore facilities of the fixed disk system. Whenever a file has been changed the archive bit is set on; when the file is backed up, the bit is turned off. So this bit is used to record which files have been changed, but not yet backed up.

## The IBM Fixed Disk System

The IBM fixed disk system is a winchester-type hard disk system, with a capacity of over ten million bytes of storage. It is a sealed disk system, and the disks cannot be removed from the disk drive, which is why IBM refers to it as a fixed disk system. Physically the fixed disk system is designed to occupy the same space as a diskette drive.

The fixed disk is organized in a manner similar to the use of diskettes. Where our diskettes have 40 tracks numbered 0 through 39, the fixed disk has 306 cylinders (the equivalent of tracks) numbered 0 through 305. Cylinder 305 is normally reserved for diagnostic use, so only cylinders 0–304 are active. The fixed disk has two disk platters, so there are four sides, 0 through 3, for each cylinder. Each of the four sides at each cylinder is a track, with 17 sectors in the track, where a diskette has eight or nine sectors per track. The sectors remain the same size, 512 bytes.

Thus, the total raw space on the fixed disk system is 512 bytes, times 17 sectors, times 4 sides, times 305 cylinders, for a total of 10,618,880 bytes.

The fixed disk system may be divided into as many as four "partitions." The purpose of the partitions is to support operating systems other than DOS. Therefore, it is possible to have DOS, and CP/M-86, and the UCSD p-System, and some other operating system all resident and working on the fixed disk. However, IBM's support of systems other than DOS, which was weak in the past, seems to have totally atrophied. So most PC fixed disks will have only one partition, dedicated to DOS. The number and size of the partitions is set by the FDISK command; they can't be changed without wiping out everything on the disk. The only way to change the partitions and still keep your data is to unload and later reload your data—a laborious process.

The first sector on the disk is the "master boot" record, which contains a table of partitions for the disk. While an ordinary boot record has the job of starting up the operating system, the program on the master boot record has the task of looking to see which disk partition is marked as "active," and then passing control to the boot record for that partition. Which partition is active can be changed at any time by using the FDISK command.

For a DOS partition, the size of the FAT, the root directory and the number of sectors per cluster will vary depending upon the size of the DOS partition. There is no published formula for how each of these will vary with the partition size. When the DOS partition is the entire disk, which is the usual situation, DOS's FAT is eight sectors big (taking up 16 sectors for the two copies of the FAT), and the directory is 32 sectors long, with room for 512 directory entries. The combined overhead on a fixed disk is thus 50 sectors: one master boot record, one DOS boot, eight FAT sectors twice, and 32 directory sectors. The size of a cluster, the units in which disk space is allocated to files, is eight sectors, or 4,096 bytes. With this minimum file size, there is a limit of about 2,500 files per disk.

It may strike you that it is very wasteful to allocate disk space in chunks as big as 4 K bytes. Certainly each of us has many small files—batch processing files, short programs, and so forth—that use only a small fraction of the 4096 bytes given to hold them. But on the average, each file will have 2 K bytes more allocated to it than needed, and that is only 1/50 of 1% of the disk's total space wasted for each file.

To give you some idea of the practical capacity of the IBM fixed disk, we can look at my experience, hoping that it is typical. My fixed disk system is 81% full, with 787 files. My files average about 10 K in size, and the total amount "wasted" by allocating space in clusters of 8 sectors is about 15% of the total disk space. I have room for about another 175 files before I have to either get another disk, or move my least important data off the disk.

The rotation speed of the fixed disk is 3600 rpm, or six times faster than diskettes. The speed of moving from track to track is twice as fast as a diskette, and does not require any "head settle time" after moving (which on diskettes, can be a major factor in the effective speed of access). In practice, the fixed disk system averages about five times faster access than diskettes achieve.

There is one more odd bit of interesting but useless information to relate about the fixed disk system. Because of the faster rotation speed of the fixed disk, the sectors are "interleaved" by a factor of six, which means that the 17 sectors on a track are not stored in the order 1, 2, 3. Instead, they are staggered, to reduce the average waiting time for a sector to swing into place. So the actual order that sectors are stored in is 1, 4, 7, 10, 13, 16, 2, 5, 8, 11, 14, 17, 3, 6, 9, 12, 15.

As with diskette drives, IBM has turned to outside suppliers for its fixed disk system. Several different manufacturers are known to be supplying disk drives to IBM, and the quality and performance of the different drives seems to be uniformly excellent.

## The Expansion Units for the PC and XT

Both the original PC and the XT version have expansion units available. The expansion units are the same for both computers, and contain the 130-watt power supply, eight expansion slots (6 long, 2 short), and room for two disk drives. (The apparent difference between the expansion unit for the PC and the one for the XT lies in the fact that the expansion unit for the original PC includes a controller board for the fixed disk unit, which the XT already has; the expansion units themselves are identical.)

There are restrictions on what expansion boards can be placed in the expansion unit, apparently because of speed limitations on communications between the system unit and its expansion unit. All memory additions, and any display adapters (which contain memory), must be in the system unit, not in the expansion unit

The original PC requires that any fixed disk system be placed in an expansion unit, simply for power supply reasons. If a second fixed disk unit is added to an XT, both fixed disks must be in the expansion unit, so the XT's original fixed disk must be moved out of the system unit.

Only one expansion unit may be added to a PC or XT, and no more than two fixed disks can be used. There can be up to four diskette drives in a system, though.

## The New Flavor of DOS 2.00

DOS 2.00 is actually a radical departure from previous versions of DOS; while the earlier versions had been evolutionary, this DOS is revolutionary. The revolution isn't obvious to the user of DOS, because when we use the new DOS, we see all of the old features, and new ones added. In short, when you use DOS it gives the appearance of having been added to, rather than radically changed. But this is deceptive.

Under the surface, DOS has been completely reorganized and redesigned. The internal changes in DOS, and many of the new features—such as "pipelining" and "redirection"—all point in the direction of the famous Unix operating system. As mentioned earlier in the book, Microsoft, the author of DOS, plans to have a series of three operating systems, with DOS on the bottom and Xenix, a version of Unix, on the top. Toward that end, Microsoft has completely restructured DOS to fit into their larger plans. From our point of view as users of the IBM/PC, this has both good and bad effects.

The good news for us is that we are gaining many of the powerful and useful features of Unix-like operating systems, and the future of our personal computers has been made more secure, because it now has a clearer path of growth and expansion—so our systems are less likely to be made obsolete. That's the good news. But the bad news is worse than the good news is good.

Because the internal workings of DOS have been completely rethought, the services that DOS provides to programs have also been thoroughly reworked. For the most part, DOS now has two complete sets of services for programs; programs can either use the old "traditional" DOS services, or the shiny new ones. This produces some horrible compatibility problems. Designers of programs must now choose whether to use the new services or the old. If a program uses the new services, it can't be used on those PCs that aren't using DOS 2.00; if it uses the old services, it doesn't take advantage of the new powers of DOS. Of course, to try to do both can create quite a mess.

The issue of new versus old DOS is made particularly bad because DOS 1.10 has not been superseded by 2.00. The main reason for this is that 2.00 uses twice as much memory as previous versions, about 24 K, instead of 12 K. In the past, 64 K was a standard size of memory for PC systems, and many programs were tailored to just fit into the 52 K that the old DOS left over. This means that, for all practical purposes, the many PC systems with only 64 K of memory cannot move to DOS 2.00. IBM has announced that DOS 1.10 will continue to be sold, so it is not a dead version of the operating system.

As a result of this, many programs will be written to work within the more limited services of DOS 1.10, and this will be a major stumbling block in the PC's march into the future. It has the effect of eliminating much of the advantages of DOS 2.00's new design.

## Making Additions to DOS: Installable Device Drivers

Of all the changes that were made to DOS, perhaps the most important is the one known as "installable device drivers." There is always a need to be able to add extensions to an operating system, particularly for new peripheral devices, such as different kinds of disks (or electronic RAM disks, which simulate a fast disk in memory).

In the past, making this kind of extension to DOS involved direct modification to the operating system. These had two grave disadvantages: first, making the modifications was a tricky, sophisticated and error-prone operation; and second, a modification for one purpose pretty much precluded using any other one.

But with DOS 2.00, a means has been provided for "device drivers" (the programs needed to support an addition to DOS) to be "installed" (incorporated into DOS) when DOS is started up. This makes it much safer and easier to add extensions to DOS, and to combine any number of separate changes to DOS.

When IBM announced its fixed disk system, it largely undercut those who had been selling hard disk additions to the PC. But at the same time, the new DOS made it possible for hard disks and other new kinds of devices to be integrated easily into the PC.

In the long term, this provision for installable device drivers will probably have the most profound effect of all the changes in DOS. This new feature opens the door to the easy addition of all sorts of new equipment for the PC. It seems likely that we will see a tremendous increase in the variety of add-on gear that is available for the PC, all because this one change to DOS has made it so much more practical.

## New Features and Services of DOS 2.00

With the far-reaching internal changes to DOS, there have been similarly extensive changes to the program services that DOS provides. There are very new changes to the existing services—almost everything new is provided in the form of new DOS function calls.

Of the changes to the old DOS services, the two most important are Ctrl-Break processing, and absolute sector addressing. In the past, as we mentioned in Chapter 2, DOS placed a rather narrow and arbitrary restriction on the handling of the Ctrl-Break interruption. Now, DOS will act on a Ctrl-Break key action whenever any DOS service is used, provided that the BREAK-ON switch has been set to activate this change.

The other change, to absolute sector addressing, is much more serious. DOS interrupt services 25 and 26 are used to read and write specific disk sectors. The rules for how a sector is specified have been changed in DOS 2.00, and changed in a way that is thoroughly incompatible with previous versions of DOS. It would have been possible to maintain the old scheme, and also provide the new one (which is clearly much better than the old) separately—maintaining program compatibility with older DOSs. Unfortunately, this was not done. Because of this, any programs that use these two DOS services will not work properly with DOS 2.00. In general, IBM and Microsoft have been very careful to keep each version of DOS fully compatible with earlier versions. Here, however, they made a small but important blunder.

The new DOS 2.00 services are all provided as function calls, which operate under interrupt hex 21. The old services used function numbers 0 through hex 2E, while the new services use codes hex 2F through 57.

There are some common factors in all of the new services. For one thing, they use a common set of error return codes, numbered 1 through 18, hex 12, which provides greater consistency, and makes error handling easier. Another major change is that the new form of file services does not make use of the old File Control Blocks (FCBs), but instead manages files internally to DOS, and refers to them through a reference number, which is called a "handle" or "token." Here is a summary of what these new services do:

Services 2F through 38 provide extended functions. These provide a variety of services, with two particularly interesting ones. Service 30 hex returns the DOS version number so that programs can detect which DOS they are running under and act accordingly. The usefulness of this service would seem to be completely sabotaged by the fact that previous versions of DOS did not have it; but apparently the three earlier versions of DOS will, in effect, report themselves as if they were DOS version zero. The other particularly interesting service is 38 hex, which reports on the country-specific variations of DOS. There are currently three variations defined: American, European, and Japanese. The information provided includes a definition of the proper format for date and time, the currency symbol (dollar sign, pound sign, etc) and the proper punctuation for numbers (e.g. "12,345.67" is the American custom, while much of Europe uses the form "12 345,67"). Considerable room is left for an expansion of this service, including a provision for subservices.

Services 39 through 3B, and service 47 provide directory operations. They include directory controlling services, 39 hex to create a directory (the equivalent of the MKDIR command), 3A to remove a directory (RMDIR) and 3B to change the current directory. Service 47 hex reports the current directory, in the form of its name as an ASCII text string.

Services 3C through 46 provide file management services. They are the new preferred 2.00 way of doing file operations, such as creating, opening, closing, reading and writing files. Among these services, 43 hex provides a service to read or change a file's attribute byte.

Services 48 through 4B provide memory management. These provide the means to allocate (or get the authorized use of) memory, release allocated memory, and change the size of an allocated block of memory. Service 4B is not strictly memory management, but is related: it will load other programs or overlays into memory. This service can be used either to make completely foreign programs act as subroutines to a master program (for example, your programs could then use DOS commands like FORMAT as if they were subroutines), or it allows programs which are too large to fit into memory in one piece to be broken into separately loaded parts, known as overlays.

Services 4C through 4F and 54 through 57 provide more extended functions. Services 4C and 4D are used in connection with program return codes, which are new to DOS 2.00. Services 4E and 4F are used for directory searches, similar to the old services 11 and 12. Service 54 hex reports the setting of the write verification switch, 56 renames files, and 57 reports or sets the date and time stamp in a file's directory entry.

## Where the XT Points

Because high-capacity disk storage is too important to the serious use of personal computers, the IBM personal computer has really come of age with the announcement of the XT model. The XT is basically what a conventional personal computer should be like.

But the XT also points to the future of personal computing, and it is interesting to notice the two most important messages that the XT has to deliver. The first message is stability. The XT model makes clear that IBM does not want the personal computer marketplace to be unnecessarily disrupted with revolutionary changes; instead, the message of the XT is evolution, and compatibility with what has gone before.

The second message of the XT is communications. It is very significant that the XT comes with an asynchronous communications adapter as standard equipment. Most of us think of the personal computer revolution as being about having our own, private and isolated computers. But that is just the opening wave of the true personal computer revolution. The real revolution of personal computing, it seems clear, will consist of personal computers hooked up to information networks. This makes communications one of the most important capabilities that personal computers can have. IBM, by making a communications adapter standard on the XT, has given the PC a strong push in this direction. It insures that anyone who buys an XT model will be able, in the future, to hook into communications networks.

# INDEX

BIOS use of memory, 35
bit, 215
bit order, power, value, 9
bits, notation for, 8
blinking cursor, 159
blinking display, 153
board, 220
Boolean, 230
boot record, 55, 57, 80, 225
boot-strap loading, 57
BP base pointer register, 37, 240
buffer, keyboard, 187
bug, 222
bus, 17, 18, 219
bus controller chip, 17
business version of PC, 22
busting copy protection, 139
BX register, 37, 128
byte, 26, 216

C language, 3
call, 229
CALL instruction, 40, 121
CALL, far, 30, 238
calling conventions, interrupt
  routines, 128
carriage-return, 94, 166, 246
carry flag (CF), 128
cassette interface, 17, 21, 45
cassette version of PC, 79
Centronics interface, 202
CF carry flag, 128
chaining space, 85
chaining, program, 62
character, 26, 216
cheating, 157
chip, 13, 220
CHKDSK command, 90
CHR$$, 3, 8
circles, three, 5
CLI instruction, 122, 193
clock generator chip, 17
cluster, 86
cluster number, starting, 84
clusters of sectors, 85
co-processor, 8087, 19, 20
Cobol, 227

code, 218
coder, 223
coding convention, 30
collating sequence, 96
color palettes, 165, 176
color, display, 153
COM files, 61, 63, 84, 91, 97
command, 218
command processor, 61, 226
COMMAND.COM, 56, 61
commands, internal and external, 61
communications, 201, 220
communications adapter, 24
compiled vs interpreted BASIC, 31
compiler, 222
composite monitor, 219
composite video signal, 144
computers, like the PC, 20
computing speed, 23
configuration switches, 19
consecutive order of sectors, 77
constants, 233
Context MBA, 153
control shift, 190
controller, 219
convention, addressing, 30
COPY command, 54, 56, 56, 95
copy protection, 73, 78, 137, 139,
  252
CP/M-86, 59, 79
Cray, 26
CRC error, 67
critical error interrupt, 66
cross-linked files, 90
CRT, 219
CRT controller, 17
CS code segment register, 30, 31, 37,
  42, 238
Ctrl shift, 190
Ctrl-Alt-Del reset, 58, 63, 193, 210
Ctrl-Break, 60, 66, 68, 69, 193
Ctrl-NumLock, 192, 193
Ctrl-Z, 95
cursor, 159
CX register, 37
cyan, 154
cyclical redundancy check, 67
cylinder, 224

# Documentation for programming access tools to accompany "Inside the IBM Personal Computer" by Peter Norton

## Contents

## Licensing Agreement

The programs contained in this diskette package are all provided as-is, without warranty of any kind, expressed or implied. All of the programs herein are © Copyright 1983, Peter Norton.

You are licensed to use these programs on a single machine, and to copy them for backup purposes in support of your use of them on the single machine.

In addition, some of the programs in this package are intended to be incorporated into your own programs; these programs are specifically listed below. For this purpose, you are licensed to incorporate the listed programs into your own programs, in either source format, object format or BLOADable format. You may then distribute the resulting programs for use on other machines, subject to the following restrictions:

1) the incorporated material must contain intact the original copyright notice;

2) you may not distribute the source format of these programs;

3) you may not distribute the object format independently, in a form which allows them to be incorporated into programs other than your own;

4) you may not distribute the BLOADable format together with information indicating how they could be utilized by programs other than your own.

The programs which you may incorporate into your own programs and distribute, subject to the above restrictions, are those which appear in the diskette files with names listed here:

| | |
|---|---|
| DIR.INC | DOSA.ASM |
| FAT.INC | DOSA.OBJ |
| | DOSA.BLD |
| DIRFAT.PAS | DOSA.INC |
| DIRFAT.OBJ | DOSP.PAS |
| DIRFAT.INC | DOSP.OBJ |
| | DOSP.INC |
| A.ASM | |
| A.OBJ | DISKA.ASM |
| A.BLD | DISKA.OBJ |
| | DISKA.BLD |
| A.INC | DISKA.INC |
| P.PAS | DISKP.PAS |
| P.OBJ | DISKP.OBJ |
| P.INC | DISKP.INC |
| PROTECTA.ASM | VIDEOA.ASM |
| PROTECTA.OBJ | VIDEOA.OBJ |
| PROTECTA.BLD | VIDEOA.BLD |
| PROTECTA.INC | VIDEOA.INC |
| PROTECTP.PAS | VIDEOP.PAS |
| PROTECTP.OBJ | VIDEOP.OBJ |
| PROTECTP.INC | VIDEOP.INC. |

## Introduction

Here is the program documentation which you need to get the best possible use of this package of software tools, which accompany the book, "Inside the IBM Personal Computer: Access to Advanced Features and Programming."

This software package comes on two diskettes (three sides). It consists of 75 files, organized into nine categories and 30 groups of programs. Over 120 programming access tools are provided, in addition to five important ready-to-use programs, and numerous demonstration programs.

This is a lot.

There is so much useful programming here, it is unlikely that anyone will make use of it all—but everyone who uses an IBM/PC will be able to get a great deal of benefit from various parts of these programs. And anyone who is doing advanced program development for the PC should find the access tools extremely useful.

If you do not yet think of yourself as an advanced user of the PC, don't turn away from these programs. There is much here that you can use immediately, and as your experience with the PC grows, the usefulness of this package will grow as well. And in this package you will find one program—the power tool DiskLook—which is extremely useful to beginners and advanced users alike, and which teaches relative novices a great deal about their diskettes.

This documentation is designed to help you get the most out of these programs, now and in the future. It is organized into eight sections, to help you quickly skip through to the parts that are of most use to you:

1) A general discussion of what is here; a quick summary will help you make sense of this complete package.

2) A list of the 75 files that make up this package, for easy and quick cross reference.

3) A description of the features and use of the power-tool utility, DiskLook.

4) A description of the features and use of several miscellaneous programs.

5) A technical description of how the access tools are organized, and how they are used.

6) A list of the access tools, arranged in two orders, for easy and quick cross reference.

7) A list of the Pascal programs which augment the access tools, arranged for easy and quick cross reference.

8) An explanation of the copy protection scheme that is included in this package.

## Section 1: General Discussion

Here is an overall summary of the contents of this software package. The parts of this package fall into nine categories:

A) Power tools

B) BASIC demonstration programs

C) Sound demonstration programs

D) Port exploration program

E) ROM exploration programs

F) Pascal access examples

G) Diskette system processing routines

H) Copy protection scheme

I) Complete access routines

Here is a brief explanation of each category; later we will list the programs in each category in more detail:

A) Power tools

This consists of the diskette display program DiskLook. A batch execution file, DISKLOOK.BAT, is provided to quickly demonstrate DiskLook.

B) BASIC demonstration programs

There are four BASIC programs here, which will demonstrate various things about the IBM/PC, including its complete character set, its display attributes, its active memory, and the control of its keyboard.

The programming techniques in these programs can be very instructive in two ways. First to illustrate modern structured programming methods, and second to show some of the programming tricks for the IBM/PC. The BASIC programming language is a clumsy one to use, and these programming examples can help you use BASIC at its best.

C) Sound demonstration programs

There are four sound generation programs here, illustrating different methods of producing sounds on the IBM/PC. A batch execution file, TONE-TEST.BAT, will demonstrate these programs. The source code for these programs explains the details of how sounds are produced.

D) Port exploration program

This program searches the IBM/PC port address space for ports which may be active. This program is interesting, but it has almost no practical value in use. Its importance to us is that it provides models for several purposes. It illustrates structured programming in Pascal, illustrates how to write an assembly-language subroutine, and illustrates how to connect Pascal and assembler routines.

E) ROM exploration programs

These two programs copy and compare the ROM storage data from IBM/PCs. The operation of these programs, and the format of their display is interesting in its own right, but it also provides a method of checking for changes which IBM makes in the future, which they may not publicly reveal.

F) Pascal access examples

These four Pascal demonstration programs sections show how to access parts of the IBM/PC system from Pascal (and indicate how it would be done in other languages). Illustrated are checking the date stamp release marker on the system's ROM-BIOS, accessing and changing the diskette control parameters (the "disk base"), and how to do direct memory mapped control of the display screens, in either character mode (which applies to both the monochrome and color-graphics systems) and graphics mode (color-graphics only).

G) Diskette system processing routines

These three Pascal program sections define the format of the diskette directory and file allocation table (FAT), and provide routines to process the directory and FAT. This is useful both to understand the diskette format, and for programming purposes such as rapid access of file data.

H) Copy protection scheme

These programs provide methods for copy protecting diskettes. A complete ready-to-use method is given, and the tools are provided to construct a customized protection scheme.

I) Complete access routines

Here, programs are provided to give access to all of the service facilities of the DOS operating system, and the ROM-BIOS. In each of five service topics, an assembly-language interface routine makes these services accessible to BASIC, Pascal and most other languages. Then, in addition, Pascal interface definitions, and support routines, make the assembler routines easier to use, for Pascal programmers.

The assembler is not needed to make use of these routines.

For BASIC programmers, these interface routines are already converted into BASIC's BLOAD format. For users of Pascal and other languages, these routines come in linkable object form.

For assembly language programmers, who may wish to adapt or customize these routines, the assembler source code is provided.

Here is a detailed listing of the thirty program groups in each of the nine categories:

## A) Power Tools

1) The power-tool program DiskLook appears in the package, in the program file DL.EXE. DiskLook provides you with a complete information and exploration source for investigating your diskettes. DiskLook will show you:

   —A complete map of the space utilization of each diskette

   —The location of any bad sectors, conflicting file allocation or temporarily unusable sectors

   —Complete directory information for each file, including information that is not otherwise available

   —A map of the location of each file, indicating space fragmentation problems

   —The names of all files erased from the diskette, and an indication if each can be recovered

   —A complete file directory listing, sorted by name, extension, date and time or file size

   —A display of any data on the diskette, shown in either hexadecimal format or text-file line format

## B) BASIC Demonstration Programs

Four BASIC language programs, which demonstrate and explore parts of the PC, are included. These programs are:

2) CHARS.BAS, corresponding to listing 1.1, will demonstrate all of the display-screen characters, including those which cannot be displayed by conventional BASIC language methods.

3) ATTRIB.BAS, corresponding to listing 8.1, will demonstrate all of the possible combinations of screen attributes, including all color combinations.

4) MEMLIST.BAS, corresponding to listing 3.1, will find and display the location of all the active memory on your PC system.

5) KEYBITS.BAS, corresponding to listing 10.1, will display the keyboard status bits, and dynamically demonstrate their action.

## C) Sound Demonstration Programs

Four assembly language programs demonstrate three variations on how to produce sounds on the IBM/PC. Each appears as a source listing (with the file name extension of ".ASM"), and as an executable program file (with the file name extension of ".COM").

6) BEEP, in the files BEEP.ASM and BEEP.COM, demonstrates a pure sound, generated by a program. This corresponds to listing 3.2.

7) WARBLE, in the files WARBLE.ASM and WARBLE.COM, demonstrates a program generated sound, altered by the effect of clock interrupts. This corresponds to listing 3.2.

8) UPSCALE, in the files UPSCALE.ASM and UPSCALE.COM, demonstrates a changing sound pitch, generated by a program.

9) A440, in the files A440.ASM and A440.COM, demonstrates a sound generated by the system programmable timer, which continues without program intervention. This corresponds to listing 11.1.

## D) Port Exploration Program

10) PORTTEST, in the executable program file PORTTEST.EXE and the two program source files PORTEST.PAS and INPORT.ASM, explores all of the ports in the IBM/PC, reporting which ones appear to possibly be active. This corresponds to listings 3.3 and 3.4.

## E) ROM Exploration Programs

Two programs are provided to read and compare the ROM-BASIC and ROM-BIOS installed in an IBM/PC.

11) ROMSAVE, in the executable program file ROMSAVE.EXE, will report the release marker on a version of ROM, and copy the complete ROM to diskette, for comparison and analysis.

12) ROMCOMP, in the executable program file ROMCOMP.EXE, will read and compare any two copies of the ROM, as produced by ROMSAVE. This program will display both versions of ROM, in hex and ASCII, and search for differences. When differences are found, the program will pause, and highlight the differences.

6

## F) Pascal Access Examples

Three program listings are provided to illustrate how Pascal is used to access three parts of the system. These programs are illustrative only, and so appear only in source format.

13) BIOSDATE, in the source file BIOSDATE.PAS, illustrates how a program can dynamically test the version of the ROM-BIOS that is being used. This corresponds to listing 6.1.

14) DISKBASE, in the source file DISKBASE.PAS, illustrates how to access, copy and modify the diskette controlling parameters in the disk base table. This corresponds to listing 7.1.

15) VIDEODEM, in the source file VIDEODEM.PAS, illustrates how to do direct memory-mapped output to the display screens in Pascal. This corresponds to listing 8.2.

16) GRAPHDEM, in the source file GRAPHDEM.PAS, illustrates how to do direct memory-mapped graphics output to the display screens in Pascal. This corresponds to listing 9.1.

## G) Diskette System Processing Routines

Three program listings are provided to give Pascal access to the diskette directory and file allocation table (FAT). These programs provide a thorough set of tools to access the diskette directory, decode the directory and FAT, trace file allocation, and more.

17) DIR/FAT/DIRFAT, in the Pascal source files DIR.INC, FAT.INC, DIRFAT.PAS and DIRFAT.INC, and the linkable object file DIRFAT.OBJ provide the diskette processing tools. This corresponds to listings 5.1, 5.2 and 5.3.

## H) Copy Protection Scheme

This set of Pascal and assembly programs provides a simple but workable means of making diskettes copy protected. The method is not state-of-the-art, and every method that I know of can be relatively easily broken by readily available programs intended to bust copy protection. These programs, though, will give you an ordinary and usable degree of copy protection for your diskettes.

18) PROTECTA, in the source file PROTECTA.ASM and the assembled object file PROTECTA.OBJ, provides the assembly language service routines needed to do copy-protected formatting, data storage and data retrieval. This corresponds to listing 7.103.

19) PROTECTP, in the source file PROTECTP.PAS and the compiled object file PROTECTP.OBJ, provides the Pascal language service routines needed to do copy protection, giving access to the facilities of PROTECTA for your own programs. This corresponds to listing 7.104.

20) PROTECT, in the source file PROTECT.PAS and the ready-to-use program file PROTECT.EXE, provides a complete copy protection service which can be used to copy-protect batches of diskettes quickly. Naturally, when

7

you copy-protect a diskette, your programs must check the copy-protection when they are run, and the Pascal source file PROTECT.INC provides a routine which your programs can use to do this.

## I) Complete Access Routine

These five sets of Pascal and assembly-language routines provide complete access to all of the features of the ROM-BIOS and DOS. The programs are organized to correspond to the chapters of this book; they may be used in that form, or you may combine separate parts of these programs to get just the sections that you need in a compact form.

Each of the programs listed below contains numerous usable routines within it.

21) DOSA provides assembler access to the many DOS service routines. The source file DOSA.ASM and the object file DOSA.OBJ give the routines themselves, while the source file DOSA.INC provides the Pascal declarations needed to use these routines. This corresponds to listing 4.101.

22) DOSP provides Pascal support routines to make the use of the DOSA routines easier and more effective. The source file DOSP.PAS and the object file DOSP.OBJ give the routines themselves, while the source file DOSP.INC provides the Pascal declarations needed to use these routines from your programs. This corresponds to listing 4.102.

23) DISKA provides assembler access to the ROM-BIOS diskette service routines. The source file DISKA.ASM and the object file DISKA.OBJ give the routines themselves, while the source file DISKA.INC provides the Pascal declarations needed to use these routines. This corresponds to listing 7.101.

24) DISKP provides Pascal support routines to make the use of the DISKA routines easier and more effective. The source file DISKP.PAS and the object file DISKP.OBJ give the routines themselves, while the source file DISKP.INC provides the Pascal declarations needed to use these routines from your programs. This corresponds to listing 7.102.

25) VIDEOA provides assembler access to the ROM-BIOS display service routines. The source file VIDEOA.ASM and the object file VIDEOA.OBJ give the routines themselves, while the source file VIDEOA.INC provides the Pascal declarations needed to use these routines. This corresponds to listing 8.101.

26) VIDEOP provides Pascal support routines to make the use of the VIDEOA routines easier and more effective. The source file VIDEOP.PAS and the object file VIDEOP.OBJ give the routines themselves, while the source file VIDEOP.INC provides the Pascal declarations needed to use these routines from your programs. This corresponds to listing 8.102.

27) KEYA provides assembler access to the many ROM-BIOS keyboard service routines. The source file KEYA.ASM and the object file KEYA.OBJ give the routines themselves, while the source file KEYA.INC provides the Pascal

declarations needed to use these routines. This corresponds to listing 10.101.

28) KEYP provides Pascal support routines to make the use of the KEYA routines easier and more effective. The source file KEYP.PAS and the object file KEYP.OBJ give the routines themselves, while the source file KEYP.INC provides the Pascal declarations needed to use these routines from your programs. This corresponds to listing 10.102.

29) MISCA provides assembler access to the miscellaneous ROM-BIOS service routines, including those for the cassette, printer, asynchronous communications adapter, print-screen, system-reset, ROM-BASIC and others. The source file MISCA.ASM and the object file MISCA.OBJ give the routines themselves, while the source file MISCA.INC provides the Pascal declarations needed to use these routines. This corresponds to listing 11.101.

30) MISCP provides Pascal support routines to make the use of the MISCA routines easier and more effective. The source file MISCP.PAS and the object file MISCP.OBJ give the routines themselves, while the source file MISCP.INC provides the Pascal declarations needed to use these routines from your programs. This corresponds to listing 11.102.

## Section 2: File List

This software package comes in 75 files, which is quite a bit to wade through. To make it easier to find any desired part, here is a list of the files, with the diskette they appear on, their file name and extension, the corresponding listing number from the book, and a short description.

| Disk | Filename | Ext | Book Listing Number | Description |
|---|---|---|---|---|
| 1 | DISKLOOK | BAT | | DiskLook demonstration batch file |
| 1 | DL | EXE | | DiskLook (executable) |
| 1 | CHARS | BAS | 1.1 | character set demonstration |
| 1 | ATTRIB | BAS | 8.1 | attributes of display demonstration |
| 1 | MEMLIST | BAS | 3.1 | memory search demonstration |
| 1 | KEYBITS | BAS | 10.1 | keyboard control bits demonstration |
| 1 | TONETEST | BAT | | sound demonstration batch file |
| 1 | BEEP | ASM | 3.2 | sound demonstration program (assembler source) |
| 1 | BEEP | COM | 3.2 | sound demonstration program (executable) |
| 1 | WARBLE | ASM | 3.2 | sound demonstration program (assembler source) |
| 1 | WARBLE | COM | 3.2 | sound demonstration program (executable) |
| 1 | UPSCALE | ASM | | sound demonstration program (assembler source) |
| 1 | UPSCALE | COM | | sound demonstration program (executable) |
| 1 | A440 | ASM | 11.1 | sound demonstration program (assembler source) |
| 1 | A440 | COM | 11.1 | sound demonstration program (executable) |
| 1 | PORTTEST | EXE | 3.3/4 | port demonstration program (executable) |
| 1 | PORTTEST | PAS | 3.3 | port demonstration program (Pascal source) |

9

| Disk | Filename | Ext | Book Listing Number | Description |
|------|----------|-----|--------|-------------|
| 1 | INPORT | ASM | 3.4 | port demonstration program (assembler source) |
| 1 | ROMSAVE | EXE | | ROM exploration copy program (executable) |
| 1 | ROMCOMP | EXE | | ROM exploration compare program (executable) |
| 1 | BIOSDATE | PAS | 6.1 | ROM-BIOS date checking illustration (Pascal source) |
| 1 | DISKBASE | PAS | 7.1 | diskette parameter change illustration (Pascal source) |
| 1 | VIDEODEM | PAS | 8.2 | character screen output illustration (Pascal source) |
| 1 | GRAPHDEM | PAS | 9.1 | graphics screen output illustration (Pascal source) |
| 2 | DIR | INC | 5.1 | directory definitions (Pascal definitions) |
| 2 | FAT | INC | 5.2 | FAT definitions (Pascal definitions) |
| 2 | DIRFAT | PAS | 5.3 | directory and FAT processing tools (Pascal source) |
| 2 | DIRFAT | OBJ | 5.3 | directory and FAT processing tools (linkable object) |
| 2 | DIRFAT | INC | 5.3 | directory and FAT processing tools (Pascal definitions) |
| 2 | PROTECTA | ASM | 7.103 | diskette copy protection tools (assembler source) |
| 2 | PROTECTA | OBJ | 7.103 | diskette copy protection tools (linkable object) |
| 2 | PROTECTA | BLD | 7.103 | diskette copy protection tools (BLOADable object) |
| 2 | PROTECTA | INC | 7.103 | diskette copy protection tools (Pascal definitions) |
| 2 | PROTECTP | PAS | 7.104 | diskette copy protection tools (Pascal source) |
| 2 | PROTECTP | OBJ | 7.104 | diskette copy protection tools (linkable object) |
| 2 | PROTECTP | INC | 7.104 | diskette copy protection tools (Pascal definitions) |
| 2 | PROTECT | PAS | 7.105 | diskette copy-protector (Pascal source) |
| 2 | PROTECT | EXE | 7.105 | diskette copy-protector (executable) |
| 2 | PROTECT | INC | 7.105 | diskette copy-protector (Pascal source for checking) |
| 2 | PROTECT | BAS | 7.105 | diskette copy-protector (BASIC source for checking) |
| 2 | DOSA | ASM | 4.101 | DOS services access tools (assembler source) |
| 2 | DOSA | OBJ | 4.101 | DOS services access tools (linkable object) |
| 2 | DOSA | BLD | 4.101 | DOS services access tools (BLOADable object) |
| 3 | DOSA | INC | 4.101 | DOS services access tools (Pascal definitions) |
| 3 | DOSP | PAS | 4.102 | DOS services access tools (Pascal source) |
| 3 | DOSP | OBJ | 4.102 | DOS services access tools (linkable object) |
| 3 | DOSP | INC | 4.102 | DOS services access tools (Pascal definitions) |
| 3 | DISKA | ASM | 7.101 | diskette services access tools (assembler source) |
| 3 | DISKA | OBJ | 7.101 | diskette services access tools (linkable object) |
| 3 | DISKA | BLD | 7.101 | diskette services access tools (BLOADable object) |

| Disk | Filename | Ext | Book Listing Number | Description |
|---|---|---|---|---|
| 3 | DISKA | INC | 7.101 | diskette services access tools (Pascal definitions) |
| 3 | DISKP | PAS | 7.101 | diskette services access tools (Pascal source) |
| 3 | DISKP | OBJ | 7.101 | diskette services access tools (linkable object) |
| 3 | DISKP | INC | 7.101 | diskette services access tools (Pascal definitions) |
| 3 | VIDEOA | ASM | 8.101 | video services access tools (assembler source) |
| 3 | VIDEOA | OBJ | 8.101 | video services access tools (linkable object) |
| 3 | VIDEOA | BLD | 8.101 | video services access tools (BLOADable object) |
| 3 | VIDEOA | INC | 8.101 | video services access tools (Pascal definitions) |
| 3 | VIDEOP | PAS | 8.101 | video services access tools (Pascal source) |
| 3 | VIDEOP | OBJ | 8.101 | video services access tools (linkable object) |
| 3 | VIDEOP | INC | 8.101 | video services access tools (Pascal definitions) |
| 3 | KEYA | ASM | 10.101 | keyboard services access tools (assembler source) |
| 3 | KEYA | OBJ | 10.101 | keyboard services access tools (linkable object) |
| 3 | KEYA | BLD | 10.101 | keyboard services access tools (BLOADable object) |
| 3 | KEYA | INC | 10.101 | keyboard services access tools (Pascal definitions) |
| 3 | KEYP | PAS | 10.101 | keyboard services access tools (Pascal source) |
| 3 | KEYP | OBJ | 10.101 | keyboard services access tools (linkable object) |
| 3 | KEYP | INC | 10.101 | keyboard services access tools (Pascal definitions) |
| 3 | MISCA | ASM | 11.101 | miscellaneous services access tools (assembler source) |
| 3 | MISCA | OBJ | 11.101 | miscellaneous services access tools (linkable object) |
| 3 | MISCA | BLD | 11.101 | miscellaneous services access tools (BLOADable object) |
| 3 | MISCA | INC | 11.101 | miscellaneous services access tools (Pascal definitions) |
| 3 | MISCP | PAS | 11.101 | miscellaneous services access tools (Pascal source) |
| 3 | MISCP | OBJ | 11.101 | miscellaneous services access tools (linkable object) |
| 3 | MISCP | INC | 11.101 | miscellaneous services access tools (Pascal definitions) |

## Section 3: DiskLook

In this section, we'll explain the features and operation of the power-tool utility program, DiskLook.

Here is one preface warning: many people do not bother to read program documentation, since it is often a nuisance. And DiskLook is easy enough to use, that it hardly needs any documentation. Two of DiskLook's features do not appear on its menu display, and you may miss them—so be sure to read the discussion below of the two "Alt" keys, Alt-f1 and Alt-f2.

To get a quick demonstration of DiskLook, put the first of these three diskettes in your PC's "A" diskette drive, and type in DISKLOOK. A demonstration batch file will activate DiskLook.

## General Information

DiskLook is a utility which will display a wide range of information about diskettes, including formatted directory listings, complete data displays and diskette maps.

DiskLook operates on IBM/PC computers, under the DOS operating system, with 64K or more of memory, one diskette drive, and an 80-column display.

DiskLook will operate with either the monochrome display, or the color graphics display; color is used to enhance DiskLook's displays.

DiskLook will operate on double-sided diskettes, which are supported with DOS release 1.10.

DiskLook may be used with any DOS release (1.00, 1.05, 1.10), with single or double sided diskettes, and with any 80-column display.

## A Summary of DiskLook's Special Features

DiskLook is a very richly featured diskette display routine. It has the capability to show virtually everything that anyone might want to know about what is stored on a diskette.

First, DiskLook gives formatted directory listings, showing file names in order—alphabetically, or by creation date and time, or by size and other ways. Hidden files are included in the directory listing.

Next, DiskLook can display any sector on the diskette, either in the line format of an ASCII text file or in hexadecimal notation. Data can be selected for display either by what file the data belongs to, or by its location on the diskette.

Next, DiskLook will map the entire diskette's storage use, indicating where files are located, where unusable bad tracks are, and other information.

Finally, DiskLook will show the complete directory information for each file, including a display map of where the file is located.

Two special notes about DiskLook and system modifications. DiskLook is designed specifically for work with diskettes, and the version included in this package does not work on the various hard disk systems that are available. However, DiskLook will work under most hard disk system modifications, and it will work well under the JEL/JFORMAT system modification from Tall Tree Systems; in particular, it will accept drive specifications through F:.

Unusual diskette formats, including JEL 10-sector format, and some copy-protected formats, will not work with DiskLook.

## Uses for DiskLook

DiskLook has numerous uses. First, it is a major enhancement to the DOS command DIR—since DiskLook will give a directory listing that shows the files in order (alphabetically and otherwise), including all hidden files.

Second, DiskLook is a wonderful browsing tool. DiskLook allows the user to completely explore the contents of diskettes, revealing the data stored, and showing a great deal of information about how DOS controls diskettes. With its rich display and mapping abilities, DiskLook shows you information that you are looking for, and helps you learn new things about your IBM/PC computer's use of diskettes.

Third, DiskLook will help you get the best use of your diskettes, by revealing bad tracks, by showing space usage, and by indicating when file storage is fragmented. This information can make it possible for you to get faster and more effective use of the data on your diskette.

## Starting DiskLook

DiskLook is started like this: **DL [d:]**

The drive specification may be A: through F:. For convenience, the colon part of the drive specification may be left out. If the drive specification is omitted, DiskLook assumes drive B. DiskLook assumes drive B (rather than the current DOS default drive) because the most common way of using the diskette drives is to place program diskettes in drive A and data diskettes in drive B.

## Operating Information

DiskLook is self-explanatory in use. The information below summarizes the operation of DiskLook, and gives details on some of the operations.

**Menu:** DiskLook's menu outlines the operations which can be performed. When a menu is displayed, the function keys are highlighted to indicate which operations are permitted.

The menu may be displayed at any time, by using function key f1.

**Function keys:**

f1 : skips to the menu, and skips back to the display before the menu.

f2 : reads directory information from a new diskette; this function key is only used if the diskette is changed after the previous diskette has been read; the diskette is read to determine single or double sided formatting, and to learn the file directory. Note: f2 is pressed after the diskette has been changed, not before.

f3 : begins a sorted directory display; another function key is pressed to select what order the file names are to be listed in—by name, by the extension to the name, by creation date and time, by file size or by the file attribute (normal, hidden etc). The directory listing may show the names of existing files (odd function keys) or the names of erased files (even function keys). Erased files may be recovered with the utility UnErase, part of the Norton Utilities.

f4 : displays the complete directory information for a file; if a file has been selected (with f8), that file is shown, otherwise the first file in the directory is shown. The display includes all directory information, even information that DOS commands do not reveal. If the file shown is an existing file, a map of its location is given; if the file is an erased file, a message indicates whether or not it is likely that the file can be recovered.

f5 : displays a sector's data in the line format of an ASCII text file (ASCII files are used by the DOS editor EDLIN, most word processors, and by compilers; BASIC programs are in ASCII format when the "SAVE ,A" command is used). Data displays may be quickly switched between the f5-line and f6-hexadecimal formats. Note—before f5 is used, a sector must be selected for display with f7 or f8.

f6 : displays a sector's data in hexadecimal format, showing both hexadecimal and character coding. Data displays may be quickly switched between the f5-line and f6-hexadecimal formats. Note—before f6 is used, a sector must be selected for display with f7 or f8.

f7 : begins the process of selecting a sector by its absolute location. When selecting a sector, backspace may be used to correct an error.

f8 : begins the process of selecting a sector by file. A list of all of the files on the diskette is displayed.

f9 : displays a map of the complete diskette space usage.

f10 : ends DiskLook, displays the elapsed time and date, and returns control to DOS.

### Alternate function keys:

Alt-f1 : DiskLook makes full use of the IBM/PC's color capabilities; however, when the color-graphics adapter is used with a monochrome display (not the IBM monochrome display, but another one, connected to the color-graphics adapter), color signals often result in a screen that is not legible. Pressing Alt-f1, after DiskLook displays its starting menu, will tell DiskLook to suppress its use of color.

Alt-f2 : The "print screen" operation, with the PrtSc key, can be used with DiskLook at any time. However, the screen information may contain characters that are also printer control codes, which will interfere with the printing of the screen data. Pressing Alt-f2 will tell DiskLook to convert its current screen display into a format which can be printed; all characters which might not be printable are converted into periods.

**Directory displays:** When DiskLook gives a directory listing, the file names appear in the chosen order. Creation date, size or attributes are shown for those display orders. When erased file names are shown, the first character of the file name is shown as a question mark ("?"), since erasing a file destroys the first character of the name.

If there are more files than can be shown on the screen at one time, it is indicated with a message. The left and right arrow keys can be used to shift the display one column left or right to show the rest of the files.

**Sector displays:** When DiskLook displays a sector, the sector location is given on the top line. If the sector belongs to a file, the file name is given on the second line. The sector data is displayed, in either line or hexadecimal format; if the line format is used, and the data appears to DiskLook not to be an ASCII text file, a message is given. The left and right arrows can be used to display the prior and next sectors (of the diskette, when the sector was selected with f7, or of the file when a file was selected with f8); for a selected file, home and end may also be used.

**Diskette map:** When the diskette map is displayed, all storage use is shown, indicating categories, such as in use, in use by a hidden file, and so forth. The location of bad tracks is shown. If there is a conflict in storage allocation (a very rare occurrence), that is shown. If space is shown as temporarily unavailable, that means that it is allocated, but does not belong to any file; this can happen occasionally, particularly with the IBM Pascal compiler. The DOS utility CHKDSK will recover any temporarily unavailable space, and also repair conflicting storage allocation.

**Directory information displays:** When the complete directory information is displayed for a file, the directory data is both decoded to indicate its meaning and also shown in hexadecimal. Any errors or unconventional information is indicated. For existing files, the location of the file is mapped, which will indicate if the file is fragmented or poorly located for fast access. For erased files, no map is possible, but an indication is given if it is likely that the file can be recovered by UnErase, which is part of the Norton Utility package.

## Section 4: Miscellaneous Programs

Five ready-to-use programs are included in this package: DiskLook, PORT-TEST, ROMSAVE, ROMCOMP and PROTECT. This section explains how to use the last four.

PORTTEST requires no special operating instructions, or diskette files; you run it simply by entering its name. If you wish a printed copy of the data that PORTTEST displays, turn on the printer-echo feature of your computer, by pressing Ctrl-PrtSc.

ROMSAVE reads the ROM programs, both BASIC and BIOS, and stores them in a diskette file, for later use. When you invoke ROMSAVE, you must provide a diskette file specification, indicating where you want the data stored. The primary purpose of ROMSAVE is to prepare ROM data for ROMCOMP to inspect.

ROMCOMP reads from diskette two copies of the ROM data, and displays them on the screen. Whenever any difference is found, ROMCOMP pauses, and highlights the differences. When you invoke ROMCOMP, you must provide two diskette file specifications, indicating the two versions of ROM to be compared. If you do not have copies of the ROM's from two computers, you may get a demonstration of ROMCOMP's operation by using ROMSAVE to produce one copy of a ROM, and then run ROMCOMP, giving it the same file name for both of its input files.

PROTECT is used to modify diskettes for copy protection. It reformats track 39, side 0 to have an unconventional sector 8. PROTECT performs its work on drive B only. PROTECT reads any existing data on track 39, and returns it to the re-formatted track. PROTECT indicates its progress as it is operating, and reports any difficulties to you. Its operation is largely self-explanatory.

# Section 5: Technical Discussion of the Access Tools

The access tools in this software package are organized into five groups, by subject: DOS service routines, diskette services, video services, keyboard services and miscellaneous services, plus a sixth group created specially for copy protection.

A common format is provided for all of the service areas. In each case, there are a number of services provided by the DOS operating system or the ROM-BIOS, which are not directly accessible from high-level programming languages, such as BASIC and Pascal. Normally they must be invoked from the assembly language level. The purpose of these access tools is to make the services usable to high-level languages.

For each service, these access tools provide an interface routine which allows high-level programming languages to invoke them. Special provisions are made for the use of BASIC and Pascal. Any other language which uses a compatible calling structure can also make use of these routines.

For each of the five groups, there are seven files, all beginning with the same identifying letters, such as "DOS" for the DOS services. Here are the names of the seven files, and their purposes:

xxxA.ASM — This file contains the assembly language source code for the interface routine. It has two purposes. For everyone who uses these interface routines, the comments at the head of the program provide the primary source of technical information about the routines that are provided. For those who work with assembly language, the source code also makes it easier to modify, adapt or re-group the services.

xxxA.OBJ — This file contains the assembled object code for the "xxxA.ASM" program. This is a form of the interface routines which can be linked together with compiled programs, such as Pascal, compiled BASIC, and other languages. Because of this object file, it is not necessary for you to have the IBM Macro Assembler to make use of these interface routines.

xxxA.BLD — This file is the "xxxA.OBJ" object code, converted into the BASIC language BLOAD format. This equivalent of the OBJ file must be used for interpreter BASIC, and it may be used for compiled BASIC.

xxxA.INC — This file contains the Pascal language definitions of the assembler interface routines. Any Pascal program which uses those routines must have them declared. This file can be included into a Pascal program, to automatically provide the necessary definitions.

xxxP.PAS — This file contains the Pascal language source code for support programs for the assembler interface programs. The assembler routines are not in the most convenient form for Pascal to use, and in most cases they can be usefully augmented by some supporting programs. This file provides those services, in source format. The source code is useful both to help understand what is being done, and to make it convenient for you to adapt or customize these services.

xxxP.OBJ — This file contains the compiled object code for the "xxxP.PAS" module. If you are using Pascal, then you could compile these programs yourself, but as a convenience, and for consistency with the assembler interface routines, the object code is provided.

xxxP.INC — This file contains the Pascal language definitions of the Pascal support module. As with the assembler routines, the Pascal routines must be declared in any program which uses them. This file can be included into a Pascal program, to automatically provide the necessary definitions.

To help you fully understand these access tools, we'll discuss their calling conventions, and how they are used in BASIC and Pascal. Finally, this section ends with some reference and access notes.

## Calling Conventions

All of the assembler interface routines operate under the same calling conventions, which are tailored to the limited calling mechanisms of BASIC.

All parameters appear in the form of two-byte words or integers, and they are made accessible and changeable by passing their data segment offsets through the stack. This is the only form of parameter passing available to BASIC, and it is the form used by Pascal, when a parameter is declared in the format "var x : word". Most languages use this calling form, since it is the most primitive and dangerous available.

To make it possible to manipulate the parameters in nearly any language, the two-byte word/integer format is used. In most instances, the values being passed are non-negative integers, so this form is appropriate anyway. BASIC can manipulate this format with "%"-type integer variables; Pascal can treat them declared as either INTEGER, or, for fewer problems, WORD.

When TRUE/FALSE values are needed, one is used for TRUE and zero for FALSE, which is consistent with both BASIC and Pascal usage.

When address values are needed, either in offset or segmented format, the word format serves as well, and is consistent with both BASIC's usage of DEF SEG and VARPTR, and also Pascal's treatment of ADR, ADS and the ".R" and ".S" components of segmented addresses.

## Basic Usage

To use these routines from interpreter BASIC, you must follow the usual rules for accessing assembly language routines. An appropriate location must be found to load them, it must be indicated with a DEF SEG statement, and the routine must be loaded with a BLOAD statement. The offset into the assembler module must be assigned to a variable, and that variable name must be called.

It is essential that the correct number of parameters is passed, and that they are all in the integer format.

A fuller discussion can be found in the IBM BASIC manual, appendix C, "Machine Language Subroutines".

A working example of the mechanics of doing this can be found in the file PROTECT.BAS. You should read it closely, if you need guidance in how to use assembly language routines from BASIC.

The offsets necessary for calling these services within each module can be found in the next section, along with the names of each service.

For compiled BASIC, two calling options are available. Either the interpreter BLOAD mechanism can be used (in which case the CALL statements must be converted to the CALL ABSOLUTE format), or linkage CALLs can be used. In the case of a linkage call, the same rules used by Pascal apply: the external name of the service appears in the CALL statement, rather than the name of a variable containing the routine's offset location, and the OBJ object module must be added to the linker parameters.

Some warnings are in order. Although all of these services are made accessible to BASIC for completenesses sake, not all of them are compatible with the way that BASIC does business. This partly stems from the nature of BASIC on the IBM/PC: it was converted, somewhat in haste, from other versions of BASIC, and also it is not fully integrated into the DOS and ROM-BIOS way of doing things.

In principle each of these assembler interface routines has been made usable by BASIC, but you should carefully test the usability of any service before committing yourself to its use.

## Pascal Usage

Use of these assembler interface routines is more straightforward in Pascal. Each routine takes the form of an external procedure, which takes parameters in the word format. All parameters are passed in the reference format, declared with the prefix "var". Any values returned are passed back through modified variables.

This calling convention is not the most convenient for Pascal users, but it is necessary for compatibility with BASIC and other languages. It does have one advantage, which is ruthless consistency. There is no question about which parameters must be variables, rather than expressions: all parameters must be variables, whether it is convenient or not.

Likewise, all values returned are via the parameter list: there are no function values returned (BASIC would not have access to them).

To make life easier for the Pascal user, the declarations in the "xxxA.INC" files eliminate much of the tedium of setting up for these services, and the additional support services in the "xxxP" programs make these routines even easier to use.

One exception is made to the otherwise universal declaration of all parameters to the assembler interface routines being in word form. When an address offset value is needed (without a segment prefix), the parameter is declared as ADRMEM, which allows use of the ADR function without conversion to word format. If you prefer a completely consistent parameter format, these declarations may be converted to word format, which is functionally the same.

For models of how to use these routines, you can inspect the code in the file "PROTECT.INC" (which is the Pascal equivalent of the BASIC "PROTECT-.BAS" program file), and also the coding in the support modules, which are in the "xxxP.PAS" files. If there is any uncertainty about the coding conventions used, refering to these files should answer your questions.

## Reference and Access Notes: Where to Turn, How to Use

It should be pretty clear that the use of these access tools, and any similar mechanisms, is not for beginners. But they should not be reserved for use by only the most advanced and technically oriented programmers.

The format and presentation of these access tools has been adjusted to an intermediate level of sophistication, so that the greatest number of appropriate program developers can make good use of them. We have avoided a complete tutorial explanation of these tools, for fear that it might mislead some into getting in well over their heads.

In preparing these access tools, I have followed the IBM Pascal compiler's example—and an excellent example, I believe—of presenting material with everything that is necessary to see how to use it, without laboriously explaining everything.

This can lead, however, to some confusion of where to turn to understand what these tools are, and how to use them. Here is the "where to find it" for these access tools.

First, for a simple outline of how to make use of these tools, read and follow the example found in the source modules, PROTECT.BAS, and PROTECT.INC and PROTECT.PAS as well.

To understand what the function of each access tool is, read the discussions in the corresponding chapter of "Inside the IBM Personal Computer." For notes on any peculiarities of each access routine, see the comments in the assembler source file, xxxA.ASM. For a list of the parameters which each function takes, see either the assembler source file, xxxA.ASM, or the Pascal definitions in the source file xxxA.INC. The names given to the parameter variables make clear their purpose.

If more detailed technical information is needed, beyond what is provided by the comments in the source files, and in the discussion in the book, you can turn to the IBM Technical Reference manual (particularly to the comments buried in appendix A, the ROM-BIOS listing) and to the appendices to the DOS manual.

## Section 6: Access Tool List

Here is a list of the 90 assembler interface routines, which provide access to DOS and ROM-BIOS services, for easy cross reference. First, here is a list of the descriptive routine names, and the modules in which they appear, in order by routine name:

| Routine Name | Module Name |
|---|---|
| BOOT-STRAP | MISCA |
| CASSETTE-MOTOR-OFF | MISCA |
| CASSETTE-MOTOR-ON | MISCA |
| CASSETTE-READ-BLOCKS | MISCA |
| CASSETTE-WRITE-BLOCKS | MISCA |
| COMM-GET-ONE-CHAR | MISCA |
| COMM-GET-STATUS | MISCA |
| COMM-SEND-ONE-CHAR | MISCA |
| COMM-SET-PARAMETERS | MISCA |
| CURRENT-SHIFT-STATE | KEYA |
| CURRENT-VIDEO-STATE | VIDEOA |
| DOS-ALLOCATION-TABLE-ADDRESS | DOSA |
| DOS-AUXILIARY-INPUT | DOSA |
| DOS-AUXILIARY-OUTPUT | DOSA |
| DOS-BUFFERED-KEYBOARD-INPUT | DOSA |
| DOS-CHECK-KEYBOARD-STATUS | DOSA |
| DOS-CLEAR-KEYBOARD-INPUT | DOSA |
| DOS-CLOSE-FILE | DOSA |
| DOS-CONSOLE-INPUT-NO-ECHO | DOSA |
| DOS-CREATE-FILE | DOSA |
| DOS-CREATE-PROGRAM-SEGMENT | DOSA |
| DOS-CURRENT-DISK | DOSA |
| DOS-DELETE-FILE | DOSA |
| DOS-DIRECT-CONSOLE-IO | DOSA |
| DOS-DIRECT-INPUT-NO-ECHO | DOSA |
| DOS-DISK-RESET | DOSA |
| DOS-DISPLAY-OUTPUT | DOSA |
| DOS-FILE-SIZE | DOSA |
| DOS-GET-DATE | DOSA |
| DOS-GET-TIME | DOSA |
| DOS-KEYBOARD-INPUT | DOSA |
| DOS-OPEN-FILE | DOSA |
| DOS-PARSE-FILENAME | DOSA |
| DOS-PRINTER-OUTPUT | DOSA |
| DOS-PRINT-STRING | DOSA |
| DOS-PROGRAM-TERMINATE | DOSA |
| DOS-PROGRAM-TERMINATE-F | DOSA |
| DOS-RANDOM-BLOCK-READ | DOSA |
| DOS-RANDOM-BLOCK-WRITE | DOSA |
| DOS-RANDOM-READ | DOSA |
| DOS-RANDOM-WRITE | DOSA |
| DOS-RENAME-FILE | DOSA |
| DOS-SEARCH-FOR-1ST-FILE | DOSA |
| DOS-SEARCH-FOR-NEXT-FILE | DOSA |
| DOS-SECTOR-READ | DOSA |
| DOS-SECTOR-WRITE | DOSA |
| DOS-SELECT-DISK | DOSA |
| DOS-SEQUENTIAL-READ | DOSA |
| DOS-SEQUENTIAL-WRITE | DOSA |
| DOS-SET-DATE | DOSA |
| DOS-SET-INTERRUPT-VECTOR | DOSA |
| DOS-SET-RANDOM-FIELD | DOSA |
| DOS-SET-TIME | DOSA |
| DOS-SET-TRANSFER-AREA | DOSA |
| DOS-SET-VERIFY | DOSA |

| Routine Name | Module Name |
| --- | --- |
| EQUIPMENT-LIST | MISCA |
| FORMAT-TRACK | DISKA |
| FORMAT-TRACK | PROTECTA |
| IF-KEYED-CHAR | KEYA |
| MEMORY-SIZE | MISCA |
| PRINTER-GET-STATUS | MISCA |
| PRINTER-RESET | MISCA |
| PRINTER-SEND-OUT-CHAR | MISCA |
| PRINT-SCREEN | MISCA |
| READ-CHAR-ATTRIB | VIDEOA |
| READ-CURSOR-POSITION | VIDEOA |
| READ-DISKETTE-STATUS | DISKA |
| READ-DOT | VIDEOA |
| READ-LIGHT-PEN-POSITION | VIDEOA |
| READ-NEXT-KEYED-CHAR | KEYA |
| READ-SECTORS | DISKA |
| READ-SECTOR-ANY-SIZE | PROTECTA |
| READ-TIMER | MISCA |
| READ-DISKETTE | DISKA |
| ROM-BASIC | MISCA |
| SCROLL-PAGE-DOWN | VIDEOA |
| SCROLL-PAGE-UP | VIDEOA |
| SELECT-ACTIVE-PAGE | VIDEOA |
| SET-COLOR-PALETTE | VIDEOA |
| SET-CURSOR-POSITION | VIDEOA |
| SET-CURSOR-TYPE | VIDEOA |
| SET-TIMER | MISCA |
| SET-VIDEO-MODE | VIDEOA |
| VERIFY-SECTORS | DISKA |
| WRITE-CHAR-ATTRIB | VIDEOA |
| WRITE-CHAR-ONLY | VIDEOA |
| WRITE-DOT | VIDEOA |
| WRITE-SECTORS | DISKA |
| WRITE-SECTOR-ANY-SIZE | PROTECTA |
| WRITE-TELETYPE | VIDEOA |

Next, here is a list of the routines, with their interrupt and service codes:

| Interrupt & Service Code | Routine Name |
| --- | --- |
| INTERRUPT-05 | PRINT-SCREEN |
| INTERRUPT-16-00 | SET-VIDEO-MODE |
| INTERRUPT-16-01 | SET-CURSOR-TYPE |
| INTERRUPT-16-02 | SET-CURSOR-POSITION |
| INTERRUPT-16-03 | READ-CURSOR-POSITION |
| INTERRUPT-16-04 | READ-LIGHT-PEN-POSITION |
| INTERRUPT-16-05 | SELECT-ACTIVE-PAGE |
| INTERRUPT-16-06 | SCROLL-PAGE-UP |
| INTERRUPT-16-07 | SCROLL-PAGE-DOWN |
| INTERRUPT-16-08 | READ-CHAR-ATTRIB |
| INTERRUPT-16-09 | WRITE-CHAR-ATTRIB |
| INTERRUPT-16-10 | WRITE-CHAR-ONLY |
| INTERRUPT-16-11 | SET-COLOR-PALETTE |
| INTERRUPT-16-12 | WRITE-DOT |
| INTERRUPT-16-13 | READ-DOT |

| Interrupt & Service Code | Routine Name |
| --- | --- |
| INTERRUPT-16-14 | WRITE-TELETYPE |
| INTERRUPT-16-15 | CURRENT-VIDEO-STATE |
| INTERRUPT-17 | EQUIPMENT-LIST |
| INTERRUPT-18 | MEMORY-SIZE |
| INTERRUPT-19-00 | RESET-DISKETTE |
| INTERRUPT-19-01 | READ-DISKETTE-STATUS |
| INTERRUPT-19-02 | READ-SECTORS |
| INTERRUPT-19-03 | WRITE-SECTORS |
| INTERRUPT-19-04 | VERIFY-SECTORS |
| INTERRUPT-19-05 | FORMAT-TRACK |
| INTERRUPT-20-00 | COMM-SET-PARAMETERS |
| INTERRUPT-20-01 | COMM-SEND-ONE-BYTE |
| INTERRUPT-20-02 | COMM-GET-ONE-BYTE |
| INTERRUPT-20-03 | COMM-GET-STATUS |
| INTERRUPT-21-00 | CASSETTE-MOTOR-ON |
| INTERRUPT-21-01 | CASSETTE-MOTOR-OFF |
| INTERRUPT-21-02 | CASSETTE-READ-BLOCKS |
| INTERRUPT-21-03 | CASSETTE-WRITE-BLOCKS |
| INTERRUPT-22-00 | READ-NEXT-KEYED-CHAR |
| INTERRUPT-22-01 | IF-KEYED-CHAR |
| INTERRUPT-22-02 | CURRENT-SHIFT-STATE |
| INTERRUPT-23-00 | PRINTER-SEND-ONE-BYTE |
| INTERRUPT-23-01 | PRINTER-RESET |
| INTERRUPT-23-02 | PRINTER-GET-STATUS |
| INTERRUPT-24 | ROM-BASIC |
| INTERRUPT-25 | BOOT-STRAP |
| INTERRUPT-26-00 | READ-TIMER |
| INTERRUPT-26-01 | SET-TIMER |
| INTERRUPT-32- | DOS-PROGRAM-TERMINATE |
| INTERRUPT-33-00 | DOS-PROGRAM-TERMINATE-F |
| INTERRUPT-33-01 | DOS-KEYBOARD-INPUT |
| INTERRUPT-33-02 | DOS-DISPLAY-OUTPUT |
| INTERRUPT-33-03 | DOS-AUXILIARY-INPUT |
| INTERRUPT-33-04 | DOS-AUXILIARY-OUTPUT |
| INTERRUPT-33-05 | DOS-PRINTER-OUTPUT |
| INTERRUPT-33-06 | DOS-DIRECT-CONSOLE-IO |
| INTERRUPT-33-07 | DOS-DIRECT-INPUT-NO-ECHO |
| INTERRUPT-33-08 | DOS-CONSOLE-INPUT-NO-ECHO |
| INTERRUPT-33-09 | DOS-PRINT-STRING |
| INTERRUPT-33-10 | DOS-BUFFERED-KEYBOARD-INPUT |
| INTERRUPT-33-11 | DOS-CHECK-KEYBOARD-STATUS |
| INTERRUPT-33-12 | DOS-CLEAR-KEYBOARD-INPUT |
| INTERRUPT-33-13 | DOS-DISK-RESET |
| INTERRUPT-33-14 | DOS-SELECT-DISK |
| INTERRUPT-33-15 | DOS-OPEN-FILE |
| INTERRUPT-33-16 | DOS-CLOSE-FILE |
| INTERRUPT-33-17 | DOS-SEARCH-FOR-1ST-FILE |
| INTERRUPT-33-18 | DOS-SEARCH-FOR-NEXT-FILE |
| INTERRUPT-33-19 | DOS-DELETE-FILE |
| INTERRUPT-33-20 | DOS-SEQUENTIAL-READ |
| INTERRUPT-33-21 | DOS-SEQUENTIAL-WRITE |
| INTERRUPT-33-22 | DOS-CREATE-FILE |
| INTERRUPT-33-23 | DOS-RENAME-FILE |
| INTERRUPT-33-25 | DOS-CURRENT-DISK |
| INTERRUPT-33-26 | DOS-SET-TRANSFER-AREA |

| Interrupt & Service Code | Routine Name |
|---|---|
| INTERRUPT-33-27 | DOS-ALLOCATION-TABLE-ADDRESS |
| INTERRUPT-33-33 | DOS-RANDOM-READ |
| INTERRUPT-33-34 | DOS-RANDOM-WRITE |
| INTERRUPT-33-35 | DOS-FILE-SIZE |
| INTERRUPT-33-36 | DOS-SET-RANDOM-FIELD |
| INTERRUPT-33-37 | DOS-SET-INTERRUPT-VECTOR |
| INTERRUPT-33-38 | DOS-CREATE-PROGRAM-SEGMENT |
| INTERRUPT-33-39 | DOS-RANDOM-BLOCK-READ |
| INTERRUPT-33-40 | DOS-RANDOM-BLOCK-WRITE |
| INTERRUPT-33-41 | DOS-PARSE-FILENAME |
| INTERRUPT-33-42 | DOS-GET-DATE |
| INTERRUPT-33-43 | DOS-SET-DATE |
| INTERRUPT-33-44 | DOS-GET-TIME |
| INTERRUPT-33-45 | DOS-SET-TIME |
| INTERRUPT-33-46 | DOS-SET-VERIFY |
| INTERRUPT-37 | DOS-SECTOR-READ |
| INTERRUPT-38 | DOS-SECTOR-WRITE |

Finally, here is a list of the routines, with their module offsets, which are needed for them to be used by BASIC, after BLOADing module.

For the routines in the PROTECTA module:

&H0020 — FORMAT-TRACK
&H005E — READ-SECTOR-ANY-SIZE
&H009C — WRITE-SECTOR-ANY-SIZE

For the routines in the DOSA module:

&H0020 — INTERRUPT-32 / DOS-PROGRAM-TERMINATE
&H0022 — INTERRUPT-37 / DOS-SECTOR-READ
&H004D — INTERRUPT-38 / DOS-SECTOR-WRITE
&H0078 — INTERRUPT-33-00 / DOS-PROGRAM-TERMINATE-F
&H007C — INTERRUPT-33-01 / DOS-KEYBOARD-INPUT
&H0090 — INTERRUPT-33-02 / DOS-DISPLAY-OUTPUT
&H00A0 — INTERRUPT-33-03 / DOS-AUXILIARY-INPUT
&H00B4 — INTERRUPT-33-04 / DOS-AUXILIARY-OUTPUT
&H00C4 — INTERRUPT-33-05 / DOS-PRINTER-OUTPUT
&H00D4 — INTERRUPT-33-06 / DOS-DIRECT-CONSOLE-IO
&H00F1 — INTERRUPT-33-07 / DOS-DIRECT-INPUT-NO-ECHO
&H0105 — INTERRUPT-33-08 / DOS-CONSOLE-INPUT-NO-ECHO
&H0119 — INTERRUPT-33-09 / DOS-PRINT-STRING
&H0129 — INTERRUPT-33-10 / DOS-BUFFERED-KEYBOARD-INPUT
&H0139 — INTERRUPT-33-11 / DOS-CHECK-KEYBOARD-STATUS
&H014D — INTERRUPT-33-12 / DOS-CLEAR-KEYBOARD-INPUT
&H0163 — INTERRUPT-33-13 / DOS-DISK-RESET
&H0168 — INTERRUPT-33-14 / DOS-SELECT-DISK
&H0181 — INTERRUPT-33-15 / DOS-OPEN-FILE
&H019A — INTERRUPT-33-16 / DOS-CLOSE-FILE
&H01B3 — INTERRUPT-33-17 / DOS-SEARCH-FOR-1ST-FILE
&H01CC — INTERRUPT-33-18 / DOS-SEARCH-FOR-NEXT-FILE
&H01E5 — INTERRUPT-33-19 / DOS-DELETE-FILE
&H01FE — INTERRUPT-33-20 / DOS-SEQUENTIAL-READ
&H0217 — INTERRUPT-33-21 / DOS-SEQUENTIAL-WRITE
&H0230 — INTERRUPT-33-22 / DOS-CREATE-FILE
&H0249 — INTERRUPT-33-23 / DOS-RENAME-FILE
&H0262 — INTERRUPT-33-25 / DOS-CURRENT-DISK
&H0276 — INTERRUPT-33-26 / DOS-SET-TRANSFER-AREA

```
&H0286    —    INTERRUPT-33-27  /   DOS-ALLOCATION-TABLE-ADDRESS
&H02B0    —    INTERRUPT-33-33  /   DOS-RANDOM-READ
&H02C9    —    INTERRUPT-33-34  /   DOS-RANDOM-WRITE
&H02E2    —    INTERRUPT-33-35  /   DOS-FILE-SIZE
&H02FB    —    INTERRUPT-33-36  /   DOS-SET-RANDOM-FIELD
&H030B    —    INTERRUPT-33-37  /   DOS-SET-INTERRUPT-VECTOR
&H0328    —    INTERRUPT-33-38  /   DOS-CREATE-PROGRAM-SEGMENT
&H0338    —    INTERRUPT-33-39  /   DOS-RANDOM-BLOCK-READ
&H0356    —    INTERRUPT-33-40  /   DOS-RANDOM-BLOCK-WRITE
&H0374    —    INTERRUPT-33-41  /   DOS-PARSE-FILENAME
&H03A9    —    INTERRUPT-33-42  /   DOS-GET-DATE
&H03C0    —    INTERRUPT-33-43  /   DOS-SET-DATE
&H03D5    —    INTERRUPT-33-44  /   DOS-GET-TIME
&H03EC    —    INTERRUPT-33-45  /   DOS-SET-TIME
&H0401    —    INTERRUPT-33-46  /   DOS-SET-VERIFY
```

For the routines in the DISKA module:

```
&H0020    —    INTERRUPT-19-00  /   RESET-DISKETTE
&H0025    —    INTERRUPT-19-01  /   READ-DISKETTE-STATUS
&H0039    —    INTERRUPT-19-02  /   READ-SECTORS
&H007D    —    INTERRUPT-19-03  /   WRITE-SECTORS
&H00C1    —    INTERRUPT-19-04  /   VERIFY-SECTORS
&H0105    —    INTERRUPT-19-05  /   FORMAT-TRACK
```

For the routines in the VIDEOA module:

```
&H0020    —    INTERRUPT-16-00  /   SET-VIDEO-MODE
&H0030    —    INTERRUPT-16-01  /   SET-CURSOR-TYPE
&H0045    —    INTERRUPT-16-02  /   SET-CURSOR-POSITION
&H005F    —    INTERRUPT-16-03  /   READ-CURSOR-POSITION
&H0093    —    INTERRUPT-16-04  /   READ-LIGHT-PEN-POSITION
&H00CE    —    INTERRUPT-16-05  /   SELECT-ACTIVE-PAGE
&H00DE    —    INTERRUPT-16-06  /   SCROLL-PAGE-UP
&H0107    —    INTERRUPT-16-07  /   SCROLL-PAGE-DOWN
&H0130    —    INTERRUPT-16-08  /   READ-CHAR-ATTRIB
&H0154    —    INTERRUPT-16-09  /   WRITE-CHAR-ATTRIB
&H0173    —    INTERRUPT-16-10  /   WRITE-CHAR-ONLY
&H018D    —    INTERRUPT-16-11  /   SET-COLOR-PALETTE
&H01A2    —    INTERRUPT-16-12  /   WRITE-DOT
&H01BC    —    INTERRUPT-16-13  /   READ-DOT
&H01DD    —    INTERRUPT-16-14  /   WRITE-TELETYPE
&H01F7    —    INTERRUPT-16-15  /   CURRENT-VIDEO-STATE
```

For the routines in the KEYA module:

```
&H0020    —    INTERRUPT-22-00  /   READ-NEXT-KEYED-CHAR
&H0032    —    INTERRUPT-22-01  /   IF-KEYED-CHAR
&H0049    —    INTERRUPT-22-02  /   CURRENT-SHIFT-STATE
```

For the routines in the MISCA module:

```
&H0020    —    INTERRUPT-05     /   PRINT-SCREEN
&H0023    —    INTERRUPT-17     /   EQUIPMENT-LIST
&H0033    —    INTERRUPT-18     /   MEMORY-SIZE
&H0043    —    INTERRUPT-20-00  /   COMM-SET-PARAMETERS
&H005F    —    INTERRUPT-20-01  /   COMM-SEND-ONE-BYTE
&H007B    —    INTERRUPT-20-02  /   COMM-GET-ONE-BYTE
&H0092    —    INTERRUPT-20-03  /   COMM-GET-STATUS
```

```
&H00A9   —   INTERRUPT-21-00  /   CASSETTE-MOTOR-ON
&H00AE   —   INTERRUPT-21-01  /   CASSETTE-MOTOR-OFF
&H00B3   —   INTERRUPT-21-02  /   CASSETTE-READ-BLOCKS
&H00E5   —   INTERRUPT-21-03  /   CASSETTE-WRITE-BLOCKS
&H0105   —   INTERRUPT-23-00  /   PRINTER-SEND-ONE-BYTE
&H0125   —   INTERRUPT-23-01  /   PRINTER-RESET
&H0140   —   INTERRUPT-23-02  /   PRINTER-GET-STATUS
&H015B   —   INTERRUPT-24     /   ROM-BASIC
&H015D   —   INTERRUPT-25     /   BOOT-STRAP
&H015F   —   INTERRUPT-26-00  /   READ-TIMER
&H0183   —   INTERRUPT-26-01  /   SET-TIMER
```

## Section 7: Pascal Access Tool List

Here is a list of the 33 Pascal support routines, which assist the use of the assembler interface routines. For easy reference, the list is given by descriptive name, together with the name of the module in which each routine appears (which also indicates its subject area):

| Routine Name | Module Name |
| --- | --- |
| change-disk-base | PROTECTP |
| char-from-word | DOSP |
| convert-keyboard-word | KEYP |
| decode-cluster-into-sector | DIRFAT |
| decode creation | DIRFAT |
| decode-diskette status | DISKP |
| decode-equipment-and-memory | MISCP |
| decode-printer-status | MISCP |
| decode-time | MISCP |
| display-string-at | VIDEOP |
| display-window-bottom | VIDEOP |
| display-window-top | VIDEOP |
| dos-sector-number | DOSP |
| encode-and-write-fat | DIRFAT |
| endode-time | MISCP |
| filename-in-display-format | DIRFAT |
| find-diskette-format | DIRFAT |
| first-sector | DIRFAT |
| fortmat-7-8 | PROTECTP |
| get-keystroke | KEYP |
| if-keystroke | KEYP |
| next-sector | DIRFAT |
| read-256 | PROTECTP |
| read-and-decode-fat | DIRFAT |
| read-and-store-directory | DIRFAT |
| read-sector | DOSP |
| reset-disk-base | PROTECTP |
| set-hidden-and-system | DIRFAT |
| test-for-hidden-and-system | DIRFAT |
| word-from-char | DOSP |
| write-256 | PROTECTP |
| write-directory | DIRFAT |
| write-sector | DOSP |

# Section 8: Copy Protection Scheme

Copy protection is one of the messier issues in personal computing. Unauthorized copying of programs—software theft—arose almost as soon as personal computers appeared, and copy protection of programs appeared immediately afterwards.

You may wish to copy protect programs which you supply. Here, we will provide you with a two-stage copy protection mechanism for you to use.

Before explaining how our scheme works, let's consider why you might not want to copy-protect your diskettes, and what alternatives there are to copy-protection.

Everyone hates copy protection. It is a nuisance to seller and buyer alike. It increases the cost of software, and reduces its ease of use. One factor that you must consider in deciding to copy-protect, is how much it may reduce your customer's satisfaction and good will.

Another reason against copy-protecting is the appearance of copy-busters. With programs available to copy "copy-protected" diskettes, the value of copy protection is reduced.

Finally, perhaps the most important argument against copy protection is transfer to other media. With more and more personal computer systems using hard disk mass-storage, it becomes increasingly important for users to be able to transfer programs. If your customers cannot move your programs to hard disk, they may turn to other programs.

There are some alternatives to copy protection, which will reduce your exposure to software theft. Reasonable pricing reduces the motivation for unauthorized copying. A useful and large set of printed documentation helps, since it is not as convenient to copy pages as it is to copy diskettes. And anything which bonds the user to the supplier, such as the need for periodic updates, or assistance by telephone, should reduce theft.

But if you wish to copy protect diskettes, the mechanisms provided in this package will make it possible for you to do so. The method provided here is not state-of-the-art by any means, but it is a workable copy protection scheme, for those who wish to use a simple one.

The copy protection scheme provided here is available in two levels. At the higher level, a complete ready-to-use mechanism will protect your diskettes. At the lower level, a set of protection tools make it possible for you to produce your own customized protection scheme, based on the methods given here.

## High-Level Method

The high-level method consists of a program to add copy protection marking to batches of diskettes, and program fragments to test for this marking, in either BASIC or Pascal. (The method can be easily adapted to other languages.)

The complete executable program PROTECT adds protection marking to diskettes. After you have produced the diskettes which you wish to copy-protect, run the PROTECT program, and give it your diskettes, one by one. PROTECT will reformat the last, 39th, track on the first side of the diskette, to contain one odd-sized sector, which cannot be read by conventional DOS methods. While doing this, PROTECT will preserve any data you have on the 39th track. When PROTECT is running, it provides you with messages explaining its operation.

Any diskette which has been modified by PROTECT will not be successfully copied by either of the standard DOS copying tools, DISKCOPY and COPY.

To complete the copy protection, your programs must test for the marking that PROTECT leaves. The program source code necessary to do this is found in the file PROTECT.BAS, for BASIC, and PROTECT.INC, for Pascal. Each program will use the object code in the PROTECTA module. BASIC programs will BLOAD the file PROTECTA.BLD, while Pascal programs must be linked with PROTECTA.OBJ.

To see how to use the testing programs, read the comments inside the source code files PROTECT.BAS and PROTECT.INC: they make clear how they are used, and they can be very easily incorporated into your own programs.

## Low-Level Method

While the high-level method explained above is convenient to use, its methods are as available to any other buyer of this package, as they are to you.

To get a greater degree of copy protection, you can produce your own customized copy protection, which could require more effort to break.

To do this, you can make use of the services provided in the PROTECTA module. One will format a track to any specifications, so that you can produce copy-resistant sectors in a location and size of your own chosing. The others will read or write unconventionally sized sectors. This will enable your programs to place key data on copy-resistant sectors, and check for this data.

See sections five and six for the discussion of the specifics of how to access and use these services.